Teaching Undergraduates

The Educational Psychology Series

Robert J. Sternberg and Wendy M. Williams, Series Editors

Teaching Undergraduates

Roger L. Dominowski

University of Illinois at Chicago

LEA

LAWRENCE ERLBAUM ASSOCIATES, PUBLISHERS

2002   Mahwah, NJ   London

Lawrence Erlbaum Associates, Inc., Publishers
10 Industrial Avenue
Mahwah, New Jersey 07430

Cover design by Kathryn Houghtaling Lacey

Library of Congress Cataloging-in-Publication Data
Dominowsi, Roger L., 1939–
    Teaching undergraduates / Roger L. Dominowski.
       p.   cm. — (The educational psychology series)
    Includes bibliographical references and index.
    ISBN 0-8058-2989-X (hard : alk. paper)
       1. College teaching.   2. College teachers.   3. First year teachers.   I .Title.   II Series.
 LB2331.D58   2001
 378.1'25—dc21

                                                                2001023471

Books published by Lawrence Erlbaum Associates are printed on acid-free paper, and their bindings are chosen for strength and durability.

Printed in the United States of America
10   9   8   7   6   5   4   3   2   1

Table of Contents

Preface

This book is intended to help college teachers plan their undergraduate courses and deliver high-quality instruction. It is based on research on human learning, memory, thinking, and problem solving as well as studies of teaching and less-formal reports of teaching practices. The book offers practical advice about all aspects of college teaching, from textbook selection through lecturing, test construction, and writing assignments to grading policies and socializing with students. The theme of the book is that teaching is a creative, decision-making, idea-testing enterprise whose purpose is to facilitate student learning in all of its facets. My goal is to help instructors understand the multiple kinds of learning taking place in their courses so that they can select, modify, and invent techniques to teach effectively.

New college instructors are the primary audience for this book, whether they are advanced graduate students about to teach for the first time or new faculty members coping with the demands of their jobs. The book can also be useful to more experienced faculty who would like to reflect on their teaching practices and consider the possibility of making some changes. Much of the material is quite relevant to the tasks of teaching assistants even though they often lack control over the choice of topics and reading materials. Likewise, the ideas are pertinent to teaching graduate courses until the format becomes joint exploration of a topic by near-equals.

The book arises from a course on teaching that I offered for two decades to advanced graduate students in psychology, just prior to their teaching a course for the first time. Over the years, my notes on teaching evolved, decidedly influenced by our discussions of teaching issues. The course was quite successful, based on the student-teachers' comments and their students' very positive reactions to their teaching efforts. I have tried to capture the substance of that course in this book. It's important to point out that psychology includes a wide variety of undergraduate courses—biopsychology, statistics, personality, history of psychology, laboratory courses, and others. This book concerns issues and ideas that are relevant to teaching courses of different types, in any discipline.

OVERVIEW

The book is divided into four parts. Part I contains just Chapter 1, on course planning. This chapter outlines the many decisions instructors face in defining courses as "theirs" and discusses the larger issues that shape a course and constrain more specific choices. Selecting course content, choosing learning goals, deciding how to pace a course, scheduling tests, are some of these issues. A workable timetable for preparing a course is included.

Part II is a mini-course on human learning, memory, and thinking. It provides the conceptual foundation for making teaching decisions, for selecting instructional techniques and especially for inventing new techniques that might particularly fit a specific course. Chapter 2 concerns attention and working memory, the processing of information on an ongoing basis, as in a classroom. Understanding how human attention functions and the limitations students must cope with in a classroom provides a basis for alleviating problems and increasing comprehension. Chapter 3 focuses on learning and long-term memory, the factors that affect learning and what influences forgetting and remembering. Chapter 4 summarizes research on thinking, which is, roughly, doing more with knowledge than just remembering. Applying concepts to new examples, solving problems, and working through complex arguments are difficult tasks, and learning to succeed at them requires special teaching arrangements. This section promotes viewing teaching in terms of what and how you want the students to learn and what can be done to nurture that learning.

Part III deals with what might be called the "nitty-gritty" of college teaching. Much of this material is informed by the principles and findings discussed in Part II, although many specific ideas are added. Chapter 5 considers how to choose a textbook, a critical decision for an instructor because of its heavy influence on the definition of a course. Chapter 6 discusses the many facets of lecturing and conducting classroom discussions. Chapter 7 covers writing assignments, their types and purposes, and how to structure and evaluate them. The unpleasant issue of plagiarism is also addressed. Chapter 8 describes different kinds of tests, multiple-choice, essay, and so on. The relation of tests to learning goals, the strengths and weaknesses of different test types, and guidelines for constructing good tests are included. Chapter 9 is about grading systems, which have great impact on the character of a course. A grading system tells students how to allocate their efforts and can encourage cooperative learning or competition.

Part IV addresses professional issues of importance and consequence to instructors. Chapter 10 concerns ethical issues, of which there are many deserving the attention of instructors. The requirement of fair treatment of students permeates multiple aspects of teaching, with advance consideration of possible issues as a wise step to take. Accommodating students with disabilities also is discussed. Chapter 11 considers student evaluations of instruction, their role in education, and how to use them in efforts to improve instruction.

Because this book comes from a long-term accumulation of ideas, many people have participated in its development—undergraduates, graduate-student teachers, and colleagues, to all of whom I am grateful. I especially want to thank Pamela Ansburg and Holly Rice for the many refreshing and beneficial conversations we have had about teaching. Acknowledgment is due the University of

Illinois at Chicago for being a research university that gives recognition and support to teaching.

I am beholden to my wife, Carol DeBoth, for her advice and encouragement to get this book underway and to see it through to completion. Thanks go to Michael Frankovic for his help with library research in the early stages of writing. Finally, I am indebted to Naomi Silverman of Erlbaum and Robert Sternberg of Yale University for their support and comments, which contributed significantly to making this book a reality.

Roger L. Dominowski
Professor Emeritus
UNIVERSITY OF ILLINOIS AT CHICAGO

I

Introduction

1
Course Planning

What's Needed Before Your First Class
Course Content: What Will the Course Cover?
Determining Course Goals
Choosing a Course Format
A Planning Timetable

Course planning serves two purposes: First and most important, it allows an instructor to organize the course to promote the goals that the instructor has for the course. Second, it encourages preliminary work that will reduce stress when the course is taught. Many decisions must be made and materials created before you hold the first meeting of your course. Here is a reasonably complete checklist. The purpose is to give you some perspective on planning a course.

WHAT'S NEEDED BEFORE YOUR FIRST CLASS

Let us assume that the scheduling of the course has been taken care of. Here are the other items deserving attention. They are listed approximately in the order in which they need to be considered.

1. Selection and ordering of a textbook and other reading materials.
2. Deciding what the course requirements will be:
   A. Exams
      (1) Number
      (2) Coverage: Will each cover a specific section or will one or more be cumulative? What weighting will be given to classroom and reading material?
      (3) Format: What kinds of questions to include; whether exams will be open/closed book; will any take-home exams be used?
      (4) Scheduling when exams will be given.
         (a) Determining policy/procedures for makeup tests.
   B. What other projects will be required? (Papers, etc.) See 1–4 under A.
   C. What rules will you have regarding class attendance, participation, and homework (if it will be assigned)?

3. Constructing a grading system.
   A. General form ("curve," pre-set criteria)
   B. Weights to be given to various course requirements
   C. Any opportunities for bonus points? On exams? Assignments?
   D. Any penalties for late tests, assignments?
   E. What will be your policy regarding incomplete grades?
4. It is very advantageous to create, for your own use, a day-by-day plan for all class meetings, filling in holidays, exams, reviews of exams, any special events, and the topics you intend to cover (one per day). Coordinate the reading assignments (typical is one standard chapter per week). You must decide on the relation between assigned readings and class content—that is, where there will and won't be (how much) overlap. Expect to change this several times, and probably again when you teach your course.
5. Prepare lecture outlines for at least the first two weeks of class. Include materials you will need for your lectures, such as handouts or overheads.
6. Construct questions sufficient for the first test, from the assigned readings and the first two weeks of class. Test construction is quite time-consuming, so the more you can do before classes start, the less stress there will be when teaching.
7. Prepare a course syllabus to be given to students on the first day of class. Preliminary drafts of the syllabus can be made while planning a course, but the final, official version is perhaps the last task completed before a course begins.
8. You'll need a course evaluation form to be given to students at the end of the term. It's also feasible to ask for student feedback during a course, a topic we'll discuss later. This task is perhaps one that could be delayed until later.

All of these topics will be discussed in this book. Much of the book is intended to help you be prepared for the first class meeting of your course. Some chapters concern topics that occur repeatedly when teaching, such as organizing lectures, and others cover issues that might arise very infrequently if at all, such as discipline problems. Course planning logically proceeds from general issues to details. So let us begin by considering matters that concern the whole course.

An instructor needs to determine three general features of a course that will give a course its particular "flavor" or slant. These are course content, learning goals, and course format. The choices one makes about these features distinguish a particular instructor's version of a course from others with the same name and number. We'll consider each in turn.

COURSE CONTENT: WHAT WILL THE COURSE COVER?

At first glance it might seem that course content is well determined by course title, but a title and catalog description greatly underconstrain what a course will actually be when it is taught. The degree of constraint on an instructor's choices depends on the course's role in the curriculum. Specifically, if you are teaching a course that is prerequisite to another, constraints increase because teachers of the subsequent course will reasonably expect that certain topics have been covered, and you need to satisfy such programmatic expectations. Even here, considerable latitude remains. For courses that are not the earlier part of a sequence, you need only cover topics consistent with the course title and catalog description; here the range of options is enormous.

How do you choose the topics to cover? A reasonable starting point is your own identification of the important topics subsumed by a course title. It is of course sensible and helpful to seek professional consultation by asking experienced teachers of the course for copies of their syllabi. Discussing the course with an experienced instructor whose teaching you admire can be extremely helpful.

It is worthwhile to adopt the view that your course might well be the students' only exposure to the topic area. If so, what topics do you want to be sure to include? In thinking about this question, it is essential to keep in mind the level of course, or the type of student that one will be teaching. Let me distinguish three kinds of courses or student groups: general education, majors, and majors who expect to pursue graduate study. Students taking a course to fulfill a general education requirement probably know very little about the area and might well never take another course in this discipline. Their knowledge and instructional needs are quite different from those of majors. Even though majors might know little in detail about the subject of a more advanced course, they bring a body of relevant knowledge to the class. They should more readily learn new concepts and should desire and acquire deeper understanding of the material. Even so, only a subset of majors will pursue graduate study. When teaching undergraduates who are headed toward graduate school, it is understandable and appropriate to focus on research and attention to details, and to introduce the level of information found in journal articles. In general, as the level of course goes up, it makes sense to go a bit faster, covering more topics per unit time, or to increase the depth of topic coverage, considering more details. Novice instructors, primed by their own, recent graduate courses, can be biased toward using a graduate-course approach when teaching an undergraduate course. The result is that they cover too much, in too much detail, and assume too much background knowledge—they present a course that is "over the heads" of their undergraduate students, who suffer and usually don't learn much. Being forewarned should help to avoid the problem; more later.

DETERMINING COURSE GOALS

Having decided what content to cover, it is still necessary to determine what you want the students to learn about the material. This decision can be made for the course as a whole, or many times with different outcomes as you proceed through the course topics. For most course topics, there are several different orientations that might be adopted for presenting the material and simultaneously for choosing what students should learn. Let me give an example.

Suppose I choose to cover the topic of perceptual learning in a course on child development. The course goal question is: What do I want the students to learn about perceptual learning? Here are some possibilities:

> The basic concepts and terms regarding perceptual learning.
> The major theories about perceptual learning and how they compare to one another.
> The most important, most reliable findings regarding perceptual learning.
> How different theories account for the major findings. Which findings pose problems for which theories.
> Examples of perceptual learning from both research and everyday life.
> Identify new examples of perceptual learning.

The point of emphasizing that any of a variety of learning goals might be adopted for any course topic is to stress both the choices available to an instructor and the need to use different learning techniques depending on what students are supposed to learn.

There are multiple kinds of learning, even within the relatively restricted domain of classroom material. Learning basic terms, comparing concepts, identifying new examples, and solving novel problems are different types of learning and call for different teaching strategies. So, the essential question for an instructor is: Once I have decided what I want the students to learn about this particular topic, what would be a good way to present the material? What tasks should I give the students to do in order for them to learn what is desired? Chapters 2 through 4 discuss the various aspects of learning that can occur in college classes and provide the foundation for selecting and creating instructional techniques.

Different kinds of learning outcomes lead to different forms of assessments. Stated another way, different course requirements or methods of assessment imply different course goals and varying types of knowledge. Although it might be claimed that any aspect of a body of knowledge could be assessed by using, say, multiple choice tests, it is difficult to support this position over the full range of possible course requirements. For example, essay versus multiple choice questions seldom if ever tap precisely the same knowledge. Requiring students to read multiple sources and to organize that knowledge and present it in a paper is asking for different learning and knowledge gaining activities than requiring them to answer questions on a test. Overall, instructors can decide to use one kind of requirement or assessment method in the service of one course goal while using a different kind of requirement for another course goal. We discuss various types of assessment methods later in the book. In planning a course, however, it is useful at the outset to think about what kinds of emphasis you want to give to course material.

CHOOSING A COURSE FORMAT

The question here is how your course should be structured. The focus is on the organization and pacing of course material, the number, nature, and timing of tests, the use of other assessment techniques, and the choice of lecture/discussion procedures. These considerations typically alter the way in which a course is organized on the basis of content and learning goals alone. In part, one needs to incorporate tests and other kinds of assignments so that the course runs smoothly. Perhaps more fundamental questions concern students' mastery of course material and the issue of individual differences.

To what extent do you want students to master course material? It is extremely easy for anyone to assert their strong desire that students learn everything, that as instructors we would be so pleased to observe such high levels of accomplishment. But I mean the question seriously. Taking seriously the question of student mastery means that an instructor makes decisions about the rate at which material will be presented, about how often and in what ways students' learning will be assessed, and about what will and won't be done to accomodate students individual learning needs. Let me explain. An instructor assigns a certain amount of material to read for a topic and presents in class particular material about that topic. If everything went perfectly, all of the students would know about that topic what the instructor wants them to know. Probably, this scenario never happens in a classroom. Therefore, the question for an instructor is what if anything should be done when some students have not mastered the material after the initial study/teaching/learning episode has been completed.

It's important to notice what is involved here. We can take for granted that an instructor would have chosen a reading assignment and precisely what to present in class. The first real issue arises with respect to finding out that at least some students haven't mastered the material. If an instructor waits too long to obtain information about students' learning, it will not be possible to take useful corrective steps to improve students' mastery. The implication here is that an instructor needs to decide how often, and how formally to check students' learning.

An instructor will decide, formally or informally, on the relative importance of different aspects of knowledge about a topic. That is, for any topic in any course, an instructor will care more or less about whether students learn one or another aspect of topical material. For example, instructors are likely to care very much that students learn basic concepts. Instructors might well care not as much that students, at the undergraduate level, can explain a theory. So an essential part of inquiring about student learning is to make judgments about what is more or less important in the course material.

An instructor makes an initial decision regarding the amount of material to cover in a specified time period. Alternatively, the instructor decides how much time—both study time and class time—to allot to a specified amount of material.

Assuming that the instructor has some indication of students' mastery of the material, the question is how little mastery should lead to some kind of remedial activity rather than proceeding ahead with the next course topic.

A critical facet of considering students' learning is deciding how many of the students in a class need to master some item of course material in order for the instructor to be satisfied. Suppose an instructor has 50 students in a class. If the initial presentation of material results in only four or five students achieving the desired level of learning, what good reason could there be for continuing on to the next topic? In contrast, if only one student does not grasp the material, stopping the course progress to rectify that student's deficiency would be unfair to the other students. These are examples of two extremes of pacing the coverage of course material. In one case, the course is geared to the best students, a pace that will leave the vast majority of students in a state of inadequate knowledge. At the other extreme, the course proceeds only as fast as the slowest student. In this case, all the other students are bored and their learning time is not properly used. Most college classes fall between these extremes. No matter what pace an instructor chooses initially, that pace will be too fast for some students, too slow for others. If the class goes too quickly, too many students will be left behind. It is easy, if an instructor pays no attention to students' learning, to simply choose a pace for presenting course material and stick to it, making no changes whatsoever. Finding a proper level at which to initially cover material is not easy, and deciding how to adjust and adapt a course to students' learning rates is more difficult. Nonetheless, the problem needs to be faced rather than ignored.

Instructors should, even if only informally, monitor their students' comprehension of course material. Assuming they do so, instructors need to decide what level of noncomprehension will lead them to go over material a second time. Pacing the course slowly will minimize the need to repeat material in one way or another. If the course pace is slow, however, what opportunities will be made available for additional learning to those students who could learn the material more quickly? As the course pace quickens, the likelihood of needing to repeat coverage of course topics will increase. Of course, fewer students will be bored and more will find the required rate of learning to be reasonably challenging.

The way in which an instructor deals with this issue might vary with the particular course being taught. One issue is the extent to which earlier material must be mastered in order to learn later material. For example, in a broad survey course, there might be little connection between topics covered early in the course and those covered later. In this case, an instructor might be more willing to accept a lower level of mastery of a topic in order to proceed to the next material and to come close to covering all of the material that was initially planned for the course. For a contrasting case, consider a statistics course in which failure to reasonably learn early material will make later learning extremely difficult if not impossible. Here, one can sensibly ask whether proceeding to the next topic makes sense if a substantial part of the class has not mastered the current topic. Clearly, an instructor needs to define "substantial" for a particular set of circumstances.

An instructor must formulate an initial plan for proceeding through course material as well as deciding what to do when students' learning "in general" does not match expectations. The question of when to modify the initial plan for the entire class has been discussed above. There is also the issue of dealing with individual differences in learning rates. Let's consider several course formats to illustrate alternative ways of dealing with these differences.

Fixed-Pace Learning

This approach is the simplest. Essentially, the instructor makes initial decisions regarding the pace at which material will be covered, when tests will be administered, and when other assignments will be due. All students are required to meet course requirements at the same rate. What about students who do not perform well at the chosen pace? Ordinarily, seeking help is left to the students' initiative, and any remedial activities will take place outside of class sessions. Students consult with either teaching assistants or the instructor during office hours. This approach can work if the number of students who need help is small, and if those who need help take steps to obtain it. Obviously, the availability of teaching assistants will affect the feasibility of providing effective help. There will inevitably be limits on the amount of tutoring that can be provided to students who need it; usually, the limitations are severe relative to need.

This scenario is unfortunately descriptive of many college courses. The majority of students do not really master the content as the course proceed—students achieving grades of D, C, and even low B are passing the course but are not learning adequately with respect to considerable course material. Only a fraction of the students who could profit from additional help are likely to seek help, and only some of those getting extra help show clear gains. One reason for inadequate results from extra help is reliance on student initiative for seeking assistance. If, for example, a student struggles with a course for five weeks, performs poorly on an exam, and waits one or two more weeks before asking for help, it is likely that the student will be so far behind that providing adequate treatment will be impossible. To avoid this state of affairs, instructors might try to devise ways to encourage students to seek assistance. Early and frequent assessment of students' progress will also alleviate the problem.

Student-Paced Learning

A completely different approach is to let students proceed through course material at their individual rates. This is what regularly happens when people take individual lessons of many different sorts—learning a foreign language, to play the piano, to play tennis or golf; or to fly a plane. One starts at "the beginning" and does not advance to the next stage until the current stage has been reasonably mastered. A critical difference between these learning situations and college courses is that, in college, a student does not have an individual tutor.

A minimal version of a student-paced course would be something like the following. An instructor assigns a textbook (or other study materials) and constructs a test of some sort for each chapter. Students are told to read the first assigned chapter and to arrange for a test when they believe they are ready.

If a student meets the required criterion on the test, he or she proceeds to the next reading assignment. Students who do not meet the test criterion are told to study more and take the test again; this cycle would be repeated until the criterion is met.

This course description illustrates the most basic elements of what is known as the Keller Plan (Keller, 1968) or the Personalized System of Instruction (PSI). Course material is divided into units; the study material for a unit could be just a reading assignment, or it could include exercises to work through. Study guides are provided to direct students' work through the first and subsequent units. Students take a unit test when they think they are ready and must meet a usually high mastery criterion to be allowed to proceed. Retesting continues until the mastery criterion is met. When the criterion has been met, the student moves on to the next unit.

These courses are not completely student paced, however. At the vast majority of colleges and universities, courses last a specified period of time, one semester or one quarter. Therefore, there is an overall time limitation on courses based on the idea of student-paced learning. What typically happens is that students' grades are based on the number of units that they successfully complete during the term. As a consequence, students proceeding at a slower rate encounter less of the course content.

Comparison.   In a student-paced course, there is unequal exposure to course content, as just noted. Also, because the units are relatively large in number but small in size, students take fairly frequent tests. In a standard fixed-pace course, students are all exposed to complete course content. They differ in terms of how much of that content they learn. So an instructor has a choice: to allow students to encounter varying amounts of the course content, while ensuring a reasonably high level of learning for the units that are attempted; alternatively, to ensure that students are exposed to all course content even though they will learn it to varying degrees. There have been many comparisons of these two approaches. Students sometimes give higher ratings to student-paced courses and perform better. Because student-paced courses involve more frequent testing than the usual fixed-pace course, it has been suggested that the better learning occurs for this reason. Goldwater and Acker (1975) found that adding weekly quizzes with a mastery criterion to a fixed-pace course improved student learning.

Also, the role of an instructor is different in the two types of courses. In a student-paced course, because students will be at different points of progress, class lectures or discussions are difficult to schedule. Consequently, lectures play little or no role, and students learn course material largely on their own. Instructors might offer lectures on different topics, but every lecture will be appropriate for only a fraction of the students. Unless recorded lectures are available on an ad lib basis, they cannot be major sources of instruction under this format. Comparisons of the two systems have been limited to students' learning of their common reading material, in other words, the textbook. A criticism of student-paced formats is that they tend to focus on lower level content (Caldwell, 1985) because of their reliance on textbook-based, do-it-yourself exercises.

Modifications.   There is, of course, no reason to limit oneself to a particular course format. There are many ways to organize and deliver a fixed-pace course, just as a student-paced course can take on multiple variations. With the standard fixed-pace format, a critical factor for identifying individual differences in learning is the frequency with which learning assessments take place. If there is just a midterm and a final exam, there will clearly be little opportunity for students or instructors to find out who is having difficulty with the course. If the instructor gives weekly quizzes, on the other hand, students' differences in acquisition will be apparent earlier to both the instructor and the students themselves. Also, weekly quizzes help students learn (Goldwater & Acker, 1975) and so should reduce problems. Instructors can employ techniques to increase the likelihood of students' seeking help. For example, a colleague of mine requires students to come for a five-minute interview at the start of the course. His purpose is both to find out something about the students' reasons for taking the course and to make it easier for them to come to him for help if they should need it later. An instructor could have the rule that anyone who gets less than some specified grade on a test must come to see either the instructor or a teaching assistant.

Just as there is an overall limit to the time allowed for a course, an instructor using a student-paced format could place time limits regarding the completion of course units. For example, if there were 15 units for a course lasting one semester, the expected rate might be one unit per week. Students proceeding quickly would simply be allowed to do so and finish the course before the semester is over. To prevent students from taking too much time on any unit, the instructor could, say, allow a maximum of two weeks for any unit. This would clearly be a modified version of a student-paced course, but it would still allow for considerable variation in learning rate.

Forced Mastery

An interesting scheme for using a fixed-pace format was called "programmed motivation" by Lamberth and Knight (1974), but I prefer the label "forced mastery." The way in which this differs from a standard fixed-pace format is in the use of a required retesting scheme. Somewhat like a typical student-paced format, the course must be divided into enough units so that tests may be given frequently. It is not necessary to use weekly tests, but I will use this plan as an example. The essential idea is that, on every test, those who do not reach a required criterion must retake the test, as many times as needed, within a short specified time period until they achieve at the criterion level. For example, suppose a test is given on Friday and the criterion is 90% correct. Tests are graded over the weekend and students receive their scores on Monday. Those with scores less than 90% must then go to a specified place, the retesting room, within specified hours on, say, Monday and Tuesday, to retake the test until they score at least 90%. The final deadline for meeting this standard might be four o'clock on Tuesday afternoon.

Three questions arise immediately. Do these students keep taking the original test or are they given new versions? Which test score is used in determining grades, the original one, the last retest, or something else? What happens if a student does not meet the criterion by the final deadline? In this plan, variations are readily available. Central to the idea is that only original test scores are used in determining grades, and retesting is done to avoid a more severe penalty. In one interesting version, retesting used the original test, which was posted outside the retesting room, with answers. If students failed to meet the criterion on time for any test, the penalty was to fail the entire course. The reported results of using this scheme were that students managed to meet the criterion for a test by the deadline, the number of students requiring retesting decreased over the term, students did extremely well on comprehensive final examinations and gave positive ratings to the retesting requirement.

When Lamberth and Knight (1974) initially used this technique with large introductory psychology classes, the tests were multiple choice, so that students who were retesting needed to do nothing more in principle than memorize the answers to the test items. One might ask, why should this method produce better scores on comprehensive final examinations when students could satisfy the retesting requirements on the basis of such simple memorization? Lamberth and Knight's answer was that taking retests is a noxious experience for students that they will try to avoid by studying well enough for later tests so that they meet the criterion when the test is given for the first time. I would add to this idea the benefit of learning the correct answer to test items that were missed; in other words, I believe that students will do more than memorize multiple choice answers when they look at the test with feedback.

I have used this method in statistics courses where test items were never multiple choice. Rather, students were required to work out problems or write answers to questions about the material. In this application, students who were retesting at least had to learn something about the content of the tests in order to successfully complete the testing. My own experience with this technique has been quite positive. Like Lamberth and Knight, I found that students completed retesting, did very well on a comprehensive final exam, and evaluated retesting quite positively (Dominowski, 1998). Also, the number of students taking retests decreased over the term. Students' reactions to test feedback were quite interesting. Consistent with Lamberth and Knight's motivational hypothesis, students would sometimes express their delight in having scored high enough to avoid retesting. In addition, another change occurred as students went from being required to retest to not needing to do so; a sense of confidence and satisfaction appeared. Occasionally, a student would remark something to the effect that "I think I am really understanding this stuff," perhaps with a look of slight surprise.

This technique is labor intensive because of the need to grade tests quickly so that students can receive feedback and know if they have to take retests. Just as with a student-paced format, the use of frequent tests and retesting adds to the workload. Tests that are easy to grade, such as multiple choice tests, reduce the grading and feedback workload. As noted above, the technique has been used with problem solving and written answer tests, which makes the workload quite high. In an attempt to reduce the workload, we tried a scheme in which, if students did not achieve a grade of A on an exam, they were required to submit correct answers to all missed problems and questions within two days of receiving their graded exams (which were graded over weekends). No retesting was involved; students prepared error corrections as homework, and checking their corrections could also be done as "homework." Because nearly all corrections were in fact correct, checking was relatively easy. Student achievement was just as high as when retesting was required, and students were happy with the scheme (Dominowski & Rice, 1999).

Instructors frequently must make choices or compromises when they lack resources to employ a procedure that they think might work best. So also in this case; the instructor needs to use a type of test that seems appropriate, a number or frequency of tests that is high enough to do the job, while working within the constraints of the teaching resources available. As suggested earlier, a good strategy for an instructor is to try out various formats with the goal of obtaining good student performance without overloading available resources.

Undergraduate Teaching Assistants

Having teaching assistants can significantly reduce an instructor's workload and enrich the course. In departments with graduate programs, graduate students often serve as teaching assistants, at least for larger classes. Whether or not graduate assistants are available for a course, instructors can improve their classes with the help of undergraduate teaching assistants. These assistants can increase student participation by conducting small-group discussion sections and can serve as tutors, especially for students who are having some difficulty with a course. Informally, an instructor can encourage students doing well in a course to help others; however, such a scheme ordinarily can't be initiated until a substantial part of a course has already been completed. To have an assistance plan in place at the start of a course, the assistants must come from outside the course. An excellent source of assistants is the select group of students who have recently completed the course (ideally, with the same instructor) and done extremely well. More broadly, assistants can be sought among the honors students in a department.

Using undergraduate assistants is beneficial to both the students in the course and the assistants themselves (McKeegan, 1998). The assistants can enroll in a seminar on teaching or directed study with the course instructor; in addition to studying the literature on teaching, they will greatly improve their own knowledge of course material and develop interpersonal skills. Using undergraduate assistants as tutors has led to improved achievement by the students they tutor (Landrum & Chastain, 1998). As discussion leaders, undergraduate assistants have received higher evaluations than graduate assistants (White & Kolber, 1978). Students might find it easier to interact with assistants who are more similar to themselves in age and status. Likewise, students might be more willing to seek help from undergraduate assistants. In general, students have quite positive reactions to undergraduate assistants.

Tutor training on interpersonal and communication skills is helpful to undergraduate assistants (Brandwein & DiVittis, 1985). During the course, weekly meetings should be used to prepare assistants for the week's activities and ensure their understanding of relevant course material. Undergraduate assistants can be useful sources of information about trouble spots in a course and suggestions for different ways to cover material effectively. One suggestion made by the undergraduate assistants for my statistics course was that tutoring sessions were more effective when two tutors worked jointly. They reported that the social interaction between tutors relaxed the students and increased their participation; also joint tutors could help each other with difficult material as well as offering the students additional forms of explanation. Undergraduate assistants can help students with a variety of course tasks, including library usage, computer assignments, and textbook comprehension. They constitute a resource that is worth using.

A PLANNING TIMETABLE

Course planning can and often does continue right up to the first day of class (perhaps the day before the first class day); decisions made after a course starts are called revisions. Outlined below is a suggested schedule for tackling planning tasks that will yield substantial plans at a reasonable pace. The time headings refer to the amount of time remaining before the first class day.

Four or More Months.   Engage in global thinking about the course and prepare to select textbooks and other reading materials. Collect syllabi from other instructors, review and evaluate possible textbooks. Think about the general characteristics you would like the course to have, and what orientations toward course content you would like to emphasize. Discuss the course or teaching itself with experienced instructors whom you admire. The broad goal is to begin forming your conception of the topic area and the course you will teach. Textbook evaluation must be done seriously because an early decision will be required.

Three or More Months.   Select and order textbooks and other reading materials. College bookstores and publishers want considerable lead time to fill instructors' requests. Bookstores typically name deadlines by which they want faculty orders submitted; these dates typically strike instructors as far too early. Nonetheless, I'd advise trying to meet them because no instructor wants to face the "disaster" of textbooks not being available when a course starts. Bookstores want to know whether reading materials will be required or only recommended; they ordinarily will order fewer copies of nonrequired items. It's worth checking that a proper number of copies of required books has been ordered; a departmental secretary or business manager can often help with these interactions.

Three Months.   Begin laying out the course. This is best done by starting at the most general level and gradually working in details. I suggest constructing a small series of course descriptions, allowing yourself reasonable time between successive levels. Remember that this is planning material that can be changed, and changed again, as you continue working on the course. As you include more constraints, the task will become harder, and you might be led to reconsider the more general description you had decided on. Within a few weeks, however, you should have a pretty good idea of the overall look of your course. Here are the levels of description.

1. List the major course topics. Limit this list to a maximum of 15 topics (if your course lasts a semester) or 10 (for a quarter-length course). Listing just two or three is not enough; going over the suggested maximum likely means that you're too ambitious or that some topics are not "major."
2. Draft a weekly plan; include weekly topics and reading assignments; insert exams and due dates for assignments. As a rough guide, assigning about one chapter per week is a common practice, although instructors frequently require more than this amount of reading.
3. Draft a daily plan; name a topic for each class meeting, include quizzes, exams, due dates for assignments, special events (a movie?), and holidays. Keep in mind the probable need to discuss the nature of assignments or to provide feedback; these activities do take class time and are worth noting. If you will be giving three, four, or more quizzes/exams (which is recommended), life will be simpler for the students if these occur on the same

day of the week. If exams occur during the first class meeting of a week, for example, Mondays, students have the weekend to prepare for them. Of course, giving exams during the last class of a week, for example, Fridays, allows the weekend to be used for grading them, if one desires to do so.

Two Months.   Prepare lecture plans for at least the first two weeks of classes. Create materials that you will use in class, such as handouts or overheads. Try out (parts of) your lectures on test audiences if you can find willing volunteers. See if you can arrange to give a guest lecture in a current offering of the course you will teach. The purpose here is not only to develop your public-speaking skills but also to allow you to check your estimates of how long it will take to cover a particular amount of material.

Six Weeks.   Construct test items for at least the first test. Consider both textbook and lecture content. Items for later textbook chapters can be developed even though corresponding lecture content has not yet been fixed. Get a critique of your tests from a knowledgeable person.

Two Weeks.   Prepare the final version of your course syllabus, to be distributed to students at the start of the course. Also, construct any handouts that will be needed, such as instructions for required assignments. If you wish to think far ahead, draft a course evaluation form (see Chap. 11).

The Course Syllabus

A course syllabus is a description of all important aspects of a course, to be distributed to students on the first day of class. It is a form of contract between the instructor and students and should be prepared with care.

Appleby (1994) points out that a syllabus, in addition to providing necessary practical information, gives an impression of an instructor's approach to teaching. It indicates what kinds of activities are considered important, and even the tone of the syllabus might suggest how approachable you are. In addition to describing assignments and methods of evaluation, Appleby suggests that instructors consider the skills they will require of students and indicate whether they will be taught during the course, assumed to exist already, or expected to be acquired independently.

A course syllabus should include the following information:

1. The name and number of the course, the term, and days, times, and locations of class meetings. Although some of this information might seem unnecessary, it is useful to students.
2. The instructor's name, office number, business phone number, and e-mail address. Instructors are notoriously difficult to contact by phone, and

spontaneous office visits can be fruitless or disruptive. Using e-mail allows fairly rapid responses while minimizing intrusion and might encourage students to ask questions they otherwise would keep back; its use should be encouraged.

3. Authors, titles, edition numbers, and publication dates of textbooks and any other assigned readings. Optional or recommended readings may also be described. Where the readings will be found should also be indicated.

4. A week-by-week schedule of course topics and reading assignments. Use dates rather than "Week 1, Week 2, ..." Although I strongly urge instructors to develop a class-by-class schedule for their own use, I don't recommend publicizing that level of detail so that day-to-day adjustments can be made without confusing students. Also, students reasonably might be expected to address the question of what they should be doing for a course on a weekly basis, but except for special events (tests, for example), expecting class-by-class attention might be optimistic.

5. Dates of tests, exams, due dates for papers and other assignments should be included in the weekly schedule and perhaps repeated in their own section. Other special events, such as holidays, should also be included. It is advantageous to make these items stand out visually so that students will notice them. For example, a part of a hypothetical syllabus:

Week of	*Topics*	*Reading Assignment*
Oct.14	Early Intervention	Chap. 7

***Monday, Oct. 14: Second Exam

6. The relations between lectures and required readings and their relations to the content of exams. Also, expectations regarding student preparation for and participation in class meetings should be stated.

7. Description of the course requirements. If a points system is used for grading, the description should also indicate the maximum number of points for each requirement.

8. Any opportunities for extra credit, and their point values.

9. A summary of the grading system, which includes a possibly redundant statement of requirements and their point values or new information about the weights assigned to requirements, plus the way in which grades of A, B, and so forth will be determined.

10. A statement of policies regarding late assignments, makeup tests, and grades of incomplete. Will late assignments be accepted, and with what time frame and penalties? Will makeup tests be allowed, and if so, under what circumstances? If a student will miss an exam, what must the student do to arrange a makeup? Will any makeup be different from the regular exam?

As can be seen, a syllabus is a complex document that captures a great deal of thought. It is the students' guide to the course and provides procedural protection for both students and instructors. The syllabus describes how things will be done in a course, and if that is the way they are done, no one has a valid basis for complaint.

Although the emphasis in constructing a syllabus is properly on clear and sufficiently complete description of course components, attention should also be given to visual appearance. Students should be able to easily locate important information, such as test dates and due dates for assignments. Also, it's handy if the syllabus can be contained on one sheet of paper, which seems more feasible by keeping in mind that two-sided printing doubles the capacity of a sheet. If an assignment requires lengthy, detailed instructions, it is best to describe these in a separate document, rather than trying to include them in the syllabus.

The first day of class should be devoted to giving an overview of the course and reviewing the course syllabus, explaining the reasoning that went into designing the course, and answering any questions students might have. Doing so usually takes most of a class period and gives the students an excellent introduction to the course.

SUMMARY

Instructors mark their ownership of a course not just by what they do in the classroom but also through the many decisions they make regarding the structure of a course. Planning a course proceeds from general issues to details. Course content should be appropriate to the knowledge level of the students in a course. Learning goals include acquiring specialized vocabulary, making theoretical comparisons, applying course concepts to new situations, and developing special skills, and the choice of goals influences the teaching techniques, assignments, and assessment methods to be used. A course format delineates the pacing of a course, how individual differences in learning will be accommodated, and the level of mastery that will be expected. Some methods that facilitate learning are labor intensive, but instructors can obtain help by arranging for and supervising undergraduate teaching assistants. Ideally, course planning should begin more than four months before a course begins. The course syllabus reflects the many decisions made in organizing a course and serves as a practical and intellectual guide to the course.

II

Learning, Memory, and Cognition

2

Understanding Attention and Working Memory

Attention
Working Memory
Long-Term versus Short-Term Memory

The essential goal of teaching is to change students' minds, by giving them new knowledge and helping them to think in new ways. By understanding the kinds of mental activities that occur during learning, the limitations that hinder learning or produce forgetting, and both the obstacles and strategies that affect the use of new knowledge, a teacher is better able to devise effective teaching techniques.

Processing Current Information. The desired effects of completing college courses are long term. Instructors hope that students will remember what they have learned, that students will make use of what they have learned for years, perhaps for the rest of their lives. But, the simple fact is that any change, no matter how long it might last, stems from one or more brief events in which the person deals with current information. Just as a journey begins with the first step, reading a book involves a great many small "acts of reading," and understanding a lecture involves a large number of listening and thinking events. Consequently, the ways in which people process current information have serious implications for the long-term changes that might take place. We consider three aspects of current processing: attention, working memory, and controlled versus automatic processing.

ATTENTION

"Pay attention!" has been uttered by many people in the role of instructor or behavior-change agent, typically when a learner appears not to be acting in the desired manner. What does it mean to pay attention? I focus on two aspects of attention: alertness and selectivity.

Alertness

Our sensitivity to environmental events changes over a very wide range, and fluctuates at a rapid rate. Each of us can think of many examples of such variation—our relative lack of reaction to what's going on when we are "half-asleep" or just dozing off, or how we miss what someone says because we are "distracted," thinking about something we have to do. Daydreaming is a classic example of turning our attention toward internal, mental events and away from what is going on around us.

There are natural changes in our alertness as we go through waking and sleeping cycles. Alertness is also affected by health, eating, drugs, pain, and other physical influences. Alertness fluctuates even within our generally alert phases; peak alertness can be maintained for less than a second (Posner & Boies, 1971). These fluctuations can be illustrated by the effects of a warning signal. Think of runners about to start a race; they know that at some point they will position themselves at the starting line and that they should begin running when the starter's pistol sounds. They want to begin running as soon as possible when the starting signal is given. In the usual procedure, the runners are told to move to the starting line; then the starter says "ready" and very shortly thereafter fires the gun. If the ready signal were not given—if the runners position themselves at the starting line and the gun is fired sometime later with no warning—their reactions to the gun would be slower. The simple warning increases alertness for a brief time so that reactions are quicker. If there is a long interval between ready and start signals, there will be no effect; in a generally alert state, warning signals raise alertness for only a few seconds.

Alertness is nonspecific; it refers to one's sensitivity to any kind of environmental event. Similarly, warnings can be nonspecific—"look out" doesn't name what should be looked out for, but it will increase a person's attention to most any environmental event. Warnings don't have to be obvious, such as "pay attention" or "look out." More subtle indications that something is about to happen can be effective. For example, after a pause, crisply saying "now" will briefly raise students' attention to whatever comes next, whether it is spoken or presented visually.

From a teacher's perspective, alertness is most directly related to classroom behavior. An instructor needs to understand that students' alertness will inevitably vary during a lecture, that students cannot be expected to stay maximally alert for an extended time. Instructors should try to avoid situations that induce low levels of alertness, such as low-volume, monotonous speech.

Instructors can employ various techniques to raise alertness when it is most important for students to pay attention, for example, by giving warning signals. Instructors can help students maintain alertness by providing input with variation—by changing location from time to time, changing the loudness and pitch of their voices, and varying what is emphasized, for example, what is being said, or what is written on the board or what is on a video screen. Students might even be given brief rests (a few seconds, perhaps even 10 to 15 seconds) so they can refresh themselves and then return to class material with greater alertness. With a long class period, a break to allow stretching and "waking up the body" can be very beneficial. Comprehending lectures requires more than just alertness, of course, but basic facts about alertness do suggest useful teaching practices. The keys are to avoid monotony, employ variation, allow brief rests periodically, and cue attention at appropriate times.

Selectivity

The environment around us contains an enormous amount of potential information. Our senses are constantly bombarded with inputs, most of which change rapidly. It is a simple fact that we cannot attend to everything at once. Some of these limitations are physical; for example, one cannot look to the left and to the right simultaneously. Even without such obvious constraints, we attend to only part of the input our senses provide. This is so even though we possess sensory memories that, for a very brief time, hold presumably complete copies of immediate input. It is as if we had a temporary tape recording of auditory input, or photograph of visual input, that is gone in a moment. These memories decay so rapidly that it is difficult to give an everyday example of their functioning. Perhaps you have had the experience of having someone say something to you that you did not quite hear, and just as you start to say so, it is as if you listen a second time to the person's speech and realize that you do know what they said. In typical circumstances, one moment's representation is overwritten by the next, so that only a fraction of the potential information is available to us.

Selectivity is inevitable in processing current information. In any set of circumstances, we are more likely to attend to some things rather than others. There are, in general, two types of influences on selective attention, features of environmental input and our expectations or intentions.

Environmental Influences.   Some environmental events command attention. For example, in most circumstances, moving objects attract attention. If something moves across your field of vision, it is very difficult to keep from looking at it. Similarly, loud sounds and bright, vividly colored things attract attention and are hard to ignore. Loud, bright, or moving things are common examples of attention getters, but perceptual inputs need not be strong to capture the spotlight. A general principle is that those things that stand out from their surroundings will receive more attention. Difference from other environmental features or change from what has been experienced attracts notice. If nearly all the words in a sentence are printed in lowercase, then one word PRINTED in all capitals draws attention. BUT IF ALL THE WORDS ARE PRINTED IN CAPITALS, THE WORD IN lowercase STANDS OUT. If a person has been speaking at a normal loudness level, increasing loudness (shouting) or quickly decreasing it (a dramatic whisper) will attract notice.

These basic influences on attention occur frequently in regard to learning and instruction. Lecturers can induce students to focus on selected aspects of what is being said by using emphasis and other changes in vocalization. Visually, more important material can be made to stand out by making it different from and more noticeable than secondary information. CAPITAL LETTERS, **bold print**, *italics*, and color changes are used to draw attention to particular words or phrases. Perceptual influences on attention can also work against focusing on a lecture; for example, a loud tie or flamboyant gestures might capture attention to the detriment of listening to a lecture.

Expectations and Intentions.   We have just seen that attention is directed or driven by variations in what occurs in a person's environment. But what we perceive and how we perceive environmental events also depend on what is already happening in our heads. In many circumstances, our attention is goal directed. This means that we have some intention or expectation about what we will perceive or the way in which we will encode environmental information. These effects cover a wide range, from simple unconscious influences through quite deliberate intentions.

The way in which we respond to or encode environmental inputs is strongly influenced by expectations or intentions. Imagine a potential buyer and a potential burglar looking at the same house; because their goals are different, they would attend to different features of the house and interpret a particular feature in different ways. For example, a door might be seen as beautiful by a potential buyer, whereas a potential burglar would see the door as easy to break into. The prospective buyer might focus on the oak frame, whereas the burglar notices the glass next to the lock. These influences on what or how we perceive also include inputs from the environment. For example, a road sign indicating that a narrow bridge will soon be encountered clearly affects what we attend to and our interpretation of what we see. A very general and powerful influence on our attention is instructions we receive from others.

In a classroom, an instructor can not only direct students' attention toward specific information but also guide the way in which they will perceive it. If you are presented with a table containing many numbers, the instruction to look at the top row and to notice how the numbers in that row increase from left to right will have a powerful impact on what you perceive. This can be stated differently; if students in a classroom are shown a display of even moderate complexity, they might have no clear idea about what they should do in looking at the display. An instructor who provides suitable direction therefore helps students to attend to appropriate information and encode the important aspects of that information. Instructors might usefully consider themselves as conductors, directing and guiding students' attention toward useful interpretations of important information.

WORKING MEMORY

Short-term or working memory is concerned with keeping information available while we are doing something with it or until we need it "in a short while." The classic example of short-term memory is looking up an unfamiliar phone number and then dialing it. Sometimes, we forget the number before we finish dialing. Because we know that we might forget the number very quickly, we often repeat it to ourselves until we complete dialing, or we might write it down. If we are successful in dialing the number but need to dial it again a short while later, we are likely to be unable to recall it. This example illustrates several important characteristics of short-term memory:

1. The risk of very rapid forgetting.
2. The use of rehearsal to prevent forgetting.
3. The use of external memory aids.
4. The lack of longer term memory even when short-term recall was successful.

It is clear that there is a limit to how much we "can hold in memory"; overloading memory is easy to do. George Miller (1956) proposed that the average adult can hold about five to nine things in memory at any one time. A traditional method for testing short-term memory is a memory span test, in which a number of digits or letters are presented one at a time, after which the person is asked to recall the items in order. "3, 5, 8" is easy, whereas "6, 2, 9, 5, 2, 7, 1, 8, 4" is beyond most people's ability to recall after one presentation. The average adult will succeed in recalling about seven digits or letters; relatively few people can successfully recall much longer strings.

Short-term memory limitations are not limited to special tests—far from it. In listening to someone talk or in reading, long complex sentences are difficult to understand (see the discussion of textbook difficulty in Chap. 5). Such sentences are difficult because they require too much information to be held in short-term memory until enough additional information has been provided to make sense of the sentence.

It's not hard to overload short-term memory by presenting too much material, but there is also a more subtle influence of amount of material. Longer words are harder to maintain in memory than shorter words because they're more difficult to mentally rehearse. With longer words, memory span performance declines and reading speeds are slower (Baddeley, 1999). When listening to a lecture, students cannot slow down their hearing to compensate for longer words, so they're more likely to make mistakes in remembering. College instructors tend to use a lot of longer words, which often are also unfamiliar to students. Lecturers who adjust their speech rate allow brief pauses for students to process what they're hearing; lecturers who repeat difficult items increase the chances that students will understand what is being said.

Similarity Effects.   Short-term memory is also affected by the similarity of items to one another. For short-term recall, a kind of similarity that is very important is acoustic similarity, or similarity of sounds. For example, B, J, S, and U are acoustically dissimilar; in contrast, B, C, D, and T share a common sound. High similarity makes them confusable and hurts performance, especially when item order must be maintained (Conrad, 1964). Although students are not required typically to perform short-term memory tests, they must, of course, complete many such tasks while listening to lectures. If a lecture contains similar sounding items, memory problems and comprehension problems will occur readily. Suppose an instructor introduces a new term that has several similar-sounding syllables or several new words that are acoustically similar—students might well have little idea what was said. These circumstances definitely call for a memory aid, namely a visual record of the new terms, on the blackboard or projection screen.

Chunking

We've seen that there is a limit to how much a person can hold in short-term memory. Earlier, reference was made to a typical limit of about seven items. But what is an item? Is it a letter or a digit as in the memory span test? Sometimes. But as Miller (1956) pointed out, the best measure of short-term memory is in terms of what he called chunks. A chunk is a cohesive unit. In some circumstances, a single letter might be a chunk; but larger chunks also exist and reflect in part the person's knowledge about the material being presented. For example, most people have no trouble recalling the following string of items in order: *dog boat red girl.* Notice that in recalling this string, a person would recall 14 letters, far beyond the typical memory span. The essential point, of course, is that in this case the person is not recalling letters directly but rather is recalling familiar words. Here, the words are the functional units or chunks. Chunking can be produced even in arbitrary ways; for example, we usually don't try to remember telephone numbers as long strings of individual digits. Rather, the total string is divided into sections so that little chunks of digits are created, easing the memory task. Compare the difficulty of remembering 6308471203 to the chunked string 630 847 1203. Perceptual grouping can produce chunks, and a person's knowledge about the presented material might allow chunks to be generated; in either case, the use of chunking reduces the load on short-term memory.

Knowledge reduces short-term memory loads by facilitating chunking. This statement applies even to low-level knowledge such as vocabulary. Students and instructors understandably tend on focus on higher level learning goals, but gaining high levels of familiarity with new vocabulary items is worthwhile. Practice with new items results in their being easier to pronounce (Dominowski, 1969) as they form more cohesive chunks. A desirable consequence is that they become easier to listen to. Time in a college classroom can't be devoted to vocabulary practice, but students should be encouraged to use new terms in class discussions and to use some study time to developing facility with new terms. Understanding lectures will become easier.

Processing Demands

So far, we have focused on simple memory tasks where the person is trying to do nothing but remember presented material. It is easy to get the impression of short-term memory as a container of a certain size, with new items pushing out old ones. But, as Posner and Boies (1971) pointed out, the situation is more complex. The basic idea is that dealing with current information can involve a number of different processes that compete for available resources and therefore can interfere with one another. In simple terms, it is often hard to do more than one thing at a time. Remembering recently presented information is one kind of processing that might be needed—most likely, a person will try to rehearse the material to remember it. But, as in listening to a lecture, rehearsing recent material can compete with attending to currently presented information, with the result that one or both processes will be degraded.

Many kinds of processing might be required by different tasks, and the level of processing demand is important. Here are two examples. First, compare the task of remembering the numbers 23, 46, 68 to the task of adding those numbers "in the head." Just remembering the numbers is much easier than addition—why? Adding the numbers requires remembering the original three numbers plus "doing the addition" and holding partial answers. We would not be surprised if a person succeeded in adding the first two numbers together but then had forgotten what the third number was. Imagine asking a person to multiply the numbers "in the head"—this task would clearly overload working memory.

For a second example, consider the task of comprehending a sentence. One must encode each word but also grasp relations among the words, and also relations among phrases or clauses if the sentence is complex. Word meanings must be held in working memory while attempts are made to identify interword relations. Beginning readers, asked to read aloud a simple sentence, often exhibit working-memory overload. The child might slowly and effortfully read each word, only to have no idea of sentence meaning when the last word is read. Beginning readers arrive at word meaning by determining how the printed word is pronounced; the printed words are unfamiliar to them, and their decoding skills are weakly developed. They must devote so much processing to get the meaning of a word that they have insufficient resources for holding prior words' meanings and identifying interword relations. So their comprehension suffers.

This example has direct relevance to college-level learning. Although college students are relatively skilled readers and listeners, they are regularly required to learn new, often technical words and to acquire new concepts as well as relations of increasing complexity. If a student falters even slightly in generating the meaning of a new word or symbol, comprehension of what is being said about that item might suffer. Difficulties would be especially likely when a lecture is given with a fast rate of speech.

Lectures involving mathematical symbols and equations are particularly problematic because familiarity is low and complexity is high. Suppose an instructor writes a symbol on the board as part of a derivation to be presented. If a student requires time, say, 30 to 40 seconds, to identify the symbol, to think of its defining equation, that student is already significantly behind the lecture and might be lost for a long time. Students are often satisfied when they are able to generate a meaning or defining equation and do not appreciate the importance of quickness. Skilled performance, such as skilled reading, involves both accuracy and speed (LaBerge & Samuels, 1974); as with vocabulary, becoming facile with symbols, equations, and operations is an important study goal.

Automatic versus Controlled Processes.   Some processes occur rapidly and do not seem to require attention or monitoring; they seem to just happen—these are called automatic. For example, recognizing that one's name has been said occurs effortlessly; we are not aware of "doing anything" to recognize our names; rather, the recognition just happens. Other processes are slower, subject to disruption, and require attention and monitoring; these are called controlled processes. Many processes fit this description; in general, if we are doing things that are relatively new to us, or things that seem a bit complex, attention and monitoring are likely to be required, and disruption is a real possibility. Some everyday examples involve perceptual-motor skills: Learning to ride a bicycle or to drive a car, there are so many things to be monitored, and frequent errors occur. These examples also illustrate another phenomenon: With a lot of practice, these activities become more automatic.

In general, automatic processes neither interfere with nor are disrupted by other processes. Controlled processes compete for attention and monitoring resources and therefore tend to disrupt one another. Increasing the automaticity of a process not only makes that process more reliable but also frees up resources for other processes. Many processes can be made more automatic; extensive practice with an emphasis on speed as much as accuracy is critical (Schneider & Shiffrin, 1977; Spelke, Hirst, & Neisser, 1976). Two kinds of changes occur with extensive practice. If processing requires multiple steps or stages, these become compiled into larger units that are less disruptable and run faster and more reliably (Anderson, 1982). In some cases, processing might be reduced to rather simple retrieval. For example, compare the processing required of someone who must work out the answer to "$25 \times 25 = ?$" to that for a person who simply knows that $25 \times 25 = 625$ and retrieves this as a fact, automatically. The first person is engaged in heavy mental work whereas the latter has the answer and stands ready for further processing.

There are clear advantages to increasing automaticity; however, substantial practice is required to do so. Educational settings, by definition, involve new terms, new ideas, new ways of doing things. We should therefore expect students to have attention and monitoring failures, to be mentally unreliable in dealing with new material. One or two practice opportunities are unlikely to yield trustworthy performance. Students should be encouraged to learn basic material, such as the meanings of new terms, so well that they can retrieve the meanings automatically. New procedures should be practiced until they can be executed smoothly. In such "simple" ways, students can become better able to deal with larger issues and more complex processing.

LONG-TERM VERSUS SHORT-TERM MEMORY

In this chapter, I've been focusing on the processing of current information, which includes remembering things for brief time periods. A common technique for holding information in short-term memory is rehearsal, specifically simple repetition of the material. Craik and Lockhart (1972) called this maintenance rehearsal. Although it is possible to create a long-lasting representation through simple repetition, Craik and Lockhart argued that maintenance rehearsal is a very inefficient way of developing long-term memories. Rather, what they called elaborative rehearsal is typically required to create mental representations that will be viable over longer time periods. Elaborative rehearsal usually involves dealing with the meaning of the material, or adding meaning to the material, in general, relating what you are trying to remember to what you already know. The next chapter will concern long-term learning and memory. At this point, it is worth noting that "trying to memorize something," which usually means simply repeating it to oneself, is a poor strategy for long-term success. This information should be conveyed to students. In the next chapter, we consider a number of learning techniques that promote long-term memory.

SUMMARY

Attention and short-term memory play important roles in college learning, most noticeably in the classroom. A student's alertness varies throughout the day and during a class session; variation in presentation and cuing important points help students attend to lectures. Instructors can use visual, vocal, and movement cues to recapture students' attention and guide their perception and interpretation of presented material. Verbally presented information, such as lectures, can be forgotten rapidly, especially when unfamiliar, confusable terms are involved. Moment-to-moment mental processes such as attending, remembering, and comprehending compete for limited resources and can easily become faulty. Providing visual memory aids that remain in view alleviates these problems. Learrning lower level material such as new vocabulary so well that recognition and accessing meaning are automatic reduces the load on working memory and allow more resources to be devoted to higher level learning.

3

Learning and Remembering

The Nature of Long-Term Memory
Factors Influencing Learning
What Affects Remembering?

Learning is commonly defined as a change in performance that stems from practice or study. As ordinarily used, both learning and remembering involve long-term memory because the time frame is on the order of minutes, hours, days, weeks, even years. Over such time periods, people are not actively rehearsing the material that is remembered; rather, they clearly stop active processing of the material and engage in many other tasks. One-trial learning refers to what is acquired through one exposure, practice trial, or study episode. Multiple-trial learning involves remembering from trial to trial as well as acquiring new learning on each trial. It is useful to distinguish changes that take place over time filled with practice or study (learning) from what happens after practice has stopped: What remains is remembered or retained, what appears "lost" is forgotten. So, a person might learn 10 Italian words by studying until all 10 words are correctly spoken when shown appropriate pictures. On a test a day later (with no further study), the person might get seven words correct (retention) while being incorrect for the other three (forgetting). Before discussing the factors that affect learning and remembering, let's briefly consider how long-term memory functions.

THE NATURE OF LONG-TERM MEMORY

Long-term memory is assumed to be limitless; that is, learning something new will not "overload" long-term memory and push something else out. As discussed in Chapter 2, not everything that a person experiences will yield a long-term memory, rather, forming long-lasting representations takes time (at least a few seconds) and appropriate processing. Long-term memories usually are also assumed to be permanent; that is, they are not expected to decay simply with the passage of time. As we frequently fail to remember things we once knew, what then is responsible for forgetting? The general answer is to attribute forgetting to problems of retrieval. The idea is that the desired information exists but it cannot be found on the basis of the cues presently available (Tulving & Osler, 1968). Long-term memory includes vast amounts of knowledge, with many kinds of relations and organizational schemes influencing the chances of completing a connection between one component (the cues) and another (what one might remember). Some theorists have emphasized that memories can be modified by later experiences so that in this sense a memory might not be re- trievable in its original form.

Long-term memory includes different kinds of memories. Episodic memories reflect our personal life histories; these are memories of events that are marked by time and place. Semantic memory refers to our general knowledge; this cate- gory is often divided into declarative knowledge (general facts and conceptual knowledge) and procedural knowledge (how to do things). An implication of these distinctions is that different principles of learning and memory might apply to the various types (Tulving, 1986). It is sensible to assume that different phenomena are emphasized from one type to another.

People will inevitably acquire episodic memories as they go through their lives. The goal of a college education is to increase a person's general knowledge. Much college instruction seems to stress declarative knowledge, the acquisition of terms, facts, concepts, and theories, with a heavy verbal component. But, proce- dural knowledge includes both perceptual-motor skills, such as hitting a golf ball, and mental skills, such as solving algebraic equations. Some disciplines, such as mathematics, clearly concern both declarative and procedural content. But per- haps all courses include mental procedures that need to be learned for thorough knowledge to exist. For example, we can distinguish between being able to give the verbal definition of a concept (declarative knowledge) and being able to identify which examples do or don't fit the concept (procedural knowledge). A person's demonstrating one kind of knowledge does not guarantee that the other has been acquired. This chapter focuses on declarative knowledge; in the next chapter, topics that include procedural components are considered.

FACTORS INFLUENCING LEARNING

What follows is a summary of the results of a great many studies of learning. Most of the research concerned the learning of verbal materials, often lists of words, or word pairs (similar to learning new language equivalents), or text ma- terials more like typical coursework. The general statements offered here apply reasonably to the learning of any type of verbal material. In the majority of the studies, the learners were college students.

Amount of Study

A very powerful determinant of how much will be learned is, quite simply, the amount of study or practice that takes place. In research studies, practice or study time is carefully controlled so that a clear picture of learning can be obtained. The material to be learned might be words, word pairs (as in learning foreign-language equivalents), or some other useful unit. Commonly, a relatively short "basic study trial" is used so that more study means more trials. For example, there might be 20 items to learn, with each item presented for three seconds, so a basic study trial would be $20 \times 3 = 60$ seconds. Increasing study time would mean repeating the basic study trial some number of times, so that we can describe differences in the amount of study in terms of the number of study trials given. Also, study trials might be alternated with test trials that are given to assess how much material has been learned. With alternating study and test trials, it is easy to see the course of learning in the changes that occur across the test trials.

The function relating amount learned to amount of study varies across learning situations. Sometimes the relation is approximately linear, with each additional period of study yielding an equal improvement. Other times, it is negatively accelerated, which means that successive study trials yield smaller increments in performance. Regardless of the specific form of the learning curve, the fundamental fact remains that more practice means better performance.

Here are three comments about this basic fact: First, smooth, regular learning curves are seen only when measurements are averaged over a number of learners. Individual learning curves have this general trend, but with more fits and starts; changes from trial to trial are variable, and one even might observe a decline in performance from one trial to the next. Clearly, most changes will be positive. Second, one cannot take self-reports of amount of study time to be accurate. All of us are aware of having more-or-less studied for, say, two hours, with so much distraction, daydreaming, perhaps nodding off, that actual study time is much less than the reported time. Students might benefit from taking a page from the researchers' handbook, defining a reasonable basic study trial and completing it, then taking a brief rest before another, and so on.

The third comment is related to the material to follow. Having established that more practice leads to better performance, we now consider other variables influencing learning. Suppose the variable is meaningfulness of the material; there would be at least two levels of meaningfulness, say, high and low. There are two ways to study the variable: Either provide the same amount of study for both high and low meaningful material and compare how much has been learned, or establish a standard of performance (e.g., 90% correct) and compare how much study is required to reach that level for material of different meaningfulness levels. It doesn't really matter which technique is used, as the same effect is indicated by either more learning in a fixed amount of study or less study required to reach a specific level of performance. The point is simply to emphasize that to say that some change aids learning means either more learning (better performance) after a fixed study period or less study being required to reach a specific level of performance.

Meaningfulness

Material that is more meaningful is easier to learn. This statement applies at multiple levels. Material that has some meaning will be learned more readily than nonsense material (Postman & Underwood, 1973). In general, meaningfulness refers to the degree to which the material to be learned makes contact with or is related to what we already know. "Meaningless" or nonsense material essentially makes no connection with what we already know. Quite clearly, material to be learned, without being meaningless, might make more or less contact with what we already know. Several points are worth emphasizing: First, a great deal of college-course material, although intrinsically full of meaning, is relatively new to students and thus doesn't make much contact with what they already know. Second, students who have greater amounts of relevant knowledge will find new course material to be more meaningful and will learn it better or faster than students with comparatively little relevant knowledge. Third, instructors and students can make material more meaningful by deliberately relating it to ideas already familiar to the students (Reigeluth, 1983). What can be seen here is that the powerful effect of meaningfulness on learning rate depends on the nature of the material to be learned, the learner's relevant knowledge, and the degree to which connections are made between the new knowledge and what is already known by the students. With respect to instruction, the keys are to identify the course content that is likely to be least meaningful to students, and to relate new material to ideas that students already know and understand.

Concreteness

There is ample evidence that, in a wide variety of cognitive tasks, people perform better with concrete material than with abstract material (Paivio, 1971, 1991). Concrete material has sensory referents whereas abstract material does not; concrete items can also be more specific. The basic difference is easily grasped by comparing concrete words such as car, strawberry, girl to abstract words such as truth, theory, idea. Concrete words are read faster and remembered better than abstract words; concrete sentences are more readily understood. Much college-level content is abstract and thus can be expected to be relatively difficult to understand, learn, and remember.

The essential technique for making abstract material more concrete is to provide examples. To be effective, examples need to be clear and well chosen; they should clearly exemplify the abstract ideas to which they are related. It is advantageous for the instructor to point out how the example illustrates the abstract idea. Here is a simple example to demonstrate this point: I was watching a TV show in which an expert was analyzing a person's office; the expert's thesis was that clutter in an area meant weakness in the related aspect of work. At one point, the expert turned and pointed to a particular spot, saying "This is the power zone, and the clutter you see means that this person will not effectively use influence." I could see the clutter, no problem, but I sat wondering "Why is that the power zone? Is it because it's a sort of work table, or because it's behind the person's desk chair, or ...?" Examples that are obvious to the example-giver can be misleading to the example-getter. Making the connection between the appropriate concrete features of the example and the abstract idea is critical.

Another way in which abstract material is made more concrete is by using analogies or physical models. At one time it was proposed that the brain functioned like a telephone switchboard; more recently, the brain has been likened to a computer. A person might say that a political campaign is like a boxing match, going on to point out proposed correspondences between the two. As with examples, using analogies will work if the analog is well understood, if the analogy fits reasonably, and if points of correspondence are identified. The function of an analogy is to aid understanding of the structure of the new material, so the emphasis should be on similarities of structure (Halpern, Hansen, & Reifer, 1990).

What about pictures, drawings, diagrams? There is evidence that recognition memory for pictures is better than that for concrete words (Standing, 1973). It is, however, difficult to equate the information in pictures with that in words; usually, pictures are more complex. There is no question that certain kinds of information are more readily presented in pictures or diagrams than in words. Similarly, discussion of a piece of music is likely to be aided by listening to it. If three-dimensional relations are important to particular course material, three-dimensional objects displaying those relations will be helpful. Comparable ideas apply to depicting motion. Using nonverbal displays to convey important information can often improve instruction. Because such very concrete items are rich in features, instructors should indicate which features are relevant to the topic under discussion. Pictures, diagrams, and the like also involve organizational issues, which we'll now address.

Organization

Organized material is easier to learn. Many kinds of organizational schemes affect the processing of presented material. Here are few examples. A well-formed sentence is easier to read, comprehend, and remember than a poorly structured sentence (Kintsch, 1986). A logical order of sentences in a paragraph will be more readily processed than the same sentences in scrambled order. Naming the players on a baseball team in order of their positions makes it easier (for someone familiar with baseball) to remember who's playing, compared to presenting the names in a random order.

Organization reflects primarily the structure that is inherent in the material to be learned. The instructor's task is to identify and highlight the basic structure, to emphasize the organization. But, there are also matters of organization that reflect more the manner of presentation than intrinsic structure. Using numbered lists increases the perceived organization of presented material even though lists are fairly arbitrary, low-level forms of organization. For example, if you want to stress, say, three points about a topic under discussion, students' learning will be enhanced if you

1. tell the students that there are three important points they should know about the topic;
2. number the points as you introduce them, for example, "First, ... Second, ... Third; ... "
3. display the list on the blackboard or on an overhead projector so that the students see the organization. For example:
   Topic
   1. Summary of point 1
   2. etc.

There are many instances in which an instructor wants to stress some number of specific aspects of a topic being discussed. The number of points and the order in which they are presented might reflect more the instructor's choice than the intrinsic structure of the material. Nonetheless, providing a simple list structure will aid students' learning.

More complex structures that can be used to advantage are the hierarchy, in which lower level material is nested under higher level categories (Bower, Clark, Lesgold, & Winzenz, 1969), and the matrix, or rows by columns table. Using the latter visual organization is helpful when comparing two or more concepts with respect to a number of issues or features. For example, suppose you are presenting two theories for which there are five points of comparison. Summarizing the similarities and differences in a two column (one per theory) by five row (one per feature) table will facilitate students' comprehension of the comparison.

An important caution applies to the learning of two or more theories or concepts. A theory-by-feature table will facilitate comparison, but we fundamentally want students to learn which features belong to which theory. If a student comes to know that, say, one theory assumes a continuous process whereas another assumes a discrete process, but doesn't know which theory assumes which process, learning is inadequate. To reduce confusion and promote clarity of understanding, it is essential for students to learn the features of the first theory or concept before introducing alternatives.

Similarity

There is an endless variety of kinds of similarity; things might be similar visually (in many ways), acoustically, rhythmically, in terms of what they're made of, how we use them, and so forth. The vocabulary of a discipline might contain terms that are similar in sound or spelling or meaning. Formulas might be similar in the terms and operators they include. Concepts or theories, as noted above, might have similar features. Similarity occurs at multiple levels, from perception to high-level, abstract meanings.

The fact that items are similar, rather than identical, means that, although they share perhaps many characteristics, they also differ. In college learning, it is usually true that the distinctions among items are important to learn. Because similar items are more confusable than dissimilar items, the net effect of increased similarity among things to be distinguished is to hinder learning (Crouse, 1971). It is advantageous for instructors to identify terms, concepts, procedures, and theories that are potentially confusable. It's to be expected that students will have difficulty with such material, and they will be helped if their attention is drawn to the critical distinctions they need to make. As mentioned earlier, learning will be easier if the first item is learned well before introducing similar items. Again, using tables to highlight critical differences as well as similarities will be helpful.

Depth of Processing

To paraphrase an old saying, bringing water to a horse doesn't guarantee that he'll drink. Analogously, presenting information to a student doesn't guarantee that any learning will occur. It is tempting to think that one must "want" to learn, "try" to learn in order to succeed. Indeed, in the typical research study on learning, participants are asked to learn and do adopt this goal. But "intent" itself might not be crucial; rather, the kind of processing that people apply to presented material determines what will be learned.

In a number of studies (e.g., Hyde & Jenkins, 1973), students were shown a list of words, one at a time. One group, the intentional learners, was told to learn the words for a memory test to be given later. For two other groups, no mention was made of learning the words or any memory test. Rather, these groups were simply given a task to do as the words were presented; group two was told to rate each word for pleasantness, whereas group three was told to count the number of e's in each word. Notice that rating pleasantness requires attending to the meaning of the words, but counting e's does not. On a later memory test, which was a surprise to the latter two groups, those who had rated pleasantness recalled more words than those who had counted e's. Furthermore, rating pleasantness and "trying to learn" led to equivalent levels of recall. Indeed, intentional learners sometimes have poorer memory scores than people who are given a cover task that requires meaningful processing, without an instruction to learn (Britton, 1978). Why would this be the case? The answer has two parts: First, meaningful processing aids learning and memory. Second, people might or might not engage in meaningful processing when instructed to learn the words. If, for example, a person tries to learn by simply repeating the words, subsequent memory will not be as good as when the words' meanings are attended to.

Craik and Lockhart (1972) introduced the concept of levels of processing as a way of thinking about learning activities. The basic idea is that learners can treat to-be-learned material in different ways, from shallow processing in which little or no attention is paid to the material's meaning to deep processing in which the material's meaning is focussed on and elaborated. The effect is that deeper processing will result in better memory representations. In Chapter 2, simple repetitive rehearsal was described as a primary means of maintaining information in short-term memory, but it was also characterized as a poor way to establish effective, long-lasting representations. Maintenance rehearsal is too shallow to be particularly effective.

There have been criticisms of the levels of processing approach, for example, the lack of good, independent measures of processing "depth." Nonetheless, the association of meaningful processing with better memory is a reliable finding. Another issue is that there are various kinds of meaningful processing that might yield different levels of learning. Craik (1979) proposed that there are two basic principles involved: Depth of processing, the idea that attending to meaning promotes memory, and degree of elaboration, which refers to the amount and complexity of meaningful processing that is performed. The elaboration principle implies that processing material in a variety of meaningful ways will lead to better learning and memory. For example, focusing on the definition of a word, comparing it to similar terms, relating the word to larger concepts, and deciding whether an example fits the word are different ways of addressing the meaning of a word. Engaging in more of these activities will enhance learning and memory (Lockhart & Craik, 1990).

WHAT AFFECTS REMEMBERING?

As mentioned earlier, learning and remembering are intertwined because learning logically requires remembering from one practice trial to the next. However, practice or study of any particular material comes to an end at some point, and we can ask what will influence how much will be remembered on a test given at some time after study has ended. In educational settings, tests of what one has learned often occur with long delays between the learning episode and the test. Consideration of what influences changes over such delays is important.

Length of the Retention Interval

As more time passes since the end of study, performance on retention tests declines. There is no single function relating amount remembered to amount of elapsed time. The "traditional" forgetting curve, initially obtained by Ebbinghaus, showed that about 75% of what was learned was forgotten one day later! However, such poor retention is found only under special, restricted circumstances (Underwood, 1957). Occasionally, very good retention has been observed over quite long intervals (Bahrick, 1984). Although no specific amount of retention can be expected for a particular time interval, we can, in general, expect retention to decrease with longer intervals. This basic fact has implications for students' test performance in courses. For example, if a student gets a score of, say, 90% correct on a test given very soon after studying the relevant material, we should expect the student to score lower on a delayed test, such as a comprehensive final exam, if the student engages in no further processing of the material. If a student, on the basis of a high initial test score, concludes that he or she "knows that material" and doesn't need to review it, a delayed test is likely to yield disappointing results. Notice that reviewing previously studied material has two beneficial effects:

1. The review provides for further learning of the material.
2. The review shortens the length of the interval between a test and the most recent study period.

These are good reasons for recommending reviews prior to tests. A good form of review is like a test, with students attempting to answer questions about the material. Performance on delayed tests is better when students have taken an earlier test (e.g., Halpern et al., 1990).

Degree of Original Learning

For any given retention interval, an excellent predictor of level of performance on a retention test is, quite simply, how well the material was learned in the first instance. If some people are given more practice or study time than others, those with more study will do better, on the average, on retention tests given at any interval after the end of study. If a number of people are given the same amount of study time, some will learn more than others, and those who learned more will also perform better when delayed retention tests are given. Fast and slow learners do not differ in the rate at which they forget once study ends; rather, fast learners will learn more in the alloted study time than slower learners. Those who learn more will also remember more when delayed tests are given, because they had more to remember initially (Bahrick, 1984).

Consider a hypothetical, numerical example. Suppose that students are given a textbook section or chapter to study, with the amount of study time controlled. Suppose further that, for this material, people will on average remember 70% of what they learned if a test is given two weeks later. The students complete the allotted study and are given an immediate test to see how much they have learned. Some score, say, 80% correct whereras others score 50%. If a retention test were given two weeks later, we would expect the first group, fast learners, to score 70% of 80%, or 56% on the average. The other, slower learners would average 70% of 50%, or 35%.

The strong influence of the original degree of learning on later retention helps to understand many observations. For example, if more meaningful and less meaningful materials are given the same amount of study time, people will learn more of the meaningful material. Later, they will show better retention of the meaningful material. It's not that "people remember meaningful material better"—the forgetting function is the same; rather, people remember more meaningful material because they learn more of it initially. In general, variables that influence the rate of learning will have indirect effects on later retention; whatever leads to more learning will, for that reason, show an advantage on delayed tests.

Instructors often can identify the harder and easier parts of a section of course material. To produce equivalent long-term retention rates, it will be necessary to devote more instructional time to the harder material. Students might not be able to judge difficulty with accuracy. If, in reading a textbook, they allocate equal study time to all parts, they will learn and thus remember less of the more difficult material. Research has shown that many students are not very good judges of how well they are learning material as they study it (Zechmeister, Rusch, & Markell, 1986). They would therefore be helped if an instructor identified the important but more difficult material that will require additional study. On occasion, a student who has performed poorly on a test might say, "I knew that material, but somehow I just couldn't remember it when I took the test." The student's implication is that something happened between study and test, or during the test, that led to the poor performance. While always allowing for such possible influences, a very good bet is that the material wasn't learned very well in the first place.

Overlearning. If learners alternate between study periods and tests to assess their learning, we will see their scores improve as study continues. If accuracy is being measured, at some point a learner will reach the level of 100% accuracy. Overlearning refers to continuing study or practice beyond the point at which 100% accuracy is first achieved. Quite clearly, during overlearning, scores won't get any better—one can't exceed 100%. But when delayed retention tests are given, those who have overlearned score higher than those who stopped studying when 100% was first reached (Postman, 1962). Further consolidation of learning takes place during overlearning, with positive effects on retention.

Retrieval Cues

Remembering something means retrieving it from long-term memory. The likelihood of success should and does depend on the retrieval cues that are presented. This principle can be demonstrated easily with a simple recall example. If asked, "What actor starred in the movie 'The Maltese Falcon'?" some people will give the correct answer but others will not. Indeed, many of those who cannot recall might say something like "Oh, I know that, but I just can't think of his name." This state is called tip-of-the-tongue. If given the addtional information that the actor's first name was Humphrey, some will quickly reply, "Humphrey Bogart, of course." These people were unable to recall the actor's name on the basis of the cues in the initial question but could do so when given an additional cue. If the first question had been "What actor whose first name was Humphrey starred in the movie 'The Maltese Falcon'?" more people would have recalled the correct answer initially. We can see that there is a fundamental ambiguity in asking the question "Do you remember?" The quality of retrieval cues that are presented is important (Tulving & Osler, 1968). The tip-of-the-tongue phenomenon shows that failure to remember does not necessarily mean absence of relevant knowledge. Commonly, people cannot remember something under current retrieval conditions but might produce the answer with better cues. For instructors, it's important to keep in mind that a student's failure to give an answer doesn't necessarily mean that the student completely lacks relevant knowledge. Rather, stronger cues might be needed to elicit what the students know. The influence of cue quality on remembering has implications for testing students' knowledge of course material, a topic covered in a later chapter.

Mnemonic Strategies

Mnemonic strategies are techniques for learning that embellish the to-be-learned material by creating an organizing structure, attaching new items to some well-overlearned knowledge, or constructing a more concrete representation. There are many mnemonic techniques, which are usually employed when learning isolated or weakly organized material, but they could also be used for course learning. Mnemonic techniques often involve visual imagery, which can provide both concrete representation and relational information. Although mnemonics usually improve memory, the effectiveness of different mnemonics varies with the learning task (Herrmann, 1987).

An example of a mnemonic technique is the method of loci. The basic idea is that one must already know, very well, a set of ordered locations, such as a walk one often takes. When learning new items, such as a grocery list or the main points of a speech to be given, one imagines the familiar walk and "places" new items in distinctive locations. When recall is needed, one takes the walk again, finding the required items in their assigned places. This technique as well as others was used in ancient Greece by orators making speeches, and mnemonic techniques have been shown to help college students as well (Bower, 1970). Even simple techniques can be used to advantage; for example, memory for word pairs is enhanced when learners create images that bind the two words together. For example, in an experiment one might have to learn the pair COUCH BANANA; imagining a banana lounging on a couch would likely aid recall. Suppose a student was learning that Einstein is the author of the theory of relativity; perhaps imagining a family portrait of one large beer mug surrounded by smaller glasses would help (ein stein with relatives), if one knew a bit of German. Mnemonic techniques are interesting because they seem to be, in a sense, unnecessary additions to a learning task. Nonetheless, they can yield more concrete, distinctive representations that bind items to one another. Material learned using mnemonic techniques is remembered better and seems to be less subject to interference from other learning (Adams & Montague, 1968).

Distributed Learning

Practice or study sessions might be clustered together (massed practice) or spread out over time (distributed practice). Quite clearly, the distinction between massed and distributed practice is relative, that is, compared to having five consecutive minutes of study, having five one-minute study periods every three minutes is more distributed; on a larger time scale, both of these schemes are closely packed. However, there is substantial evidence that distributing practice over days yields better long-term memory than confining study to one day (Baddeley & Longman, 1978). There are two clear implications of this finding for course learning:

1. Students should be told, emphatically, to engage in repeated study of course material with at least one-day periods between successive study periods.
2. Instructors should arrange class periods to allow for review of prior material with at least one-day intervals.

I recognize that "repeating (in any way) previous material" flies in the face of an orientation to cover the next material. Nonetheless, if the goal is to teach students so that they have substantial retention of course material, reviews are in order.

SUMMARY

Learning is the establishment of long-term memories. Although some memories might be modified by later experiences, long-term memories are generally assumed to be permanent, and forgetting occurs because of problems in retrieving desired information. Long-term memory includes personal history, called episodic memory, and general knowledge, which can be divided into declarative knowledge of facts and concepts, and procedural knowledge, or how to do things, including intellectual tasks. One focus of college learning is acquiring declarative knowledge of terms, facts, concepts, and theories. Learning increases directly with the amount of study. Meaningful material, which makes contact with what one already knows, is easier to learn; any material can be made more meaningful by deliberately relating it to existing knowledge, finding connections. Concrete material is easier to learn than abstract content; as much college learning involves abstractions, examples are needed to facilitate learning. Analogies, models, and diagrams are ways to make abstract content more concrete and meaningful. Organization, at both the perceptual level and the conceptual level, aids learning. Similarity among items being learned, whether new terms or theories, can produce confusion regarding their differences and calls for careful attention to appropriate distinctions. The strength of long-term memories depends on the quality of processing during learning; focusing on meaning in a variety of ways aids learning. Retention of learned material decreases over time, although the rate of forgetting is highly variable. Long-term remembering strongly reflects the original degree of learning, and those who overlearn remember better than those who end study upon first reaching a learning criterion. Remembering is influenced by the retrieval cues available, so that stronger cues can elicit memories that were inaccessible with weaker cues. Mnemonic strategies, special techniques for organizing learning materials and creating personal retrieval cues, aid remembering. Spacing study trials across hours and, particularly, days, substantially improves remembering.

4

Teaching Thinking

The Nature of Thinking
Concept Learning
Problem Solving
Reasoning
Metacognition

The discussion of learning and remembering focused on declarative knowledge such as terminology, facts, and relations among facts. The principles are relevant to learning complex materials, such as theories. However, the goal of college learning is not just to remember some material at a later time. An important emphasis is on applying knowledge to new situations, to solving problems, or to constructing sound arguments. It is commonplace and correct to say that we should teach for the future, that students should develop abilities that will enable them to use the knowledge they acquire. Such intellectual skills involve more than basic learning and memory, and acquiring them usually is not easy. This chapter focuses on these complex processes and how instruction can be structured to promote their development.

THE NATURE OF THINKING

By the time students enter a college classroom, they already know a lot about thinking, probably less than they believe they know but more than their instructors surmise. Thinking is a general term referring to a variety of activities that involve doing something in some sense new, generating an idea that is different from or more than what has been experienced. For example, suppose a student is asked to identify similarities between the American Civil War and the Vietnam War. If the student previously had read or been told a list of similarities, then the student's behavior boils down to whether he or she can remember that previously presented material. But if the student had not received such direct instruction, then the student would be required to think. Remembering facts about the two conflicts would be necessary, but much more would be required. Facts and relations among facts in the two cases must be compared, possible parallels must be abstracted from the two sets of details, and tentative ideas that are drawn need to be evaluated. These processes might be cycled through a number of times. Because of the complexity of thinking, one of its typical characteristics is a delay in responding. We would be surprised if a student immediately began discussing similarities in the example above. Alternatively, we might begin to suspect that the student is remembering answers from a previous experience rather than generating them for the first time. The response delay need not be long, but some delay is expected.

Another characteristic of thinking is that it is often less than adequate. There can be many reasons why thinking might be insufficient, as evidenced by a lack of responses or poor-quality answers. If a person lacks relevant knowledge, there's not much hope. We are well aware that we virtually never remember at any one time all that we might know about a topic; recalling "the wrong stuff" will produce difficulties. A person might use weak methods for trying to find similarities between the remembered sets of materials, or might err in judging the adequacy of a possible answer. The fact that good thinking requires overcoming a number of obstacles and that poor thinking might occur for any of a number of reasons has two implications for teaching. First, the observation that a student exhibits poor thinking about a topic does not necessarily mean that the student lacks relevant knowledge about the topic. Second, instruction that stresses remembering previously presented material is not likely to produce particularly good thinking.

The discussion of thinking here focuses on four aspects: concept learning, problem solving, critical thinking or reasoning, and metacognition, which is thinking about thinking. These activities play important roles in higher education, and they impose special demands on instructors. Indeed, trying to promote the development of thinking skills can produce conflict with the goal of covering all of the content an instructor might want to include in a course. The conflict, which is based in time limitations, will be clearer at the end of the chapter.

CONCEPT LEARNING

Concepts come in many varieties, from concrete concepts such as "chair" to abstractions such as "justice," "gene," or "irrational number." Concepts might be specified rigorously, as in mathematics, or more loosely, as are many concepts drawn from ordinary language use. In any case, concepts are critical components of knowledge and have characteristics that have important implications for instruction.

Conceptual knowledge is at the heart of college learning. The particulars of any case usually are not studied for themselves, but because they are examples of a more general phenomenon. A common form of explanation is to account for the specifics of a case by reference to more abstract ideas and principles. These are instances of conceptual thinking. Concepts allow us to treat distinguishable entities as somehow the same. A concept is an item of knowledge that refers to multiple examples, as in "Canada, Australia, and France are democracies," or "2, 4, 6, 8 (and others) are even numbers." Certainly, Canada can be distinguished from France, yet there are sensible reasons for treating them as alike. Conceptual thinking involves treating entities as similar rather than identical. By bringing together what might otherwise be unrelated entities, concepts bring order to our experience and allow powerful inferences to be made. We use concepts so much in our everyday lives that we tend to forget about the sophisticated thinking that is involved in mundane inferences and generalizations. When students try to learn new and usually abstract and complex concepts, the thought processes are more deliberate and difficult.

Although we often focus on learning or knowing a particular concept, any concept logically implies at least one other contrasting category. For example, the concept of democracy implies at least the concept of not-democracy. In other words, for any concept some things will belong and some others will not—these others will belong to some other concept, which might be given the minimum label of "not-something" or might have its own positive label. So a concept implies a minimum distinction between two sets of things—those that belong to the concept versus those that don't (the "not" category). In some circumstances, both sets might have positive labels, as in distinguishing odd numbers versus even numbers. Sometimes three or more categories might be linked in a conceptual system, such as dividing the visible spectrum into color categories red, blue, green, and so on. The essential point is that concepts involve making distinctions between two or more sets or categories. Applied to education, students must learn not only when to use a concept but also when not to use it.

It's important to recognize that concepts and their names are different entities. For example, "five" and "cinque" are different names in different languages for the same concept. People might use the same terms but mean different things by them, as when people have different concepts of justice. What this means is that they will not apply that term in the same way; there might be other differences as well for the kinds of inferences that might be made. We communicate with one another about concepts by using their names on the assumption that we mean the same thing when we use the same name. The mere fact that someone knows the name of a concept does not guarantee that they properly understand the concept, that they will apply and not apply the concept name appropriately. In teaching concepts, instructors must get students to focus on conceptual meaning, not just the name. This focus affects both teaching and assessing students' conceptual knowledge.

Concept meanings can also be distinguished from definitions, especially when verbal definitions are used, such as in a dictionary (mathematical concepts might be an exception). Verbal definitions are often vague and incomplete; although they give some information about concepts, they can be poor guides to proper use of concepts (see Bransford, 1979). Instructors and textbook writers commonly provide definitions of concepts they introduce, and doing so is sensible. However, knowing a concept's definition and being able to apply a concept are different aspects of conceptual knowledge (Hamilton, 1989); therefore, focusing on definitions is at best an incomplete approach to teaching concepts.

Positive and Negative Examples

Concepts apply to multiple examples, which means both that a concept is more abstract than the examples and that no particular example can correctly illustrate a concept. For any concept, examples that fit the concept are called *positive examples*, whereas those that don't belong are called *negative examples* (or nonexamples). Some negative examples are so "distant" from a concept that they are really irrelevant; to illustrate, "A truck is not a flower." Using the ordinary meanings of *truck* and *flower*, we can see that the statement is true, but it also seems pointless—who would ever consider a truck in relation to the category of flowers? The interesting and important nonexamples are those that are "close-in" to a concept; to illustrate, "Is a blade of grass a flower?" This question seems sensible and might require a bit of thought before answering. Because blades of grass have some similarities to flowers in appearance and typical locations, and because both are plant materials, considering a blade of grass as possibly a flower is reasonable even if the final answer is "no."

Any concept will have positive examples that fit the concept as well as near and far nonexamples. In addition, the positive examples might vary in terms of their familiarity or goodness of fit to the concept, from excellent examples all the way to examples that barely belong. Proper use of the concept requires applying the concept to the full range of positive examples as well as distinguishing nonexamples from those that belong. From this perspective, it's easy to see that effective teaching of concepts must include multiple examples.

Concepts differ in their clarity and structure. Some are clear and, indeed, have clear definitions; for example, a triangle is a closed figure with three straight sides. Others are more vague, for example, *democracy*, and their definitions are likely to be inadequate guides to proper use of the concept. There is considerable debate about different kinds of concepts and how they should be characterized (Ross & Spalding, 1994). In many circumstances, it is useful to describe concepts in terms of critical attributes, which determine concept membership. Positive examples have critical attributes, but they will also have other unimportant or variable attributes. For example, a car must have an engine among other things, but the color of a vehicle is unimportant. Learning the concept "car" involves separating the critical from the unimportant attributes. Even if it is difficult to identify absolutely necessary critical attributes for a concept, some attributes will be clearly important to classifying examples whereas others will be unimportant. For simplicity's sake, "important" attributes will be treated here as critical. Furthermore, even when concepts lack strictly necessary attributes, learners attempt to identify roughly critical features that will aid classification (Martin & Caramazza, 1980).

How do these ideas apply to teaching concepts? Having identified important concepts for students to learn, instructors need to consider the structure of these concepts. What features determine whether something fits the concept? What are particularly good examples of the concept? What are other positive examples that will illustrate the breadth of the concept? What's a good contrast example that seems related but doesn't quite fit the concept? The answers to such questions will guide the instructor in developing a set of teaching examples for a target concept.

No single example of a concept will be adequate; because it will have both critical and unimportant attributes, it can be viewed as ambiguous. The instructor can help students by pointing out why the example fits the concept. Because the reasons are typically quite obvious to instructors, we are inclined to forget to emphasize them for the students, for whom they are not obvious. It's best to start with a very good example. Other positive examples are shown both to strengthen the focus on critical attributes and to illustrate through variety which features are unimportant. A small set of highly similar positive examples can lead to students' acquiring an undergeneralized concept (Markle & Tiemann, 1970); that is, they might treat an unimportant feature as critical and thus fail to apply the concept broadly enough. To illustrate, suppose an instructor is teaching the concept of "reward" and uses two examples, both of which involve a parent rewarding a child. Students might think that the concept is restricted to parent-child relations and thus fail to see its relevance to a different situation, such as employee and boss. Alternatively, if family and work examples are both used, but in both cases the reward is administered by the more powerful person (parent, boss) to the less powerful child or employee, students might believe that the concept is restricted to such power relations. It's effectively impossible to describe all that's unimportant for a concept, so that the breadth of a concept must be conveyed through multiple positive examples. Because there's a limit to the number of examples that reasonably can be shown, it's advantageous for instructors to present a couple of good examples as well as a couple of quite different positive examples to illustrate breadth.

Near nonexamples are used to emphasize what's important for concept membership. An ideal contrast is between a positive example and a negative example that differ on only a critical attribute, thus highlighting that attribute. Ideal contrasts might be hard to come by, but they can be approximated by the instructor's creating a hypothetical near nonexample. Having shown a positive example, the instructor can point out that, if a selected critical feature were deleted or changed, the example would no longer fit the concept. It is also important to present several near nonexamples so that students can compare them to positive examples to identify the critical differences between the two types. Inadequate exposure to nonexamples leads to overgeneralization of a concept because of failure to identify critical features.

Active Processing

It's easy to think of teaching concepts as a demonstration, with the instructor presenting the various examples and commenting on reasons why they do or don't fit the concept under discussion. Indeed, such demonstrations are an important first step in teaching concepts, but students must become active participants for learning to be fully effective. Research using simple concepts has shown that encouraging students to formulate and test hypotheses about the concept facilitates their learning (Dominowski, 1973). In the classroom, after introducing the concept and presenting one or two examples, the instructor should have students try to classify further examples and explain the reasons for their judgments before receiving feedback from the instructor. Early in learning, students' hypotheses and explanations need not be accurate or well stated; the immediate goal is to get students to think about the concept. By providing appropriate feedback, the instructor can correct misconceptions and polish students' language for discussing the concept.

After an initial period of instruction, active processing can be promoted by having students compare the new concept to an appropriate contrasting concept. This form of elaboration of new concepts facilitates learning (Hamilton, 1997). Another effective technique is to have students generate their own examples of the target concept (Hamilton, 1989). These techniques strengthen students' understanding of a concept and increase their chances of using the concept appropriately in the future.

PROBLEM SOLVING

The essence of a problem is that there is a goal to be achieved, but the means of achieving it is unclear. This problem definition implies that many situations present problems, and the implication is correct. In everyday life, we face a wide variety of problems ranging in severity from small and momentary to severe and long lasting and having many different kinds of content. Finding a lost object, fixing a household appliance, constructing an efficient plan for a day's activities, and choosing the way to apologize to an angry spouse are examples of everyday problems. The kinds of problems students encounter in college classes typically are intellectual in nature and reasonably well defined—that is, their boundaries are clear and the adequacy of proposed solutions can be evaluated reliably. We normally associate academic problem solving with courses in mathematics, science, and engineering, but any task requiring students to deal with a new or uncertain situation involves problem solving.

For a task to really be a problem, it must have at least some difficulty; if a person immediately knows how to accomplish a task, it's not a problem. If I go out to the garage with the ordinary goal of starting my car and all of my usual behaviors are successful so that the goal is achieved, no real problem solving has taken place. In this situation, only if my usual behavior was not successful and I had to do something different would we refer to facing a problem. From this perspective, one effect of education can be seen as reducing or eliminating problem-solving activity. That is, if students are given enough training on a particular kind of problem so that they come to know what to do when given such a problem, they can retrieve the solution from memory rather than engaging in more complex problem solving. Such a high level of efficiency requires extensive training, more than is likely to occur in a college course. It's not feasible to give students extensive practice on every different kind of problem they might encounter. Rather, the hope is that students will be able to transfer what they have learned to new related problems. Students begin as novices with respect to the problems they encounter in a college course; instructors seek to make them better problem solvers, but not experts.

Instructors are experts with respect to the problems they give to their students. They are familiar with the problems and practiced at solving them. As experts, they view the problems very differently from their students. Instructors sometimes get frustrated when their students seem unable to solve a problem for which the solution appears obvious to the instructor. But as these are real problems for the students, hesitancy, uncertainty, and failure are to be expected, at least initially. To guide the students toward more effective behavior, it's important for instructors to understand how students approach the problems and what are their obstacles to solution.

There are three general phases to problem solving: interpretation, production, and evaluation. *Interpretation* refers to how a problem solver understands or mentally represents a problem. *Production* concerns the generation or selection of possible answers or steps to a solution. *Evaluation* is the process of judging the adequacy of possible answers or intermediate steps that are reached during attempts to solve a problem. These are not rigid stages of problem solving— rather, they are activities that a person might engage in a number of times during work on a problem. For example, someone who has difficulty generating possible answers might return to the problem statement to see if a different interpretation of the problem is possible. Difficulties can arise in any of these activities.

Obstacles to Solution

When students fail to solve a problem, it's easy to say that they "don't know how to solve it." Of course, this inference might be wrong. Just as we don't always remember all that we know about a topic, a person could succeed in solving a problem on one occasion but fail on another. So inferring a lack of relevant knowledge from failure should be done cautiously. Furthermore, if a person lacks relevant knowledge, what is missing? Is it not knowing the appropriate solution procedure? Or starting the right solution but not knowing how to continue? Or not knowing how to tell which solution procedure to use? Any failure has multiple possible explanations. Those who have taught courses in which students regularly attempt problems on tests, such as in mathematics, are aware that when a number of students miss the same problem, they do so in a variety of ways. Instructors' first inference probably is that a student does not know the solution procedure, and this might indeed often be the case. There are, however, other obstacles to finding solutions.

Misinterpretation. The structure of a problem consists of the relations among the important components of a problem. The description of a problem contains both important and unimportant or less important material, and grasping a problem structure requires identifying the important information. Typically, that structure is more abstract than the terms used in the description of the problem as presented. For example, the problem of determining the number of ways that one can select sets of three balls from five different colored balls has the same structure as selecting sets of three cards from five different cards. That one problem involves balls and another cards, or what colors the balls are, is unimportant for solving the problem. However, novices tend to interpret problem descriptions in terms of their surface features rather than their underlying structure. A problem involving cards is about cards, and so on. Novices have difficulty distinguishing what is important from what is unimportant in the description of a problem they are given, so they can easily interpret the problem in a way that will not lead to a solution. They might include unimportant material as important or fail to include important information in their interpretation.

When given an ordinary problem, experts quickly form a coherent representation, relating the problem to a category of problems with which they are familiar. Faced with a novel, more complex problem, they take time to examine the information they're given until they grasp the problem structure (Ericsson & Hastie, 1994). In contrast, novices tend to leap to action, any action, on the basis of a superficial reading of the problem. For example, given a problem that includes numbers, novices often immediately begin calculating something, without ascertaining whether calculating is required or precisely what kind of calculation is needed. In addition to learning solution procedures, students need to learn how to interpret problems. An important first step is to get them to read problem descriptions carefully. Instructing students to re-read problem descriptions can eliminate a number of what might be considered foolish mistakes (Dallob & Dominowski, 1992).

Another way in which instructors can help students to interpret problems is to include self-descriptive comments when they are presenting practice problems. Ordinarily, an instructor presents a practice problem and shows the students how the problems can be solved. What the students need to know is how the instructor decided what kind of problem it was, what the instructor paid attention to in the problem description. Providing such information can be difficult for instructors because they are so familiar with the problems they are presenting that they interpret them automatically. Nonetheless, trying to describe what they're doing and directing students' attention to what is important in the problem description can be very beneficial.

Problem Size.   Larger problems are harder (other things being equal). Although there is no generally applicable measure of problem size, the idea is easily conveyed with examples. In a mathematical proof, the number of required steps provides one index of size. With respect to choosing a move in a game of chess, the number of available moves might represent size. Imagine a scheduling problem, say, arranging a work schedule so that a number of workers can do a number of jobs efficiently. With increases in the number of workers, number of different jobs, and number of relations among workers and jobs (who can do which jobs, whether two jobs can be done independently, and so on), the problem gets larger and more difficult. Increasing the number of required steps or the number of items and relations that must be dealt with increases problem difficulty (Gagne & Smith, 1962; Polich & Schwartz, 1974).

There are several reasons why larger problems will be harder. The more information that must be processed to reach a solution, the greater is the chance that something important will be missed. Evaluating the usefulness of a possible move generally is harder in the middle of a problem than at the end, and larger problems have larger middles. When trying to cope with difficulties in the middle of a problem, a person might forget the overall goal of the problem or how the current state was reached, which makes correcting errors more difficult and can lead to useless or even detrimental solution attempts.

There are general strategies for coping with larger problems. *Planning strategies* ignore some of the details, thus creating a simpler problem. The idea is to find a solution to the simpler version and then see if it can be modified to solve the larger problem. The usefulness of this approach depends on the relevance of what is ignored in creating a simpler problem—if relatively unimportant details are ignored, then a solution to the simpler problem is likely to apply to the larger problem. So, although it is reasonable to suggest to students that they try to think of ways to make a problem simpler if they seem overwhelmed by problem details, there is a clear element of risk to this approach. Demonstration by the instructor of successful use of this technique is recommended. A generally helpful strategy for dealing with long problems is to generate *subgoals* that represent intermediate states of progress toward the final goal. The (sub)problem of reaching a subgoal is simpler than the entire problem; several subgoals might be identified so that a large problem is replaced by a set of smaller ones. To be effective, a subgoal must really lead toward the overall solution; identifying useful sub-goals seems to be feasible in many situations. The idea of breaking down a problem into smaller parts is used in computer programming, mathematics, behavioral analysis, and other realms. Again, demonstrations by instructors will help students learn the technique.

Motivation. Some instructors' immediate reaction to the topic of students' motivation might be "I wish they had more of it." The reference here is to motivation to study and work on assignments over longer periods of time such as weeks and months. My focus here is on motivation as it applies to a person trying to solve a problem. The Yerkes-Dodson law is a long-established generalization that states there is an optimal level of motivation for any task, meaning that at levels either below or above the optimum, performance will suffer. In addition, harder tasks have lower optimum motivational levels. Problems are difficult tasks and thus are best approached with a low-moderate motivational level—alert but calm. Under stressful conditions, which includes exams for many students, anxiety and fear of failure depress performance (Deffenbacher, 1978). Heightened anxiety distracts attention and elicits competing responses. Cultivating a positive attitude—a calm, reflective, task-oriented approach to problems—can help students to maximize their performance.

A subtle aspect of motivation that is important is persistence, even in the short term. Few problems are solved instantaneously. An ordinary problem will require extended effort to reach a solution, even if the time period is no more than a few minutes. Difficulty arises because working on a problem and not getting the answer (or making obvious progress) is frustrating, a negative experience in itself. Reacting to the negativity by quitting or settling for a quick, weakly considered answer allows escape from the immediate frustration but yields no or poor solutions and bodes ill for future problem solving. Reasonable persistence is a fundamental part of problem-solving skills and is based on the attitude that striving for solutions is worthwhile. Acquiring such an attitude requires some success in problem solving, including experience with extended effort prior to finding a solution.

Learning to Solve Problems

People obviously can learn to solve problems. Furthermore, it is possible to teach someone to solve a problem—to teach someone to complete a task by teaching them precisely what to do in a specified situation. This procedure is followed a great deal in industry and in education; drilling in a specified procedure to be followed in a well-defined situation gets the job done. The problem-solving issue is what the person will do when the specified procedure doesn't work or when the situation changes. A college education certainly includes learning how to do some existing, well-specified tasks. The aim, however, is to have the students learn a more flexible set of skills that will help them to deal effectively with new situations. We want students to learn solution procedures that they can appropriately generalize beyond the examples used in learning.

Unguided Practice.   The simplest way to try to get students to learn to solve problems is to give them a number of practice problems to work on their own. If the students succeed in solving most of the problems, they are likely to learn quite a bit and to be able to solve other related problems (Lung & Dominowski, 1985). The weakness in this procedure is that students often cannot solve the practice problems. This outcome not only doesn't aid learning to solve but actually produces negative effects. People who experience repeated failure in trying to solve problems perform more poorly on later, even easy problems, compared to those without such experience (Mikulincer, 1989; Rhine, 1957). There are several reasons why failure might produce negative effects. People might come to believe that problems require unusual, even bizarre solutions (which typically is not the case); failure can raise their anxiety in problem situations, which will be detrimental to performance, or they might see themselves as unable to solve the problems and reduce their efforts to solve. Regrettably, instructors can create failure experiences for their students by giving them problems that are too difficult, too early in the course of instruction. Trying but failing to solve a problem is not an effective learning experience.

When people solve a problem, ordinarily they obtain some understanding of the problem's structure because this must be done to achieve a solution. If they have found the solution by chance or luck or with only partial awareness of why the solution works, then they might learn nothing useful even though they have solved the problem. Relatively few solutions are really lucky. People who solve a problem usually do learn something about the solution so that they find the problem quite easy if it is presented a second time (Dominowski & Buyer, 2000).

Providing Solutions.   In contrast, giving people the solution to a problem or having them watch someone else do the problem is less effective. When people who've been shown a solution are later given the problem to solve, their performance is highly variable. On some problems they might do quite well, on others performance is poor; overall solution rates are only moderate (Dominowski & Buyer, 2000). The reason that providing solutions is not helpful is that the person receiving the solution need not connect the solution to information present in the problem. In courses such as mathematics and statistics, students frequently watch instructors work through practice problems. Even though they pay attention, students might not subsequently be able to solve the problem on their own. Seeing the solution might not enable them to execute all necessary steps, and they might not know which problem information cues a particular solution step.

In their attempt to help students produce a solution themselves, instructors might try giving hints or providing a part of the solution. A general weakness with giving hints is that they often don't do much good. The hint giver, who knows the solution, sees the connection between the hint and the answer. The hint receiver, who doesn't know the solution, might interpret the hint in a radically different way so that it seems meaningless or leads in the wrong direction. A good hint is one that eliminates one or more wrong approaches, including the one currently being used, without specifically telling someone the answer (Burke, 1969). In this way, the chances of the person's adopting a useful approach are increased. Constructing good hints, especially on the spur of the moment, is difficult.

Providing part of a solution usually will help a person reach the solution but can reduce learning about the problem's structure. Even though the person arrives at the solution, with some help, he or she might not understand completely how the solution relates to the problem and might be unable to solve the whole problem (Buyer & Dominowski, 1989). As these remarks indicate, trying to help someone solve a problem is a tricky business. The helper needs to provide extra information that will increase the person's chances of finding a solution while not providing too much information. The general solution to this problem is to have learners work on multiple practice problems. Initially, if necessary, considerable help might be given so that the learner in some sense arrives at a solution; on subsequent problems, the amount of help can be reduced, eventually to none at all.

Although some benefits accrue from unguided practice and providing solutions to students, these techniques can produce weak outcomes because students don't learn enough from them. There are ways to increase the benefits students obtain from practice. The basic ideas are to increase success rates on practice problems and to get students to pay more attention to how the problems are solved.

Strategy Instructions.   Giving *strategy instructions* that provide guidance in trying to find solutions can increase success on practice problems and thus on later test problems. What to include in such instructions depends on the kinds of problems to be tried and might require some testing to develop effective statements. Success has been achieved with instructions that identify an important subgoal to be sought, but more general instructions, such as to re-read a problem and look for a different interpretation, have also proved effective (Ansburg & Dominowski, 2000; Lung & Dominowski, 1985). To create strategy instructions, it's worthwhile to address the question of what advice you could give people that would help them solve the problems. The advice should be clear and stated as directly as possible; the format "If you (face this situation), then try (this approach)" can help with developing the instructions. It's reasonable to assume that some useful strategy instruction exists for any type of problem. Any instruction that increases success on practice problems will have some benefit.

Worked Examples.   Another way to improve outcomes is to include worked examples together with practice problems to be solved by students. This technique has been studied with respect to statistics, mathematics, and physics in the context of homework assignments given after an initial period of instruction. Standard homework consists of a number of problems for students to attempt; keep in mind that students have access to notes and instructional materials when doing their homework. When worked examples, which show how solutions are reached, are included with problems to solve, students often perform better on subsequent tests (Ward & Sweller, 1990). This effect is not due to different success rates on homework problems, as high levels of homework success are observed in these studies. The situation is not simple, however. Worked examples sometimes have no effect and are occasionally slightly detrimental, compared to getting only practice problems. The key is that worked examples must allow and encourage students to learn something useful that they are unlikely to learn from solving problems. For example, worked examples that emphasize important subgoals are more effective than worked examples without such emphasis (Catrambone, 1994). Ward and Sweller argue that when students work on practice problems, their focus is on the goal of finding the solution. Consequently, they might devote little or no effort to studying the structure of the problem, such as what intermediate states are reached and how operations are related to states. If worked examples make it easy for students to study the structure of solutions, then they are likely to be helpful. But if the worked examples impose a cognitive load, if considerable mental work must be done to grasp the relations between aspects of the problem and solution operations, then the examples are likely to be ineffective. Subtle differences, such as the physical layout of problem and solution information, can affect the usefulness of worked examples. Even though the odds favor getting a positive effect from including worked examples, there is a need to find a format that will facilitate seeing the structure of the solution.

Ward and Sweller (1990) point out that worked examples can be excellent materials to use in the classroom, with the instructor guiding the students through the information provided. In teaching statistics, I have found a variation on this idea to be helpful. Students are given a problem sheet that describes the overall problem and displays major parts of the solution but requires additional information to be filled in. Working one part at a time, students have the opportunity to complete a section on their own and to ask questions before seeing the instructor's answer. In this way, the structure of the solution is emphasized, students can generate parts of the solution and check their understanding, and they possess at the end a worked example. To fully use Ward and Sweller's ideas, the completed solution should be reviewed to highlight important aspects.

Giving Reasons.   When working on a problem that involves multiple steps or operations, the normal course of events is for people to focus on reaching the solution. A technique that has been shown to increase efficiency on both current problem solving and later transfer is to require people to explain what they are doing as they work. Initially, people were asked to give a reason for every move they tried in a multi-step problem (Gagne & Smith, 1962). Later studies have shown that positive effects are obtained by asking for reasons as well as other questions that make people think about how they are working on the problem, for example, "How do you know that this is a good move?" (Berardi-Coletta, Buyer, Dominowski, & Rellinger, 1995). Thinking about thinking is called metacognition. So the basic idea here is that getting people to engage in metacognition—to think about their problem solving (as opposed to thinking about the problem itself)—will make them better problem solvers. The advantage of metacognitive processing during work on practice problems has been greatest on later test problems that are more difficult than those seen during practice.

There are several interesting features of the findings regarding the effects of asking for reasons or other metacognition. For one, people received no feedback about their reasons, which means that no direct attempt was made to improve metacognitive thinking; rather, people were simply asked to engage in it. In fact, positive effects from reason giving have been obtained when students record their reasons on problem sheets that are turned in after problem solving (Dominowski, 1990). Indeed, there is evidence that people don't have to respond overtly to benefit from metacognition; simply asking them to think about their answers to the questions improved their performance (Berardi-Coletta et al., 1995). The benefit stems from problem solvers' engaging in metacognition, which leads them to construct better problem representations and to develop more sophisticated strategies.

This technique of requesting metacognition is relatively easy to put into practice. Given some practice problems, an instructor adds appropriate questions, whether asking for reasons or asking other process-oriented questions ("How are you choosing ..., deciding ..., evaluating ..."). Questions and spaces for answers, to help ensure the questions are addressed, can be included on worksheets containing practice problems. The expectation is that students will get greater benefit from their problem-solving practice.

Promoting Transfer

A minimum goal in teaching problem solving is that students can solve the examples presented and other problems that are structurally identical and very similar to the examples. If the problems are described with equations, a very similar problem uses the same equation but includes different numerical values. Another similar problem might require that the same equation be used in a different way. As a simple illustration, suppose the base equation is $c = a^2 + b$ and the training example is to find c given that a is 4 and b is 7. A highly similar problem would be to find c given that a is 9 and b is 4. A less similar problem would be to find a given that c is 15 and b is 5. Students might not be able to solve this problem as it involves different operations than the example. Of course, teaching goals are likely to be much loftier; we would like students to be able to use the solution "upside down and backwards," to recognize when the solution applies, and when it doesn't, and perhaps even to creatively modify a solution when a situation calls for it. These goals are not easy to achieve.

In studies of learning to solve problems, a frequent and disappointing finding is that learners fail to appropriately generalize what they have learned. This finding can be illustrated with a simple procedure: Students are given a practice or training problem and are either shown the solution or asked to solve it themselves (we will assume they are successful). Then a test problem is given; this problem looks different but has the same structure as the training problem and can be solved in an analogous way. A typical finding is that students fail to use the prior solution in trying to solve the new problem capital—in short, they do not transfer the solution (e.g., Novick, 1988). Novice problem solvers tend to encode a problem in terms of its surface features, the words and other details of the description they are given. When given a second problem with different surface features, they see it as unrelated to the first; therefore, the previous solution is not applied. They are capable of applying the first solution to the second problem, because they will do so if told to try it (Gick & Holyoak, 1983). The central point is that they do not spontaneously transfer the solution.

One of the striking differences between experts and novices concerns the way in which they interpret or represent problems (Ericsson & Hastie, 1994; Novick, 1988). Experts seek integrated, structural representations and are not bothered by changes in surface features, whereas novices focus on surface features and construct piecemeal representations. Novices' focus on surface details prevents them from seeing useful similarities between problems in structure and solutions. To promote transfer and develop useful skills, novices must not only learn solution procedures but also learn to detect important similarities among problems.

Exposure to multiple problems is necessary. Just as no single example can completely represent a concept, no single problem will bring about generalized understanding of a type of problem. Multiple problems, having comparable structures but varying in their surface details, form the basis of transfer-promoting training. Some of the techniques already discussed, such as strategy instructions, including worked examples, and especially requiring metacognitive processing, increase success on practice problems and encourage encoding of more general aspects of problems and their solutions, thereby improving transfer. To these can be added a very powerful technique, namely problem comparison. This method is straightforward, asking solvers to identify any similarities they can find between solutions to two problems. Over a series of problems, consecutive pairs of problems can be compared (1 with 2, 2 with 3, and so on).

Adding problem comparison to practice problems noticeably improves transfer (Ansburg & Dominowski, 2000; Gick & Holyoak, 1983). Problem comparison, in effect, forces a more abstract encoding of problems and solutions because a similarity must go beyond the details of either problem. A combination of strategy instructions, practice with feedback on problems with varying surface details, and problem comparison yielded greatly improved performance on test problems that varied considerably in their details (Ansburg & Dominowski, 2000). Problem comparison is a technique that can be readily applied to a classroom setting; its use would be expected to facilitate students' learning transferrable skills.

REASONING

Drawing inferences, reaching sound conclusions on the basis of careful thought, evaluating arguments and evidence in a logical, analytic manner, are what is meant by good reasoning. We would expect that a college education would promote the development of reasoning skills, and research indicates that this expectation is met. One year of college moderately improved students' performance on tests of evaluating evidence and distinguishing strong versus weak arguments (Pascarella, 1989). A longer term study assessed reasoning abilities of students at the beginning of their freshman year and again at the end of their fourth year of college (Lehman & Nisbett, 1990). The kind of improvement shown depended on the type of major that students had pursued. For example, psychology and social science majors improved most on statistical and methodological reasoning, whereas natural science majors showed greatest improvement on conditional reasoning (inferences regarding causal and noncausal "if, then" statements). In some instances, there was no improvement; for example, social science and psychology majors did not improve on conditional reasoning. The different patterns of change were attributed to differences in the emphases of the various curricula, with conditional reasoning improvement associated with a focus on mathematics.

These changes occurred over extended time periods and many courses taught in a variety of ways, some undoubtedly more beneficial than others. The findings suggest that some positive changes in reasoning will take place in the normal course of events, but they don't provide guidance regarding teaching techniques. There are textbooks on critical thinking (e.g., Halpern, 1997; Zechmeister & Johnson, 1992) that contain a variety of exercises instructors might use as sources of ideas for their courses. Reasoning is a particular kind of problem solving, so the earlier discussion of problem solving is relevant to teaching reasoning skills. There also are special issues that arise with respect to reasoning, and these are summarized here.

Memory Load

Reasoning tasks typically place noticeable loads on working memory because multiple pieces of information must be maintained and operated on to work through the relations needed to formulate an answer. The strong correlations between reasoning performance and working memory measures have even led some to suggest that reasoning ability might be little more than working memory capacity (Kyllonen & Christal, 1990). Of the major components of working memory, the central executive is most regularly implicated as playing a major role because of heavy "data management" demands (Gilhooly, Logie, Wetherick, & Wynn, 1993). In short, it's relatively easy to "lose one's train of thought" in the midst of trying to follow the path of an argument or to engage in less-than-thorough analysis because of competing memory maintenance demands.

Two implications stem from the importance of working memory in reasoning. First, tasks that require more maintenance or processing are more likely to lead to errors. One meaning of this statement is that longer arguments or those including more difficult acts of comprehension will be harder to follow or evaluate.

Another meaning is that tasks requiring more alternatives to be generated will be more difficult. In evaluating arguments, deciding whether a conclusion does or does not logically follow from a set of premises, some problems can be done correctly by constructing just one mental model of what the premises mean. Other problems require two or three different mental models of premise meanings to be completed correctly (Johnson-Laird & Byrne, 1991), and errors increase with the number of models required. The relevance of this idea to instruction is that more complex presentations are less likely to be fully understood by students. For example, in deriving theoretical implications or describing the rationale for an experiment, quite complex arguments are often involved; try as they might, students might not succeed in following them completely because of working memory overload. To make the students' task more manageable, such a presentation should be made slowly, with repetition of key points. In addition, memory aids should be provided, which is the second implication of working memory's role in reasoning. Visual representations of the argument being presented will help students follow the presentation (Gilhooly et al., 1993). Diagrams depicting the relations among the components of the argument are particularly useful. Tree diagrams and matrices are generally useful forms. Also, students should be encouraged to create diagrams of complex material for themselves to aid their comprehension and analysis.

Error Tendencies

Correct responding on reasoning tasks is based on logical systems. Research on human reasoning has shown that people often respond incorrectly. We've already seen that errors might arise due to memory overload. In addition, particular kinds of errors occur with noticeable frequency. Some errors depend on specific content being used and are discussed in the section on "content effects"; others, although possibly influenced by content, have been observed with different kinds of materials and are summarized here.

Accepting Invalid Conclusions. The most common error on reasoning tasks is accepting a conclusion that does not logically follow from the premises provided. Although some of these errors might be attributed to misinterpreting premises or to memory overload, there appears to be a basic tendency to draw conclusions on the basis of similarity or associative relatedness (Evans, 1989; Sloman, 1996). Accepting conclusions because the terms seem to go together is often correct, but it can lead to errors, such as treating a possible or plausible conclusion as a necessary one. Rejecting such conclusions requires more work of an analytic, rule-based nature.

Some arguments, although invalid, are psychologically inviting. Using arbitrary symbols, here's an example: All A's are B. C is a B. Therefore, C is an A. The logical fact is that the relation between A and C is unspecified by the two premises; the conclusion is invalid. Nonetheless, it is accepted by a fair percentage of college students. Seductive conclusions are compatible with the premises; that is, C could be an A—the conclusion in no way contradicts the premises. But the premises don't require this conclusion. To check on the validity of the conclusion, the test is to see if a model of the two premises' meanings can be generated that is incompatible with the conclusion—to try to create a counterexample. Of course, that can be done in this invalid case: The first premise allows the possibility that there are B's that are not A's; C could be one of these B's and thus would not be an A. Students can have trouble generating counterexamples even when explicitly asked to do so (Helsabeck, 1975). One goal of college instruction is to have students "challenge the material," which involves questioning proposed conclusions. To do this, students will need practice and guidance in generating counterexamples.

Overconfidence.   People tend to overestimate the accuracy of their knowledge and judgments; confidence in judgment exceeds judgmental accuracy. For example, on simple tests of general knowledge, when people say they are "sure" their answer is correct, they are right about 80% of the time. Overconfidence stems from the way in which people approach the task. Suppose a person could choose between two possible answers to a question. A thorough and rational way to proceed would be to consider reasons for and against choosing each alternative and select the answer favored by the weight of the evidence. Having done this, even informally, confidence in the accuracy of the chosen answer is likely to be moderate and appropriate unless the weight of the evidence is overwhelming. But people tend to be attracted to an answer and then focus on reasons for that answer being correct—hence, overconfidence. Asking people to list reasons *against* their answer before responding reduces overconfidence (Koriat, Lichtenstein, & Fischoff, 1980). Notice the similarity of considering reasons against an answer to generating counterexamples to a proposed conclusion. These behaviors do not occur automatically in students and need to be encouraged.

Hindsight Bias.   It could be argued that the "benefit" of hindsight is always wrong (apologies to historians). Once one knows the outcome of a particular scenario, it is very difficult to ignore that knowledge in estimating how likely that outcome was—it tends to be seen as the obvious, to-be-expected outcome (Fischoff, 1975). It is an example of using the ease with which something comes to mind to estimate its likelihood, which is called the *availability heuristic* (Kahnemann & Tversky, 1982). If something is easy to think of or imagine, it's seen as likely; if it's hard to imagine, it's seen as unlikely. In the case of hindsight, the outcome one knows about is made readily available, so it's seen as much more predictable than was in fact the case. In addition to promoting regret and blame for negative outcomes ("should have known better"), hindsight bias encourages an erroneous view of uncertainty. To reduce hindsight bias, it is important to consider alternative outcomes and their likelihoods *before* the outcome is known. Instructors often present research findings, which students tend to see as predictable and perhaps uninformative when they receive a description of the research and the outcome. It would be better to present the research and ask students to generate possible outcomes before describing the outcome. In this way, students should gain a better understanding of the importance of theoretical predictions and the informativeness of research.

Content Effects

It is standard practice to describe the rules of logic using abstract symbols, as the rules apply regardless of content. In contrast, performance on reasoning tasks varies greatly as the content of the task changes. The familiarity and concreteness of the material are important; high levels of these characteristics produce both positive and negative effects on reasoning, although positive effects are more common.

When people attempt reasoning tasks with arbitrary, abstract content, they typically make many logical errors. It is important to keep in mind that the reference here is to people who have not had extensive training in logic or reasoning strategies, roughly, the average college student. It is quite clear that people can learn to be very analytical and logical, and to handle abstract content with ease. The average college student has not had such training.

Compared to abstract materials, concrete content is easier to comprehend and hold in memory; in addition, people are less likely to misinterpret propositions with concrete terms. For example, compare "All *x*'s are *y*'s" to "All spaniels are dogs." People sometimes mistakenly interpret the first statement to also mean "All *y*'s are *x*'s," whereas they are unlikely to interpret the second as also meaning that all dogs are spaniels.

Although we would generally expect better reasoning with concrete materials, researchers sometimes have found no improvement (Dominowski, 1995), which has raised the question of what forms of concreteness yield improved reasoning. There are many possible variations of concrete materials, such as concrete terms with arbitrary relations (If the book is blue, then I have ice cream for dessert), unfamiliar rules (If it's before noon, then you must use the east staircase), and very familiar rules (If you drive a car, then you must have a valid license), among other possibilities. There is an ongoing debate over which characteristics are critical, and there is presently no resolution of the issue. What safely can be said is that the nature of the relation between concrete terms is important. Good reasoning is more likely as the meaningfulness and familiarity of the propositions increase. There is a related danger, however. If an instructor uses a very familiar rule as an example, students might follow the argument in that case but make mistakes when a less familiar case is encountered. Using several examples of varying familiarity and helping students to work through the arguments will reduce problems.

Belief Bias.   There is one clear-cut negative effect seen with concrete materials, which is the tendency to accept or reject conclusions on the basis of whether they agree or disagree with one's beliefs, independent of their logical validity. Rather than evaluating the quality of argument that is presented, a person affected by belief bias focuses on the fit between belief and the conclusion. Belief bias is stronger with respect to accepting belief-consistent but logically invalid conclusions (Evans, Barston, & Pollard, 1983). The operative factor is the degree of conflict between logic and belief. If a person follows a valid argument that leads to an unbelievable conclusion, the conflict is heightened—logic implies "accept" whereas "belief" implies "reject." For an invalid argument, however, a believable conclusion will be consistent with but not required by the premises, so the conflict is less. In this way, accepting believable invalid conclusions is "easier" than rejecting valid unbelievable conclusions and thus occurs more often.

The potential danger in belief bias is undue reinforcement of existing beliefs. Rather than analyzing a presented argument, a person who views an invalid conclusion as following from the premises in effect obtains another argument in favor of the belief represented by the conclusion. Of course, the support is bogus. The likelihood that belief bias might be relevant to a reasoning task clearly depends on the content; biology, psychology, and social science courses include topics that might well make contact with students' beliefs and pose problems for some students. Evans et al. (1983) found that belief bias was reduced when people focused on the premises before attending to the conclusion. Directing students' attention to the premises of an argument and to the logical development of the argument should reduce problems due to belief bias.

METACOGNITION

Metacognition concerns knowledge of cognitive processes in general and one's own cognition in particular. We have already seen several examples of the importance of metacognition, for example, that having people give reasons for their problem-solving moves improves both their current performance and transfer to new problems. Metacognitive processes of planning, monitoring, and evaluating play a major role in intelligent behavior (Sternberg, 1997). Metacognition not only aids current task performance but also is the principal means of developing generalizable, useful intellectual skills.

It is important to recognize that, in many circumstances, metacognition is optional behavior. If the task is to remember something, one tries to remember it; there is no explicit demand to think about how one is trying to remember or whether there might be good strategies for remembering. If the task is to solve a problem, efforts are directed toward finding an answer and need not include consideration of how one is trying to find an answer or what strategies might apply to the situation. Performance on tasks of any complexity is better when such metacognition guides behavior; how much people will think about what they are doing and have done varies considerably. Tasks elicit action, whereas metacognition is reflection to guide action.

Helping students to become thoughtful people includes encouraging them to engage in metacognition. Instructors can do this by simple encouragement, by requiring metacognitive activities, and by modeling metacognition for their students, as in describing how they are deciding what to do in working out a sample problem. Subtle changes in presentations can encourage appropriate thinking. For example, suppose an instructor has demonstrated the solution to a problem and will now give the students a practice problem that differs at least a little in surface features. A standard instruction would be "Now, you try this one." An alternative would be "Here's a problem for you to work out. What similarities do you see between this problem and the one I worked?" The latter instruction encourages students to engage in problem comparison, which, we can assume, some would and some would not do on their own. Problem comparison involves going beyond the specifics and plants the seed of developing useful problem categories, which are hallmarks of good problem solvers. For another example, suppose an instructor poses a question that requires more than simply memory retrieval, and a student gives a correct answer. Rather than just saying "Fine, that's a good answer," suppose the instructor added "Tell us, how did you figure that out?" The addition will elicit a metacognitive reply, which will be helpful to the respondent and to the other students; the instructor can use related questions and guiding comments to improve the quality of description, if needed. Through a variety of in-class techniques and homework assignments, instructors can promote metacognition, with the payoff of more sophisticated student behavior in the future.

Comprehension Monitoring.   One task in which metacognition is virtually required for success is reading comprehension. To understand text, a reader must develop an interpretation that sufficiently matches that of the author. At various points during reading, instances of noncomprehension will occur, for any of a variety of reasons, and these must be noticed and corrected for appropriate understanding to occur (Hacker, 1998). Better readers monitor their comprehension more closely, and encouraging students to actively do so improves comprehension. Useful techniques include constructing questions about the material, summarizing, deliberately relating new material to previously learned information, as well as establishing the meaning of any words that are initially unclear. Hacker points out that a student could construct a personally coherent interpretation of a text but still be askew, not matching the intended meaning. A good way of checking one's understanding is through dialogue and cross-questioning with other students. In addition to gaining others' perspectives on the reading material, answering other students' questions is a better test of understanding than self-testing, which can be tedious if done carefully and is subject to erroneous feelings of

"I know that." By reminding students of the importance of comprehension monitoring and describing useful techniques, instructors can raise student achievement and promote metacognitive processing.

SUMMARY

Thinking involves doing more than just remembering terms and facts. Learning concepts provides ways to organize knowledge and categorize new experiences. Learning the definition of a concept does not mean that the learner will be able to use the concept appropriately. Positive and negative examples of a concept can be used to identify critical features and the breadth of a concept. Adopting an active, hypothesis-testing approach aids concept learning. Problem solving entails interpretation of a problem situation, production of possible solutions, and evaluation of solution attempts, any of which might yield difficulty. Obstacles to solution include misinterpretation of problems, complexities due to problem size, and motivational hindrances such as anxiety. Although solutions to particular problems clearly can be learned, generalizing solutions to new problems is often difficult. Problem-solving practice is useful only if practice is successful, and providing solutions might be ineffective. Strategy instructions, worked examples, requiring reasons, using an appropriate variety of problems, and requiring problem comparisons increase transfer of problem-solving skills. Reasoning, drawing inferences and conclusions, can be difficult because of overloading working memory. Error tendencies such as accepting invalid conclusions, overconfidence, hindsight bias, and belief bias stem from processing inadequacies and undue influence of familiar content. Metacognition, attention to how one goes about cognitive tasks, is an important element of acquiring thinking skill; planning, monitoring, and reflecting are essential to intelligent behavior.

III

Implementing Instruction

5

Selecting Textbooks

Content Coverage
Lecture–Text Relations
Rating Readability
Choosing Additional Materials

Textbooks provide opinions about topic coverage for a course; they represent the authors' views of what is most important about an area. Quite clearly, different authors' conceptions of a topic will vary in their similarity to any instructor's ideas about a course. In planning a course, you can read textbooks to inform and modify your own views about what the course should cover. But the most important textbook-task for an instructor is choosing (one or more) textbooks that the students will be required to read. In selecting textbooks, instructors take large steps toward defining what their course will be like. It is therefore important to choose textbooks that are compatible with your view of the subject matter.

Textbooks must be chosen well in advance of the start of courses because of the time lag involved in ordering them from publishers and having them delivered to bookstores. Typically, book orders need to be placed 4 to 6 months before classes start to ensure that books will be available to the students. A highly undesirable situation, one to be avoided, is starting a course with students unable to obtain textbooks. Because textbooks need to be ordered early, and because they play an important role in defining a course, choosing a textbook provides an opportunity to consider the course as a whole.

It's highly advantageous to examine a number of textbooks both to compare their contents and to compare different authors' treatments of a particular topic. How to get copies? As a fast, temporary solution, borrow them from faculty colleagues. You can obtain examination copies from publishers; they will want to know your name and departmental mailing address, the course you are teaching, the expected number of students, and the date by which you must choose a text. You can contact publishers through their local representatives (if such exist) or by writing or phoning the publisher's college division (faculty might, and college bookstores will have addresses, phone numbers, and perhaps e-mail addresses). Most publishers now have Web sites that you can contact and use to request examination copies.

CONTENT COVERAGE

What are good ways to evaluate textbooks? Most instructors first look at content coverage, so let's start there. There might be useful book reviews in professional journals, but often the assessments you want will not be available. Chapter titles and tables of contents provide some information, but at this level of description most textbooks on a subject will seem rather similar. Chatman and Goetz (1985) described a fairly efficient method for performing an initial screening. The idea is first to develop a list of key concepts and major theorists; the list in its fashion characterizes important course content. Items for the list might be obtained by scanning review articles in the area, from more advanced books, by collecting colleagues' opinions, and of course by using your own judgment. Once the list is compiled, it is then used as a standard to which the index of any textbook is compared, to determine how many of these important concepts and theorists each book includes. A more refined measure can be obtained by noting the number of pages devoted to each list topic. By this method a shorter list of alternatives can be identified for more thorough analysis.

When evaluating likely candidates for adoption, it is important to read a fair amount of each book. Although this step might seem obvious, in practice instructors usually have little time to devote to reading much of textbooks that they are considering, which makes it tempting to rely on more shortcut methods such as the topic lists described above and a quick skim of each book. These techniques, although useful, do not provide information about the flow of ideas in a text, which can be grasped by reading, say, a chapter (Dewey, 1995). Dewey suggests that instructors pay attention to which books "draw them in," as such books will be informative, interesting, and well written.

LECTURE–TEXT RELATIONS

In evaluating a text's content coverage, an instructor needs to decide on what sort of lecture–text relation is desired. The issue here is the extent to which classroom lectures will cover material also treated in a textbook. Let me propose a general principle: There is no need to repeat in a lecture what is presented in a textbook unless the material is notably difficult—unless one believes that the students cannot reach the desired level of mastery from the textbook alone. When lecturers consistently repeat what is in a textbook, students learn to skip one or the other—unless the repetition is needed. For example, only a minority of students is able to master statistical concepts and techniques by reading a textbook, so redundancy between lectures and text is appropriate and welcomed by most students. New terminology, such as anatomical and physiological labels, is hard to acquire by just reading (how does one pronounce that term?), so that hearing and seeing an instructor use the terms is helpful. When research procedures and results are described in a text, students frequently will have trouble comprehending them and will benefit from the instructor's guiding them through the material. But in many circumstances textbook materials will not require repetition, and here instructors should do something different, in some way introducing new material.

When evaluating a textbook's coverage, instructors often check to see how their favorite topics are presented (I would guess that, most often, the judgment is that the coverage is inadequate). Although this tendency is understandable, more complete assessment is desirable. Relative to any instructor's list of core topics and judgments of adequacy, a textbook will cover some very well, some less well, and perhaps some not at all. As textbook coverage varies, so does the purpose of lectures. Clearly, an instructor will allocate class time to core-list topics that are not presented in the textbook. When a text provides less on a topic than an instructor would like, there will be a need to complete the coverage. When a topic is thoroughly discussed in the text, an instructor could omit the topic from lectures (see caveat on difficulty given above). Alternatively, the lecturer could present associated material, embellishments, or take a very different slant on the topic (e.g., if the text is concept-theory oriented, to discuss practical applications). Obviously, a text's coverage must be deemed sufficient to be worth considering for use; beyond minimum acceptability, an instructor's options for what to do in classes increase with the completeness of a textbook's coverage. At the same time, the fact that a text gives scant attention to an instructor's favorite topic should not cause concern—what could we be more interested in talking about?

In assessing the content of a textbook, two further issues should be kept in mind. Both concern the degree of agreement about the subject matter between the textbook author and the instructor. First, an instructor should generally agree with the views expressed by the author. If an instructor regularly corrects and contradicts what the students read in a textbook, they become confused and begin to question why they should read the text. I am not arguing here that a monolithic view should be presented; indeed, fair coverage of controversies is required. Rather, I am suggesting that overall compatibility between author and instructor is desirable. Often, points of disagreement among professionals are not relevant to the level of knowledge appropriate for undergraduate students.

Second, textbook author and instructor should generally agree regarding the order in which topics will be introduced. If reading assignments flip back and forth among textbook chapters, students are likely to have more difficulty than if the material is read in the order it was written. Authors write later chapters on the assumption that earlier chapters have been read; the chapter brought forward can thus yield comprehension problems. The likely extent of the problem will vary with the amount of text scrambling that is done.

RATING READABILITY

It is difficult to estimate the difficulty of a text to someone whose knowledge base is very different from one's own. Reading involves a tremendous amount of inference making, much of it automatic, so that we are frequently unaware of how much "filling in" we are doing in comprehending what we read. The relevant point is that an instructor, in examining a text for possible use, might find the text easy to read and be unaware of how much background knowledge is required to readily comprehend the material. It would be helpful to have a sample of students with appropriate backgrounds read text samples and provide readability information (Quereshi & Buchkoski, 1979), but this option is seldom available to instructors. There are some relatively efficient procedures that can be used to give some idea of how difficult a text will be for students to read. Most are best applied to several samples of text from different parts of the book.

Traditional measures of text difficulty focus on word length and sentence length, to which one could add paragraph length. In quickly measuring word length, concentrate on the content words (ignoring *and*, *the*, *but* and the like). Longer words also tend to be less familiar (Zipf's Law) and are harder to read. When more obscure words are used, students are less likely to understand them, and, regrettably, few of us read with careful monitoring of our comprehension and a dictionary at the ready. A certain amount of technical language is inevitable in writing a textbook; however, excessive use of jargon or using longer, less frequent words when shorter, familiar words will do the job just creates difficulties.

Longer sentences are also harder to comprehend, especially those that require a reader to hold substantial information in working memory while reading until encountering the items that make the material make sense (rather like this one). Paragraphs involve connections among sentences to construct paragraph meaning; long paragraphs can increase the difficulty of "getting the point."

Calculating the length of content words, sentence length, and paragraph length for several samples of a text can be done quickly and will provide a rough idea of text difficulty. Another way to get a general idea of readability is to have someone read a sample of text aloud and watch for hesitations, unintended pauses and stops, running out of breath, and stumbling/backtracking. These are all indicators of the reader's encountering some kind of complication. Because textbooks go through copyediting prior to publication, differences among texts on these measures might not be large.

Other indicators of textbook readability can be obtained with a bit more attention to content. In addition to presenting information, textbook authors should help students to attend to and understand important material; greater use of pedagogical aids makes a textbook less difficult to read (Griggs, 1999). New terms should be clearly defined when introduced, and it helps to draw attention to them with highlighting. Abstract material is hard to comprehend. A great deal of college-level material involves abstract concepts, so that presenting more concrete examples will help. Mathematical content is extremely abstract, and what matters is the extent to which the author "talks about" symbols, formulas, and procedures. Again, examples are important.

Students can be helped to grasp the organization of material through lists, tables, and graphs. These visual aids need to be discussed in the text itself to direct readers' attention and aid interpretation. At a more global level, chapter summaries can help readers gain an overall interpretation of the material, both as preview and review. These ideas can be summarized in a list of questions that you can apply to textbooks (They imply "yes" or "no" answers but the real meaning is typically "to what extent?"):

- Are chapter summaries provided?
- Are new terms highlighted when introduced?
- Are new terms clearly defined?
- Are examples of new concepts provided?
- Are formulas described in the text?
- Are symbols clearly explained?
- Are procedural steps described?
- Are worked-out examples provided?
- Are tables and graphs presented?
- Are these discussed in the text?

Another indicator of textbook difficulty is the frequency of citations of source materials. Such references are indicated by footnotes or, as in the style of the American Psychological Association, inclusion of the source author's name and year of publication. For example: "Giving more complete feedback has not always been found to improve performance (Smith & Jones, 1995)." The density of citations reflects the level of writing; professional journal articles have the highest frequency of source citations, whereas something written for the general public might have none at all. Professional-level publications deal with details and nuances, and require citations for use by their professional readership. Writing directed to more general audiences contains broader, "safer" statements, and close referencing isn't needed. Undergraduate textbooks should fall somewhere between professional publications and the general press. Books for introductory courses would be expected to have less-dense citations than books for advanced courses. In a basic way, citations disrupt the flow of sentences and paragraphs; professionals get used to the inclusion of citations (and are often quite interested in them). The density of citations also is an indicator of the level of detail and complexity that is likely to be found in the text. As these increase, so do the required background knowledge and reading difficulty.

Reading difficulty is also increased by including descriptions of research procedures. Textbooks that frequently present research procedures and findings are also likely to have high citation densities; both reflect the author's intention to discuss details and complexities. Describing research procedures is not easy; an adequate account might require more words and more details than the writer deems necessary. This issue is again a matter of adjusting for differences in familiarity; in my opinion, the adjustment is usually insufficient. If a textbook often describes research, expect the students to have some difficulty with comprehension.

The purpose of examining these indicators of readability is not to then select the simplest, easiest textbook for use in a course. Just as a textbook can be too complex and difficult for the students in a course, a textbook can also be too simple. The goal is to select a textbook that is reasonable to require students to read, and for instructors to be aware of how often and where students are likely to need help with textbook material. In addition to providing classroom coverage of difficult textbook material, instructors can improve students' experience with any textbook by giving students explicit guidance regarding how to read the textbook (Schallert, Alexander, & Goetz, 1985).

CHOOSING ADDITIONAL MATERIALS

Non-textbook reading materials might be employed for any of several reasons. For courses that include emphasis on learning procedural skills, such as statistics, workbooks providing examples and practice problems often accompany textbooks and can serve as learning materials. More generally, workbooks usually are intended to provide examples of concepts and to allow students to check their understanding. Another kind of supplementary reading is a casebook or collection of articles providing examples of concepts discussed more abstractly in a textbook. The goal of such publications is to present readily understood examples in some detail or to show the relevance of course concepts to everyday life. One would expect such material to be easier to read than the "average" textbook, although an instructor could use the material as the basis for assignments of any level of difficulty.

A different sort of supplement is a set of readings that represent a higher level treatment of course topics than is provided by the textbook. Reprints of journal articles are one common form of supplement. The purpose of using such material is to have the students confront greater complexity, at least for some course topics.

A question that needs to be addressed concerning nontextbook readings is whether they should be required, or associated with extra-credit projects, or merely recommended. There are no simple answers to this question; rather, the answers depend on the instructor's goals for a course. A few general remarks can, however, be offered. Recommended readings describe opportunities for personal enrichment about relevant topics but will play no real role in a course. Requiring students to read materials that are above their current level of knowledge and training is unfair unless instruction is provided to guide and support students' reading of such higher level sources. All extra-credit assignments rest on the assumption that the activity in question is worthwhile and relevant to the course but, for some reason or another, should not be required of all students. Reading more detailed, higher level sources fits the description, and because no course can possibly cover all that is relevant to a topic, so does reading material that broadens students' exposure to an area. Magazine and newspaper articles can be the basis of effective extra-credit assignments, as can books or articles dealing with relevant topics that do not receive textbook coverage.

SUMMARY

The textbook(s) for a course should cover a high percentage of the topics deemed important by the instructor, in a manner that is appropriate to the level of the course and compatible with the instructor's approach to course content. The choice of a textbook is influenced by the desired amount of overlap between textbook and lectures. Estimating the difficulty level of a textbook for students is an important but difficult task. Basic measures such as word length and sentence length give some idea of text difficulty. Pedagogical aids such as chapter summaries, clear definitions of new terms, ample use of examples, and relevant illustrations make textbooks easier to understand. Detailed descriptions of research procedures and results increase difficulty and might well call for lecture reinforcement of such textbook material. Giving students guidance about how to read the textbook is also beneficial.

6
Lectures and Discussions

Lecture Preparation
Lecture Delivery
Discussions
Good Teachers

A major theme of this book is that teaching involves many different activities—selecting textbooks, constructing exams, creating assignments, and the like. Nonetheless, when people usually think of teaching, they are referring to the instructor's behavior in the classroom. There is no question that what instructors do in the classroom is important, both for how they will be viewed by students and for their own sense of their teaching skills. Quite obviously, students can acquire information about a subject in several ways—they can read a book or article, watch a film or videotape, or use a computer in a number of ways. What sets apart classroom instruction from other techniques is that it is personal. When a student sits listening to lectures, asking or answering a question, or getting feedback from an instructor, an interpersonal exchange takes place. From a different perspective, the most direct way for an instructor to put his or her personal stamp on a course is by means of what happens in the classroom.

Although a lecture could be nothing more than a speech that, in principle, could be videotaped in a studio, adopting this approach for classroom lectures is a mistake. Compared to making videotapes, the great advantage a lecturer has is the opportunity to get feedback from the students so that the presentation of course material can be adjusted for greater effectiveness. Quite obviously, the amount of student participation can vary over a wide range, reaching a maximum when classroom activity consists of student discussion with perhaps little or no direct involvement by the instructor. In the material to follow, I will assume that a "lecture" involves at least some interaction between students and the instructor, but that the instructor does most of the talking. Class sessions (or parts of sessions) in which student participation is the major activity will be treated as discussions.

LECTURE PREPARATION

In Chapter 1, I recommended constructing a day-to-day course plan with the understanding that the plan is likely to require adjustment as a course goes along.

The overall course plan will identify a topic for a class session; preparing the lecture for a class is expanding the course plan to a greater level of detail. To the extent that the day-to-day topic plan is considered fixed, lectures must then be adapted to the amount of class time that has been allocated to a topic. If a topic is allocated one class period, the instructor must then decide how to treat that topic, what to say about it, within the temporal confines of a class period. Conversely, if an instructor wants to present enough material about a topic to take up several class periods, then other topics must receive less coverage.

What happens frequently is that an instructor intends to present, in a single class period, more material than can be covered within the time limit. Each time this happens, the instructor faces a choice: Should the material that wasn't covered today be dropped or be covered next time (requiring a modification of the topic plan)? Perhaps a compromise solution can be effected—"I'll cover just one left-over point next time and cut a little from the next topic (what to cut?)." A series of adjustments can make a course as delivered be quite different from the course as originally intended. Making changes in course plans is not intrinsically a disaster and can lead to a course being better. Nonetheless, frequently having to make adjustments in a course plan is a situation that instructors might usefully try to avoid—they have enough to do!

With respect to the decision to either drop the material that wasn't covered or carry it over to next time, there is no simple solution. Clearly, the relative importance of one subset of course material compared to another must be considered. Other things being equal, I would tilt in favor of dropping uncovered material, or more creatively, providing the information in a way that doesn't consume (much) class time, such as in a handout. The reason for this "tilt" is to minimize the need to modify students' expectations about what the course will cover and when exams will occur. "Carrying over" material to the next class can lead to progressively falling further behind the intended schedule such that, at some point, a drastic modification of the course plan is required.

In my graduate seminar on teaching, the prospective instructors had to give several practice lectures. In addition to giving the student-teachers opportunities to practice public speaking and to get constructive feedback about their performances, the practice lectures also served the purpose of developing the students' ability to estimate more accurately how much material they could cover in a fixed amount of time. Most often, they had more material than time. Despite the teacher's nightmare of "running out of material," running out of time is much more likely. Making good estimates of what reasonably can be covered in a class period is a key to smooth-running classes and better sleep.

How Much Material?

As a rule of thumb, I recommend planning to cover three main points about a topic in a one-hour (usually, 50-minute) class. A main point in this context is at the level immediately below the topic for the day. For example, suppose I plan to give an introductory lecture on cognitive neuropsychology ("mind and brain"), and an outline (through two levels) of that lecture looks like this:

Cognitive Neuropsychology
1. Main components of the brain
2. Ways of studying brain and behavior
3. Memory—using amnesia to understand memory
4. Language—what deficits tell us

Of course, there would be further entries under each of the four main headings. My prediction is that it is not likely that I'd be able to cover the four points in a 50-minute lecture. If I dropped one point, the chances of having enough time will be much greater. Quite obviously, I could take steps to assure covering all four points by talking faster, whipping through the material, neither asking or accepting any questions, but what's the purpose of doing that? As an instructor, my goal is to have students learn the material I present, which means presenting the material at a pace that they can understand, checking to see if my presentation is "getting through," and allowing at least some questions so that students' comprehension can be aided. From this perspective, if I'm limited to one 50-minute period, one of the four main points "has to go."

There is unquestionably some slippage in my rule-of-thumb—that's what a rule-of-thumb is like! If, for example, I had 10 points I want to cover under each main heading, I might not be able to finish two in a class period. If I had only a few things to say about each main point (which I think is generally unlikely), perhaps I could cover all four. Think of the first draft of a lecture as "what I might present about this topic," to be shaped and polished into "what I will present." Reworking a lecture plan is very useful to instructors because they must think about what is more and less important about a topic within the context of a course.

Using the above example, which of the four main points "should" I drop? It seems hard to skip "main components of the brain"—unless that's been covered before and all I need to do is remind the students of a few things and show them a slide depicting the components I'll be referring to. If so, number one is gone as a main point that will take substantial time, and I'm free to concentrate on the remaining three. Alternatively, maybe "ways of studying brain and behavior" is too much for my course, especially if I'd be discussing methods that won't be referred to again. On the "third hand," if memory and language are just examples of brain-cognition relations, I might use just one. How to choose? One might be a better example, or easier to describe and comprehend. However, are two examples better than one (general answer=yes)? In that case, especially if they illustrate brain-cognition relations in different ways, I'll keep them both, and something else has to be cut. The essential point of this thought experiment is that, regardless of how I alter the lecture outline, I will have done some good thinking about the topic, and I'm likely to give a good presentation.

What to Write Out and Take to Class

Instructors with inordinate self-confidence might be able to walk into a classroom without any lecture notes, but I've never known anyone who even tried to do so. Some instructors write out the complete text of what they intend to say, and this technique has even been recommended by some authors. I believe that doing so is a mistake.

Why would an instructor want to write out the complete text of a lecture? Especially when one considers that preparing complete text is very time-consuming. A likely reason is fear. If a lecturer is afraid of forgetting what to say, of hesitating, hemming and hawing, written-text lecture notes can seem to be a kind of security blanket. In fact, complete-text lecture notes can be a poor aid when seeking guidance about what to say next because the excessive amount of text makes finding any particular item more difficult. Another possible reason is a desire for precision, wanting to be sure to say the right things. This concern is misdirected because the focus is on "the words" whereas the real meat of a lecture is the ideas that are conveyed, and all or nearly all ideas can be, and often need to be, stated in more than way. There is, of course, the need to define and use technical terms accurately, so including definitions of such terms in lecture notes makes sense. But definitions, probably excluding those stated in mathematical language, allow paraphrasing. Furthermore, recording careful definitions does not require the full text of a lecture—dictionaries typically do not use complete sentences. Finally, preparing and taking to class the complete text of a lecture encourages reading the lecture to the students. Anyone who has listened to "read" lectures or convention papers knows that such presentations, with extremely rare exceptions, are deadly dull and difficult to comprehend. The reasons are numerous— monotone, a speech rate that's too fast, lack of eye contact, and others.

The most useful lecture notes constitute an augmented outline. A hierarchical outline is the base, with main points, subtopics, and related points subsumed under these. The outline is amplified by definitions, perhaps equations, graphs, and phrases that summarize the points to be made in the lecture. The amount of detail to include will depend on the material itself and on the instructor's familiarity and confidence with the material. When a lecture is given for the first time, more detail—more memory aids—might be included. After a lecturer has some experience presenting a given topic, revised lecture notes might be less detailed, for example, with single words or shorter phrases being sufficient replacements of earlier, longer notes. Typically, sentences are not needed. The idea is to prepare lecture notes that focus on the content and let the language that is used to present that content be developed, "on line," when the lecture is given.

Although much of what will be said in a lecture can be left out of lecture notes, a class of items that deserves careful preparation is *examples*. If the examples are quantitative, it is advantageous to "do the math" in advance to ensure accuracy when the example is presented in class. More generally, concrete examples of abstract concepts need to be crafted so that they are good examples. Any example has both features that are central to the concept being exemplified and features that are peculiar to the example but irrelevant to the concept. If, say, one uses a mother-daughter interaction as an example of a power struggle, there will be aspects of mother-daughter relations that students might think are important but which are irrelevant to the idea of a power struggle. It is important to think about what needs to be pointed out as relevant and irrelevant when the example is presented. As discussed in Chapter 4, multiple examples typically are needed to help students identify relevant and irrelevant features and to generalize the concept appropriately. Selecting or constructing two or three examples in advance will result in an improved presentation.

In addition to preparing an augmented outline of a lecture, critical definitions, equations, and examples, instructors need to work out everything that will be shown or given to the students. These materials include overheads and handouts. The use of these aids will be discussed shortly.

Paper and pencil, or keyboard?   To a degree, whether one literally writes out lecture notes or uses a word-processing program is a matter of taste. Creating lecture notes on a computer has two clear advantages: Computer print is easier to read than virtually any handwriting, including one's own, and keeping lecture notes in computer files makes it easier to modify them. Anything that will be shown to the students is better prepared on a computer, using a font size that will be easy to read. Word-processing packages also include options for drawing and creating graphs, which allows excellent illustrations to be prepared.

Rehearsal

What will I say in class? This is the natural question to address prior to a class period. This question is considered in preparing lecture materials to be taken to the class. Beyond that preparation, it is useful to rehearse the upcoming class "in one's head." The idea is not trying to memorize precisely what will be said, but thinking about the main points to be covered and what one would like to stress. Giving parts of the lecture to oneself is fine, subvocally or aloud, if circumstances permit. However, the focus should be on mental rehearsal rather than on the specific words to be uttered. I have found that imaginally "running through" at least the initial parts of a lecture on the way to work is quite helpful. Even more important is to set aside 10 to 15 minutes immediately prior to a class period to skim lecture notes, check all materials needed for the class, and reflect on the main points to get across. Then it's time to go to class and do it!

LECTURE DELIVERY

Being in front of a room full of students is an exciting opportunity. The students have signed up to learn something about the topic of the course, and every class session is a chance to fulfill their probably vague expectations, to increase their knowledge and understanding, and to shape the way they think about the topic at hand. If that description seems too optimistic, I suggest an attitude change. New instructors frequently have the perception, possibly affected by their experiences as teaching assistants, that undergraduate students are dull, disinterested, and disappointing. I think that this perception stems from informally comparing undergraduates to themselves, graduate students they know, and perhaps even (unconsciously) their professors. Anyone who finds himself or herself in the position of instructor must have been a top-of-the-line undergraduate student and must have an unusually strong interest in the subject matter. In short, compared to the vast majority of undergraduates an instructor will encounter, instructors are peculiar! Most of the students in an introductory course are not going to major in that subject. Most of the undergraduate majors in any department (with perhaps a few exceptions) are probably not intending to go to graduate school in that area of study. In short, the background knowledge, orientation, and goals of most undergraduates are different from those of their instructors. Students are not as interested in the course topic as the instructor is and, of course, they know far less about it. Undergraduates might well be intimidated by the topic of a course, and they are likely to be intimidated by the instructor because of the huge status difference combined with the perceived knowledge difference. As a consequence, undergraduate students tend to be passive in classes. Such passivity does not mean that they do not want to learn. By far, students prefer learning when they are in class to spending time and not learning; they just might not express that preference in ways that instructors readily recognize. If instructors assume that their students, unresponsive though they might be, do want to learn, and then challenge the students to learn and try to help them do so, classes become more productive and more enjoyable.

Keep in mind that by "lecture" I mean an interactive session in which the instructor does most of the talking. There are many aspects to instructors' behavior and their effects on students' behavior and learning. "Tips" about what to do when lecturing properly stem from what we know about attention, memory, learning, and thinking, as well as interpersonal relations. For coherent presentation, I will discuss various facets of lecturing in different sections. In an actual classroom, these features are thoroughly intertwined.

Overview

A good way to begin a class is by reviewing material from the previous class. The review provides an opportunity for distributed learning, which will improve long-term retention. Casting the review as a brief quiz (which may or may not count toward grades) encourages active processing by the students and allows their comprehension and memory to be assessed, by themselves and perhaps also the instructor. A three-questions-and-answers review could be completed in 10 minutes. A less-formal review, with questions posed publicly for anyone to answer, might take less time. A no-question review of main points by the instructor is likely to take the least time. Of course, the more time-efficient the review is, the less processing the students engage in. Many instructors do not employ reviews because they do not want to allocate class time to "old" material that otherwise could be devoted to new material. Their concern is understandable, but it does not diminish the fact that a start-of-class review is an excellent instructional device. Spaced reviews and the use of paraphrasing aid learning class material (Glover & Corkhill, 1987).

When introducing new material, it is a good idea to provide a brief outline. Think of describing the (three) main points; include brief remarks about how the new material relates to what has been covered previously. The introduction can be used to focus students on what they should learn about the day's topic ("Pay particular attention to ... "). Presenting an intriguing question or vivid example captures students' attention; of course, the lecture should provide a reasonable answer or explanation. Introductions need take no more than a couple of minutes; they can aid learning of lecture content and certainly give students an idea of how the lecture will develop.

When the main portion of a lecture is finished, ideally a brief recap would follow. The recap might include a restatement of major points, asking a few questions, or taking students' questions about the class. Frequently, instructors run out of time before any type of recap might be initiated. If feasible, encouraging students to ask their questions immediately after class will help at least a few of them. If forced to choose between an end-of-class recap and a start-of-the-next-class review, I'd recommend the review, as the delay between initial presentation and review should make the technique more effective.

Establishing Rapport. Everything works better in a classroom when students and instructors get along well. Students respond better when they perceive the instructor as interested in their learning and academic progress. That perceived interest could be general, that is, "The prof is really trying to help us learn this stuff," but rapport is improved when instructors are seen to recognize that students are individuals as well as parts of a group. One way for instructors to do this is by trying to learn the students' names. Addressing students by name makes them feel more accepted and can increase their willingness to expend effort for a course.

Walker (1980) suggested that a good way to put names to faces is to take a "class picture" at the start of a course, make a xerox copy of the print, and have students write their names near or on their pictures. Walker took the labeled print to class, glanced at it periodically, such as just before each class session, and found that he could recall about 90% of students' names after a few sessions, and there were 110 students in the class! Short of using a photographic memory aid, there are other ways to try to learn students' names: Having students each provide an interesting fact about themselves, encouraging them to make brief visits to the instructor's office early in the term "just to chat," and asking students to say their names when talking with the instructor, for example, after class, are all schemes for increasing the instructor's ability to identify individual students. Creating a small assignment to be returned to the students early in the term provides an opportunity to associate names with faces. Making the effort to learn students' names will be appreciated by them and makes teaching more fun for the teacher.

Presentation Skills

Lecturing has a lot in common with acting (Harris, 1977). The teacher stands in front of a classroom, performing a role: "myself as teacher." Many people dislike, indeed, are intimidated by the idea of speaking in front of a group of people (even from a seat in a classroom). Given the option of saying nothing, that is precisely what they do. Lecturers don't have that option. Some prospective teachers say "I'm not very outgoing," or "I'm shy," or "I don't usually say much." So be it. Teaching requires public speaking, and people with all kinds of personalities do it successfully. Many actors say that, personally, they are quite shy and quiet, that it is when they adopt a role they are playing that they can behave differently. Similarly for teachers. Each of us has many selves, or roles that we play. For those who take on the task of teaching, one of the roles they must adopt is that of classroom teacher. Doing so does not require a personality makeover or an abandonment of "self"; it does require adopting the role of teacher.

Successful lecturing does not require singing, dancing, telling jokes, or grand gestures. It does require a commitment to communicating clearly, to maintaining student interest, to being enthusiastic about course material, and to trying hard to get students to think about course material and acquire important aspects of what is presented. Students perceive and appreciate instructors' efforts to help them learn.

The best, short advice regarding classroom behavior that I can offer to new instructors is one word—relax! The underlying assumption is that the instructor is well prepared for the class session. If so, and if the instructor makes a sincere effort to "get through" to students, to help them learn the core of the material, successful lectures are likely to occur. At the same time, good intentions themselves need to be augmented by good techniques.

Vocal Qualities.   When lecturing, it's important to speak clearly and loud enough to be easily heard by the most distant students. It is also important to have a "live" voice, that is, to change the intensity and pitch of one's speech over time. As discussed in Chapter 2, varied speech helps to maintain and recapture students' attention. Vocal changes are needed to indicate emphasis as well as to convey enthusiasm and to make the lecture more interesting to listen to. In short, lecturers need to make use of all of the vocal cues the language provides. All of us speak in different ways depending on the circumstances—we speak differently in private conversations, group discussions, and when ordering food in restaurants. Lecturers need to develop a speech style that will work well in the classroom. It is advantageous to listen to tape recordings of one's voice to get an idea of what others hear. People are often surprised when they listen to recordings of their voices, saying "I don't sound like that." The fact is that we sound different to others compared to the way we sound to ourselves for the simple reason that we hear vibrations coursing through the bones in our skull that others do not hear. Consequently, recordings of our voices tend to strike us as thin and higher pitched than we "ordinarily" sound.

Eye Contact.   When lecturing, it is important to speak **to** the students. When we have a conversation with another person, we look at the person while speaking—we don't look up at the ceiling or over at a wall. Lecturers sometimes engage in such defocused speech, perhaps looking at a point a short distance above the heads of the students. If you have been in the audience when a speaker does this, I'm sure you have noticed that is difficult to pay attention to what is being said. So the basic rule is simple: Look at people when you are speaking to them.

In the classroom, it is important to distribute eye contact around the room. There are many subtleties involved in making eye contact with the group of students. For example, a bright-eyed, eager-looking student whose head nods in assent to what the lecturer is saying strikes most lecturers as a marvelous target for instruction. It is understandable that lecturers would prefer to speak toward students who appear to be paying attention than to those who seem less interested. The danger lies in falling into the habit of speaking to one's "favorite" students, thereby speaking less to the rest of the group, which encourages them to be less interested. The vast majority of students will respond positively to being spoken to during a lecture. To increase the chances of distributing eye contact throughout the class, it helps for lecturers to move around. Obviously, one can direct one's gaze to different locations with the turn of the head, but physically moving to different locations makes it easier to direct a lecture to students in various parts of the room. As a related idea, lecturers need to be careful about their positioning when they use a blackboard and when they turn away from the board to face the students. After we have written something on the blackboard, we tend to make a minimal turn to face the class, and we make the turn by moving our writing hand in an arc away from the blackboard. So right-handers spin away in a clockwise rotation, whereas left-handers turn in a counterclockwise rotation. This movement tends to leave right-handed lecturers looking to the left side of the class as they face it. This tendency can lead to the majority of the lecture being given to the left side of the class. Therefore, lecturers need to remember to "complete the turn" at some point and direct their attention to students on the other side. Changing location from time to time should correct for a turning bias and also make the lecture more effective because change attracts attention (Chapter 2).

Our speech also carries emotional information. Bored speakers do not talk the same way as those who are enthusiastic about what they are saying. Lecturers need to convey enthusiasm for and interest in the material they are presenting. Students' interest and enthusiasm will be dependent on the cues given by a lecturer.

Gestures.   Facial expressions and gestures are additional sources of information for an audience. All of us have gestures and expressions that we use regularly and automatically; these might include nervous habits that are more likely to come into play in more anxious situations, such as lecturing to a room full of students. Repetitive gestures are usually distracting and therefore do not aid communication. If the speaker is constantly twirling a pencil or piece of chalk, or brushing hair to one side with a flip of the hand, these actions provide no useful information but attract attention and thus distract listeners from what is being said. Communicative gestures and expressions are related to the content that is being presented. When one wishes to emphasize the information in a particular part of a visual display, whether it be part of a list, a table, or a figure, the simple act of pointing to the material being stressed vocally will increase the emphasis. Watching a videotape of oneself delivering a lecture can be a superb educational experience. The videotape allows us to check for any possible distracting mannerisms we might have so that we can make a mental note to try to keep these in check. The tapes also allow an assessment of how well we use gestures, facial expressions, and movement in ways that will reinforce what is being said. Look for opportunities to add visual cues to the verbal presentation.

For many people, an emphasis on a how they sound, how they talk, how they look, how they move can make them quite self-conscious. This self-analysis of presentation skills might seem to contradict the idea of relaxing in front of the classroom. Clearly, one presentation goal is to appear relaxed, self-assured, and enjoying what one is doing. Self-analysis of presentation skills should take place outside the classroom as part of the process of developing a comfortable and effective classroom technique. In the classroom, although we are always somewhat aware of what we're doing, the main goal is to deliver a lecture, to interact with the students as best we can. Self-analysis between lectures can lead to better presentations, but the classroom is an arena for action.

Humor.   What about humor? Are funny lectures better? If you're not very good at telling jokes, does that mean you're not likely to give good lectures? This is a point at which the similarity between teaching and acting is diminished. Entertaining an audience is not the teacher's main goal, and teachers can be effective whether or not they are especially humorous. Students like lecturers who use humor (Check, 1986), so there is a benefit to interactions with students from injecting a bit of humor. However, it does not appear that humor has a large effect on memory for lecture content. Humorous examples can lead to better memory for the concepts to which they are related, but memory for surrounding material is reduced (Kaplan & Pascoe, 1977). Overall, serious and humorous lectures were remembered equally well. There appears to be no need to employ humor in lectures, nor is there anything wrong with doing so, provided that attention is not seriously distracted from lecture content.

Visual Aids

An essential part of lecturing is employing visual aids that are coordinated with the verbal presentation. As discussed in Chapter 2, auditory presentations such as lectures do not provide memory aids for what was said—one utterance is followed by another. One reason for using visual presentations is therefore to provide a lasting display of information spoken by the lecturer. The visual display should contain the key ideas of what is said. Another reason for using visual displays that are redundant with verbal presentations is that they can help students to better understand what was said. At a relatively low but still important level, students might not be sure precisely what name or word the lecturer just said. There is new terminology in every course, including the names of researchers and theorists who are likely to be unfamiliar to students. Therefore, a good rule of thumb to follow is to always present new terms and important names both visually and vocally. In this way, students will both better understand the lecture and be able to connect what they read (in a textbook) with what they hear in the classroom.

Visual displays are the natural mode of presenting certain kinds of information. Pictures, diagrams, graphs, and tables provide enormous amounts of information that can be difficult or impossible to describe verbally. Visual displays are ideally suited to present relational information. This point is obvious when the information itself is of a visual spatial nature, but it applies as well to describing relations that are not intrinsically spatial (see Chap. 3). Lists, flow charts, and other diagrams can be used to display many kinds of relations. In essence, we can make use of the spatial relations available in visual displays as analogies for other kinds of relations. For example, an organizational chart shows how work and authority are distributed among workers. The higher and lower levels in the organizational hierarchy do not refer literally to positions in space. Nonetheless, the spatial relations in the chart convey very clearly the functional relations in the organization.

Visual displays not only use spatial relations but also employ visual markers to represent relations. Arrows, headings in a table, and color coding are some of the ways in which visual markers can be used to enrich visual displays. For a familiar example, consider a street map, which displays the relative positions of the roads in some location; adding the names of landmarks or places of interest to the map (or numbers associated with a list of relevant information) makes the map more useful, and marking a path through the setting to a desired location provides excellent guidance. In seeking help while traveling, I have been the recipient of both sketchily drawn but labeled maps and sequential verbal directions ("go down two streets, turn right, ... "); the maps have worked whereas verbal directions have often failed. Think of visual displays for lectures as guide maps through a knowledge setting—they can help students to follow the train of thought of a lecture. Indeed, a reasonable approach to a lecture could be to plan the visual displays and then decide what one will say about them.

What about the physical form of visual displays? The options include chalkboard, overhead projector, projection computer, and handouts on paper. Available equipment and cost considerations will affect what is feasible in any given situation. Computer presentations probably are least likely; although quite sophisticated presentations are possible, the required software and hardware might not be available or be usable in a particular classroom. Presumably all instructors have access to overhead projectors and copying machines, and I assume that all classrooms have chalkboards.

Chalkboards. Chalkboards can be used for most anything and are best used for relatively small amounts of material. A weakness of chalkboard use is that instructors must write or draw the display immediately prior to use. If the instructor is writing on the chalkboard, nothing much else goes on with respect to instruction. Entering a few words or a simple drawing, something that takes 10 to 20 seconds, poses no problem. When larger amounts of material are to be put on a chalkboard, it is best if the instructor arrives before class to enter it, to minimize "dead time" during class. If chalkboard space is limited, instructors can face the problem of having to erase what they or some students might like to continue to have available in order to create space for new material. As a consequence, instructors need to acquire chalkboard-management skills, which include consideration of the amount of board space available (general rule = use it all!) and coordination of the importance of what needs to be presented visually with the space at hand. Chalkboards are very useful for a general outline of a lecture, including a numbered list of main points, for spelling out new terms and important names, and for any visual explanation of a point that arises during a class period. When using a chalkboard, it is essential to write—I would say print—clearly and large enough to be seen by students in the distant seats. Don't count on students "shouting out" to write larger; deliberately ask if students in the back rows can read what you're putting on the board, just as you ask them if they can hear you adequately.

Overhead Projectors. Large classes in large rooms make chalkboard use more problematic. The basic issue is whether entries can be made large enough to be seen from the back of the room. Under these circumstances, many instructors abandon chalkboards and switch to overhead projection displays. Instructors also use the displays, even in smaller classes, because they deem them superior to chalkboard presentations. Overhead projectors often include a roll of clear plastic so that one can write "on" the overhead projector like one writes on a chalkboard. But most use of overhead projectors involves presenting transparencies that have been prepared beforehand. These materials typically are prepared on paper, with a copier then used to make transparencies. Lecture outlines, lists of important points, graphs, tables, examples, and illustrations all can be presented via overhead projector. Anything that can be copied can be made into a transparency, so this method can be used to display cartoons and text or graphic materials from magazines as well as instructor-prepared materials. As Lutsky (1997) points out, if one sees a newspaper article that would be an excellent example of a course concept, producing a transparency makes it easy to present the article to the students. When creating materials for transparencies, it is critical to use a large and clear font; Lutsky suggests a minimum of 1/4 inch in height. Here are examples of different font sizes:

12 example / 18 example / 24 example.

When using projector displays, keep in mind that students will need time to read what is shown. Even more time is needed if students are expected to, or choose to copy the content. In some instances, students cannot possibly record useful notes without copying substantial amounts of presented material—what good are comments about an example without the example? Statistical or other mathematical data sets are likely to require noticeable copying. These considerations suggest that instructors should consider what students will do when projected materials are presented. To minimize conflict between students' copying material from the screen and students' listening to what is being said about the material, a common technique is to use a mask over the transparency so that only part of its content may be seen. For example, if an instructor plans to show the students an outline of four main points about some topic, after saying that four points will be made, the instructor would then show only the first point while it is discussed. By moving the mask down the transparency page, successive points are presented and copying initiated at the appropriate time.

Handouts.   An alternative to using overhead projectors is providing handouts to students. Anything that can be made into a transparency can also be copied and distributed to students. Sometimes there is no real choice between the two. For example, if an instructor creates a one-or-more page discussion of a topic deemed important but not covered in the textbook, there's no good alternative to giving each student a handout. A more general question is whether it is better to project a transparency or distribute a handout when either could be used. Among the relevant considerations are ease of viewing, paper costs, and the amount of display content that is useful for students to have in their records. In some physical settings, overhead projectors might be difficult to use because there is no convenient display space or because the projector itself causes sight-line problems for a significant number of students. Whereas handouts are un-likely to have viewing problems, copies are costly to produce, with the cost increasing with the number of students.

Perhaps a good rule of thumb to follow is that handouts become preferred as the amount of material increases, especially in regard to the amount of copying that students will be likely to do from projection presentation, provided that most of the display material is important. For example, a newspaper item that has considerable text but can be usefully summarized in a few sentences would not require each student to have a copy. In contrast, a data display of critical importance that would require a lot of copying would be a prime candidate for a handout.

In teaching statistics, over time, I have made increasing use of handouts. Much of statistics instruction consists of working through sample problems. If students need to copy the data set from either a chalkboard or a projection screen, class time is spent in copying that could be better spent on course material. By giving students individual copies of the data set and information outlining the kind of analysis to be done, more efficient use is made of class time and students leave with an accurate record of the data set and their notes about the analysis on same sheet. This use of handouts illustrates the situation where considerable copying would otherwise be required and where a good record is highly desirable.

A Note on Note-taking.   Students take notes while listening to a lecture, presumably for the purpose of providing themselves with a document they can use for later review. Two questions about note-taking deserve attention:

1. What is the effect of taking notes on comprehension of a lecture?
2. How useful is review of notes with respect to later test performance?

Note-taking is an active process that might be expected to have both positive and negative effects on lecture comprehension. As discussed in Chapter 2, taking notes can compete with listening to what is being said, so that the student misses important information. On the positive side, taking notes represents more active processing of lecture information than just listening, which could aid learning. Perhaps not surprisingly, comparisons of memory for a lecture after just listening versus taking notes (with no review) can show no difference in test scores (e.g., Kiewra, 1985). Instructors can minimize conflict between listening and note-taking by reducing lecture rate, allowing pauses for note-taking, and providing a visual display of important information, all of which reduce the load on working memory (Kiewra, 1987).

With respect to reviewing notes after a lecture but before a test, it is clear that a review is better than not doing so. The best notes to review are the lecturer's! Kiewra (1985) found that students who just listened to a lecture and later reviewed the lecturer's notes scored higher than those who took and reviewed their own notes. Of course, the lecturer's notes will be more complete and better organized than students' notes. Indeed, analyses of students' notes have found many weaknesses in them.

Students' notes might include only 25% of the information in the lecturer's notes (Baker & Lombardi, 1985; Kiewra, 1985). Students are more likely to record main points than subordinate points, although their notes are far from complete, including 50% to 67% of main points. They are far more likely to record information that is presented visually on a chalkboard or overhead projection (Baker & Lombardi, 1985). Visual cuing is more effective than spoken cuing for getting students to include information in their notes (Scerbo, Warm, Dember, & Grasha, 1992). In general, material that is in students' notes and thus available for review is remembered much better than missing information. So to facilitate long-term memory for a lecture, a key step is to get students to take good notes, to have good notes for later review.

Kiewra (1987) suggests that instructors simply could provide students with notes for review. Short of doing that, instructors can help students take better notes by adjusting lecture pace and using visual displays, as noted above. In addition, handouts can be used to guide students' note-taking, as in the statistics example described earlier. Morgan, Lilley and Boreham (1988) found that providing students with handouts containing the main headings of a lecture and space for students to fill in the details produced far superior performance on both immediate and delayed tests of lecture memory.

Promoting Learning

Every instructor will try to do a good job of describing and explaining major concepts of the course being taught. This section is a brief discussion of specific techniques that instructors can use to facilitate students' learning. It is a partial recap of Chapters 3 and 4, a checklist of things to keep in mind when presenting new material.

Organization.   Organizing course material is a major responsibility of lecturers. Instructors can help students see the "big picture" by regularly relating the current topic to a larger view of the course. Instructors should also make use of any organizational cue that may apply to what they're teaching. Diagrams are excellent ways to show relations among various concepts. A numbered list of points covered under particular headings helps students remember what is presented. When assets and liabilities, similarities and differences, reasons for and reasons against a position are being discussed, a visual display with clear separation of the different categories should accompany the verbal presentation. Indeed, some suggest that when presenting, say, assets and liabilities of some theory or procedure, the lecturer might mark the distinction by changing positions—assets to left, liabilities to the right, or some comparable scheme. In short, thinking about organizing the material, conceptually and perceptually, is an everyday task for a lecturer.

Raising Questions.   It is a good idea to raise questions about course material, even rhetorical questions. Hearing a question encourages listeners to think of possible answers and to expect that an answer will be forthcoming. Introducing a section of a lecture can often be done with either a declarative statement or a question: "Now I'll discuss reasons why the Puritans settled in Massachusetts. Why did the Puritans settle in Massachusetts?" The question format is a bit more engaging; it's likely to attract more attention than the comparable declarative statement and to lead students to think a little bit about the topic. Of course, a question need not be rhetorical—one could ask the students to propose reasons why the Puritans settled in Massachusetts.

Examples.   As mentioned earlier, presenting examples is an important part of lecturing. Examples should be prepared before class and can be used in a variety of ways. One could start with an example and encourage students to think of ways of explaining it before presenting the concept and principle that it exemplified. The concept could be presented first and followed by an example or several examples to illustrate the concept. The instructor might simply explain how the example fits the concept or ask students to do this, followed by instructor feedback. If several examples are given, which is recommended, the lecturer might explain the first one to guide the students' thinking, but the students should be asked to explain the other examples. It's important to challenge students to master the material, which means that the students will have to do some work. It's rather easy to sit and watch instructors solve problems, compare theories, or explain examples. Although these instructor activities are useful, they by no means guarantee that students will be able to do these important intellectual tasks. Instructors do their students a favor when they incorporate thinking tasks into their lectures.

Checking Comprehension.   As a lecture proceeds with more and more new information being presented, it is important to check whether most if not all students are understanding the material. As mentioned earlier, day-to-day comprehension assessments can be made through end-of-class recaps and beginning-of-class reviews. But it's important to also check comprehension on an ongoing basis. Lecturers can, during their presentations, conduct "eye checks" as comprehension assessments. If one looks around the room and sees students brightly and eagerly looking back, anticipating the next point, chances are that they are understanding the lecture. If, on the other hand, one sees glazed eyes and perplexed looks on the students' faces, chances are there is a comprehension problem. In small-to medium-size classes, eye checks can be nearly exhaustive; in large classes, some sampling is required. If eye checks raise any doubt about students' comprehension, they can be asked if they are understanding what is being presented or if they have any questions about the material. When asked if they understand, students often give ambiguous responses, either because they know they don't understand but don't want to show it or because they're not very sure whether they do or don't understand. So only forthright "yes" responses and "no" responses might be taken at face value. When asked if they have any questions, most students don't ask any even though they may have one or more on their minds. One of my favorite comic strips shows a room filled with students, each of whom has exactly the same thought balloon above his or her head. The thought balloon says something like "Prof lost me about 10 minutes ago but I'm not asking a question because all the other students will think I'm stupid." Because of students' reluctance, instructors need to use techniques that are more forceful than simply asking "Any questions?"

Questions and Answers.   In 400 B.C., Socrates used a question and answer technique to sharpen his students' understanding of moral issues. In modern college classrooms, instructors typically spend little time asking questions of their students. Barnes (1983) reported that, on the average, less than 4% of class time was devoted to questioning students. This low rate of questioning applied to both beginning and advanced courses. Because questioning students is an excellent way to gauge comprehension and promotes students' learning, it is unfortunate that instructors spend so little time using this technique.

One reason that instructors ask few questions of their classes is that students are reluctant, perhaps even refuse to answer. There are several reasons why a student might not attempt to answer a question put to the class. Not knowing the answer, being afraid of being wrong, general reluctance to speak in front of groups, and boredom are all reasons for nonresponse. Barnes reported that most instructor questions asked for simple memory answers, which could contribute to boredom as a factor. One reason for answering such questions is to impress the instructor; however, some students might have the attitude that one doesn't want to look like the kind of student who's trying to impress the instructor. Certainly we can think of more reasons not to answer instructors' questions than to answer them.

To stimulate a reasonable level of class participation, instructors must try to insure that appropriate conditions exist. Very large classes introduce maximum levels of group inhibition as well as problems of hearing answers and negotiating some reasonable distribution of opportunities to respond. Therefore, questioning is more feasible in medium-sized and smaller classes. Instructors should both ask questions frequently from the beginning of the course and clearly state that answering questions is expected as well as explaining the reasons why asking and answering questions is deemed important. It is of course possible to require that students attempt to answer posed questions, to call on specific students rather than inviting volunteers, and to keep records of participation, but few instructors will be interested in such methods. A possible exception is a small, advanced seminar where a discussion format is used and class participation is fundamental to the course. In most undergraduate courses, students' participation will be encouraged rather than required.

It is of the utmost importance that instructors treat with care and consideration any reply that students give to their questions. The easiest way to suppress class participation is by harshly criticizing a student's attempt to answer a question. Negative treatment of a student will not only cancel that student's further participation but also will "teach" the other students that speaking in class is a dangerous activity that is best avoided. To encourage students to offer answers, instructors must respond gently while maintaining the goal of arriving at a good answer. If the student's reply is vague, one might say "I'm not sure I understand what you said—could you say a little more?" If the answer is partly correct, either incomplete or part right-part wrong, the instructor should note the correct part, then indicate that more is needed. If a wrong (part of an) answer is close, the appropriate comment is to say so. Improvements, additions, clarifications, or whole new answers may be requested gently from the original respondent, who will often decline, or from other students, while conveying a spirit of a group effort to arrive at a good answer. Knowing and using students' names can help to maintain a useful atmosphere.

No one likes to appear "stupid" or ill-informed in front of a group—this statement includes instructors. In the pursuit of further knowledge, guesses need to be made, and mistakes will be made, and no one knows all the answers—this statement also includes instructors. With respect to encouraging student participation, one of the most encouraging statements that a lecturer can make is "I don't know." Stated differently, the way in which students will respond to an instructor's questions will be influenced by the way in which the instructor responds to students' questions. Instructors must treat students' questions with respect, even the banal ones such as "Will this be on the test?" It is important for instructor-student interactions that the instructor make an effort to understand a student's question, asking for clarification ("I don't understand ... "), and then make a serious attempt to answer the question. Serious effort includes honestly saying "I don't know" when that statement accurately describes the situation.

Students are quite capable of asking questions for which lecturers don't know the answer, either because the question lies outside their current expertise or because the discipline offers no real solution. The worst way to respond to

a "stumper" question is for the instructor to "fake it," "saving face" by perhaps de-
meaning the question, or by bluffing with a vague non-answer, or by essentially ignoring the difficult aspect of the question and instead answering a seemingly related question for which one has requisite knowledge. Students will recognize the
fundamental dismissal of the question, perhaps even with a single episode, and
more certainly with repetition. The alternative, for instructors to publicly admit
that they don't know the answer to a question, while perhaps offering a clearly labeled "principled guess," coupled with a promise that they will try to find an answer (and fulfillment of that promise, whether the news is good or "bad"), sends a
powerful, complex, and positive message to students: "That was a good question
even though I don't know the correct response. It's okay sometimes to not know
the answer to a question. It's good to try to answer questions, even if the effort
isn't completely successful. Acquiring knowledge is a continual, ongoing activity,
even for the faculty! There are multiple sources of information available, and it's
smart to use them—that's what the faculty do." The amount of good that can be
done by an appropriate confession of ignorance is amazing!

In the preceding discussion, I have assumed that questions and answers are
both public events. The instructor poses a question, and one or more students indicate a willingness to respond, with some equitable method used by the instructor to choose which student will speak. To ask a question of the instructor, a student must also speak publicly, and the reply is also public. There is no quarrel
with the idea of instructors asking and answering questions publicly—that's
their job. There are, however, alternatives to requiring students to speak publicly. An instructor could require all students to write answers to a question, with
the responses collected and perhaps graded in some basic "okay or not" fashion.
Scanning the answers (or a sample if necessary because of class size) gives an
idea of the general level of understanding and can provide the basis for subsequent explanatory remarks. Analogously, students might submit written questions, either voluntarily or as a requirement, at a pause or the end of a lecture.
The instructor can review the questions, during a break or between class sessions, and then answer a selection of the questions when the class resumes. The
use of written questions and answers is a bit more cumbersome, but more students participate and the instructor gets more information about what's on the
minds of the students.

DISCUSSIONS

Question-and-answer periods constitute a form of discussion, albeit one in which
the lecturer is likely to do most of the talking. When the goal for a session is to
have the students do most of the talking, a clear change to a different format takes
place. Class discussions are not efficient methods for presenting new information.

Rather, their purpose is to explore a topic in greater depth, allowing students to discover and reflect on their own views of an issue and consider the perspectives of other students. Discussions will be effective to the extent that participation is widespread, ideally universal among the students, and relevant to the topic at hand. Fostering participation is the key goal, and class size is perhaps the major obstacle to success.

Discussions are difficult in large groups; the problem is more severe when a goal is to have everyone participate. In addition to exacerbating widespread inhibitions about talking in front of groups, large groups create problems of time allocation; if each of 80 people speaks for two minutes, the minimum discussion time is nearly three hours with no one having a second chance. Kramer and Korn (1996) suggest that class discussions work best with groups of four to nine students. If there are, say, 200 students in a course, more than 20 discussion groups would be needed if a desirable group size is to be used. As a practical matter, some enrollments might be too large to employ class discussions. Even a class of 20, 40, or 60 students is itself too large for a whole-class discussion. Goetz and Gump (1978) distinguish whole-class settings and part-class settings. The essential idea is to divide a class into reasonable-sized groups in which better discussions will take place. For a class of 40 students, five part-class groups would yield useful subgroup sizes. Multiple, small discussion groups can meet in the same room in which the whole class meets, in many circumstances. People talk more quietly in smaller groups, and people generally are good at focusing attention on their group's conversation and filtering out others. Consequently, space requirements for multiple discussion groups usually can be met.

To promote student participation, instructors need to minimize their own participation. Students will defer to the instructor as a participant, which works against the goal of student activity. Instructors might initiate the discussions and should observe them, perhaps offering help to facilitate progress when it seems needed. Kramer and Korn (1996) suggest that an instructor's important contribution to class discussions would take place *before* the discussions, in setting the ground rules for participation. Among the rules they list are these:

- Everyone is expected to participate.
- Dominance of the conversation by one or two people is unacceptable.
- Do not interrupt—let people finish their thoughts.
- Different views are encouraged.
- Keep the discussion focused on the assigned topic.

Kramer and Korn also suggest that instructors form discussion groups on some simple, arbitrary basis rather than letting students form groups on the basis of existing friendships, and that discussion groups be re-formed each time they are used. The hypothesis is that randomly formed groups are more likely to focus on the assignment.

It is essential to set specific goals for the discussions. A question or issue is the basis of the discussion, and groups should know what product they are to deliver at the end of the discussion. One way to both focus the discussions and promote participation is to give students an individual assignment prior to the discussion. Flanagan (1978) suggests using a brief, several-question exercise that students complete anonymously prior to group discussion, with the results compiled for later summary and comment by the instructor. More generally, students might be given a brief homework assignment in which they prepare their individual, preliminary answers to the question to be discussed. Students bring two copies of their proposals to the next class, one to be given to the instructor (to verify that the assignment was completed) and the other to be taken to a discussion group. Discussion involves comparing ideas with the goal of arriving at a group consensus position. Group ideas can then be compared in a probably brief whole-class discussion in which everyone at least has a stake. This technique can lead to very lively class sessions.

GOOD TEACHERS

Good classroom teachers are not born—they are self-made, sometimes with some help. Some people perhaps are "naturally" better speakers than others, some are more gregarious than others, and so on. But good teachers do things that make their classes interesting and informative and that help students to learn. Any instructor can learn to speak more clearly, to construct better examples, to improve any teaching behavior. Becoming a better teacher is a process in which any instructor can take part.

Large-scale surveys have been done of students' ratings of many different teacher attributes and behaviors, and their relations with judgments of teaching effectiveness (e.g., Erdle & Murray, 1986; Murray, 1985). There is no best style that must be followed to be effective, but there are characteristics that are associated with effectiveness. For a graduate course on teaching, I compiled some of the survey results to construct a "Lecture Description Profile," which is reproduced in Figure 6.1. With the exception of one item, "Reads lectures from notes," high ratings on the 25 items are associated with high ratings of effectiveness. The items are partially redundant with one another, so there is no "requirement" that one obtain high ratings on every scale; basically, one would prefer to have good ratings on a number of items. The profile can be used for self-analysis; any lecturer can complete the items with respect to self-perception and compare own ratings to those made by students. The profile is not an end-of-course evaluation scale but rather a descriptive instrument that can be used at any time to get feedback about lecture presentations. In Chapter 11, more formal end-of-course evaluations are discussed.

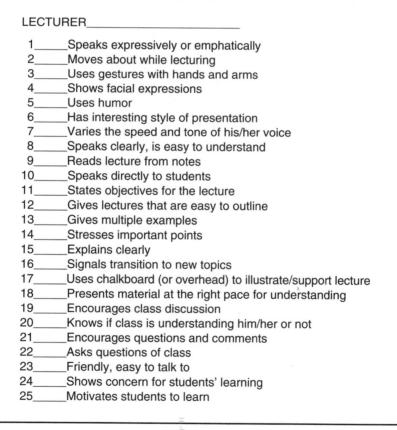

For each statement given below, decide how well it describes the lecturer you have just seen/listened to. Use this scale to indicate your judgment.

5=VERY DESCRIPTIVE
4=MODERATELY DESCRIPTIVE
3=SOMEWHAT DESCRIPTIVE
2=WEAKLY DESCRIPTIVE
1=NOT AT ALL DESCRIPTIVE

Write the appropriate number in the answer space by each statement. If a statement doesn't seem to apply to this lecture, skip it. Be sure to enter the lecturer's name in the space provided.

LECTURER_____

1_____Speaks expressively or emphatically
2_____Moves about while lecturing
3_____Uses gestures with hands and arms
4_____Shows facial expressions
5_____Uses humor
6_____Has interesting style of presentation
7_____Varies the speed and tone of his/her voice
8_____Speaks clearly, is easy to understand
9_____Reads lecture from notes
10_____Speaks directly to students
11_____States objectives for the lecture
12_____Gives lectures that are easy to outline
13_____Gives multiple examples
14_____Stresses important points
15_____Explains clearly
16_____Signals transition to new topics
17_____Uses chalkboard (or overhead) to illustrate/support lecture
18_____Presents material at the right pace for understanding
19_____Encourages class discussion
20_____Knows if class is understanding him/her or not
21_____Encourages questions and comments
22_____Asks questions of class
23_____Friendly, easy to talk to
24_____Shows concern for students' learning
25_____Motivates students to learn

Figure 6-1   Lecture Description Profile

SUMMARY

Lectures should be viewed as interactive sessions in which the instructor does most of the talking. Deciding how much material to try to cover in a class session is critical to smooth-running classes. A rule of thumb is to cover three main points in a 50-minute class. Lecture notes are best thought of as an augmented outline, and it is useful to prepare them on a computer. Examples should be prepared in advance. Prior mental rehearsal of the overall form of a lecture aids presentation. Overviews and reviews are good ways to start a class. Learning students' names increases rapport and student participation. Lively vocal quality, eye contact, movement, and appropriate gestures make lectures more effective. Visual aids provide emphasis as well as memory assistance; chalkboards, overhead projectors, and handouts have different strengths as visual presentations. Focusing on organization, raising questions, providing examples, and checking comprehension are some of the techniques instructors can use to enhance learning. The way in which instructors respond to students' questions and answers has a strong influence on classroom atmosphere. Class discussions can promote active learning and comprehension; instructors should reduce their participation and focus on preparing students for discussions. Setting specific goals, establishing rules to encourage full participation, and mixing small-group and whole-group discussions are helpful.

7

Writing Assignments

Writing and Thinking
Kinds of Writing Assignments
Setting the Assignment
Feedback, Grading, and Revising
Plagiarism

In this chapter, we'll consider assignments in which students write papers of one sort or another. The amount of text that is produced usually is greater than an answer to an essay question on a test, and the writing typically takes place outside the classroom. There are two general reasons for using writing assignments: (a) The paper serves as a report on some learning activity—it serves to demonstrate that a student has completed some task or that a student understands some designated course material. In effect, the paper serves as an alternative to answering exam questions or making an oral report. (b) A paper might be assigned because the instructor considers the act of writing to be important (Klugh, 1983). The focus here is on writing itself, rather than on some other activity that is reported by means of a paper. These two reasons, of course, are not mutually exclusive; an instructor might both assign an activity that is deemed important and require a paper based on that activity because creating the paper will contribute to the student's learning in a special way.

WRITING AND THINKING

People learn to speak and to comprehend a spoken native language through everyday living; in contrast, writing and reading involve additional symbols and rules, and mastering these skills requires extensive, focused practice that is different from basic day-to-day living. All of these skills, of course, exist at multiple levels—chatting with a friend is different from giving a speech, for example. Speaking and writing are means of communicating ideas to others as well as to ourselves. Effective communication requires thought about both the ideas to be expressed and the technique of expression; indeed, it is difficult to separate the message from the medium, perhaps especially in writing. People sometimes speak "without much thought," saying something and then commenting "That's not what I wanted to say" and correcting their statements. Well-thought-out and well-expressed oral statements can fail to yield successful communication, as indicated by listeners' responses such as "I don't understand" or blank stares. In most situations, this feedback allows the speaker to try to adjust what is said until a satisfactory reaction occurs. In addition, the listener usually can ask questions to help in clarifying the message. In writing, misstatements should be corrected by reviewing and revising the text; however, there is no opportunity to adjust to less-than-desired comprehension. Rather, the writer must anticipate the reader's level of relevant knowledge and what statements will be effective. Furthermore, writing lacks the extra-lexical cues that ordinarily accompany speech—changes in pitch and loudness, facial expressions, and gestures. Although a limited set of visual markers is available in writing, such as italics, bold print, or all caps ("NOW" seems to be shouting), and although punctuation can be used to indicate textual relations, the words in writing carry a heavier burden than the "words" in speaking. For these reasons, writing is more demanding intellectually than speaking.

Our unexpressed thoughts are often vague, incomplete, even piecemeal. Speaking about a topic encourages greater coherence, but even here we might still be vague and disorganized, relying on conversational give-and-take to produce some common understanding. In a discussion, people might not even feel a need to be organized and coherent; rather, being "relevant" might seem sufficient. Writers must move things ahead on their own, and even minimally effective writing requires some organization. Consequently, the act of writing makes people consider their thoughts more carefully than they otherwise might do. And because of the more formal character of writing, compared to speaking, writing increases the demand to be clear, organized, and coherent. In a very real sense, writing about a topic can help people formulate their thoughts on the subject. Students tend to believe that writing is just a matter of delivering the message after they have thought about the topic (Sternberg, 1988). However, the fact is that writing can and should be an essential part of thinking about a subject.

The stream of speech itself is too fleeting to ponder, and, ordinarily, one utterance is closely followed by another, making review virtually impossible. Few people have the opportunity to review audio tapes or videotapes of themselves talking. By constructing a more permanent product, writing provides an opportunity for people to reflect on their thoughts. Writing objectifies a person's thoughts. Even a cursory review of what one has written can alert a person to previously unconsidered aspects of one's beliefs or to relative strengths and weaknesses of what one has written.

To summarize, the relation between writing and thinking is bidirectional. Obviously, one cannot write coherently about a topic without thinking coherently. Grades on papers have been found to be correlated with scores on standard reasoning tests (Dominowski, Dallob, & Penningroth, 1994). The act of writing also influences thinking, as described above. One direct effect of writing assignments is that students can be required to justify or explain their choices, compared to merely selecting an answer as in a multiple-choice test. Students tend to be weak at justifying answers (Applebee, 1984). Appropriate writing assignments therefore can help students to develop reasoning skills.

KINDS OF WRITING ASSIGNMENTS

Special, creative writing classes might require students to write poems, short stories, or novels, which will not be considered here. More generally, writing assignments ask students to create expository prose, writing about a topic in some fashion. Nodine (1998) described two broad classes of assignments that are distinguished by their basic purposes. *Expressive* writing is done for the students' benefit, to help them understand a topic. *Transactional* writing has the major goal of providing information to an audience (often the instructor). Commonly used assignments such as term papers and laboratory reports are transactional in Nodine's terms. Sternberg (1988) characterizes such assignments as *persuasive* writing to emphasize the goal of getting one's point across to the reader.

Expressive Writing.   Such assignments are short and typically ungraded (Nodine, 1998). The basic idea is to have students react to and think about some topic by writing a brief paper. These are, in Nodine's terms, writing-to-learn papers. After listening to a lecture or reading some textual material, students might be asked to summarize the material, describe what they think is most interesting, or respond to a question that encourages them to think about the topic. Nodine suggests that such brief writing activities, lasting perhaps just a few minutes, should be incorporated into lectures. Because every student writes, there is greater participation than in a class discussion where only a few students take an active role. In addition, students' papers can be used to encourage subsequent discussion.

There is evidence that writing summaries can aid learning. Davis and Hult (1997) found that students who were asked to write a summary of a lecture showed better recall of lecture material on tests given after a delay of nearly two weeks, compared to those who did not write summaries. Similarly, Radmacher and Latosi-Sawin (1995) found that students who wrote weekly summaries of textbook material earned higher grades on a final exam than students who were not required to do so. Furthermore, having students write short answers to questions yields more learning than answering multiple-choice questions or just reading (Applebee, 1984). As these findings suggest, having students write briefly about course material can aid learning.

Nodine suggests that expressive writing activities should be ungraded. The emphasis should be on the ideas generated rather than on grammar or quality of exposition. She points out that the purpose is to get students' ideas on paper where they can be reviewed, that expressive writing can serve to stimulate discussion. Such papers are not finished products.

Another form of expressive writing is the journal. According to Hettich (1976), a student journal is not a diary; rather, it is a record of thoughts and experienced events that are related to course content. Entries tend to be short, ranging from only a few sentences to several pages. The central idea is to have students think about course content when they are away from the classroom. In addition to having students think more about a course, a journal can prompt students to relate course material to aspects of everyday living. As with the other forms of expressive writing, journals usually are not graded; as Hettich puts it, any entry having some connection to course material is acceptable.

These writing assignments could, of course, be graded. For example, summaries of articles, textbook sections, or lectures could be readily assessed for accuracy and completeness. Other assignments, such as journal entries, would be difficult to evaluate on a systematic basis without prescribing the form and content to be entered. However, structuring assignments and grading them beyond general, minimal compliance with assignment instructions changes the assignment drastically. Writing assignments are expressive because of their purpose, to allow students to think about course material for their own benefit, rather than to demonstrate knowledge or understanding to another.

Persuasive Writing.   The more common writing assignments require students to demonstrate that they have done one or more things well. Term papers, lab reports, book reports, and critiques all ask writers to persuade readers (instructors) that the ideas expressed are well founded and carefully argued. These assignments also reflect the completion of some activity such as collecting data or library research. This kind of writing is what people usually have in mind when referring to writing assignments, writing skills, or improving writing. Here, issues of grammar, word usage, and style do matter, and the goal is to be clear, direct, and convincing.

Four broad classes of persuasive writing assignments can be distinguished readily and were listed above. Laboratory reports, more generally research reports, are highly constrained, formulaic papers ranging from very brief, minimally written reports to mini-journal articles. The format is determined by the relevant discipline—sociology, biology, and psychology papers, for example, use different terminology and citation procedures. Nonetheless, research reports generally have four major sections: problem, methods, results, and discussion. The methods and results sections require descriptive writing, methods dealing with relatively concrete procedures and results concerning perhaps more complex analytic techniques. In their own ways, these sections reflect the writer's understanding of what was done as well as the writer's understanding of what should be described and what form descriptions should take. Problem sections, or introductions, and discussions require interpretation and inference making and are likely to concern more abstract and complex conceptual material. Overall quality of research reports therefore should be more strongly related to the problem and discussion sections than to the methods or results sections. Differences in relevant knowledge and comprehension will more likely be reflected in these interpretive sections. The expected level of quality will vary with course level; for example, introductory students cannot reasonably be expected to understand complex procedures, concepts, and theoretical issues at a level appropriate to seniors majoring in a discipline.

Book and article reports are ways for students to demonstrate that they understand something they have read and that they can discuss the material intelligently. To a considerable degree, book reports are extended summaries, which, as noted above, can be evaluated for accuracy and completeness. What else will be in a book report depends on instructors' choices. Students might be asked, in addition to summarizing the reading, to relate the reading to textbook or lecture material, to critique the author's argument, or to apply the reading to an example, among other possibilities. These reports will inevitably have a summarizing/ comprehension component, with additional factors depending on the instructor's choice of specific questions.

Term papers typically are literature reviews, and that is the form discussed here. The student selects a topic, perhaps from a list provided by the instructor, and must then find readings relevant to that topic to serve as the basis of the paper. A clear influence on the eventual quality of the paper is the quality of the set of readings that the student uses. In many circumstances, students need help with conducting literature searches. For example, university libraries now provide access to a wide variety of literature databases; giving students guidance as to how to access and use such databases can save them time and frustration. A potential problem for literature reviews concerns the number of articles (or other readings) to include. As the number of included items increases, so does the number of items to be searched, the time to scan abstracts to decide on likely inclusion, the time to read selected articles, the time to organize them—the time to complete each step in the process from topic selection to finished paper. It makes sense that undergraduates should be asked to write limited literature reviews. It further makes sense to tell the students the minimum and maximum number of readings to include. Once one abandons the goal of being "exhaustive," the appropriate number of readings is whatever number suits the assignment. Even a small number, three to five readings, can be enough for students to demonstrate that they can select a coherent set of articles and write about them intelligently. Because students' knowledge of the subject area is limited, they often have trouble selecting a coherent set of readings. In effect, their topic is too broad, so that their readings, other than being relevant to a broad issue, have little to do with one another and will not provide a sound basis for an interesting review. I have found it useful to encourage or require students to bring in the titles and abstracts of the articles they intend to use in order to receive the instructor's judgment regarding the articles' likely coherence. Such preliminary checks also can serve to identify readings that seem likely to be too complex for the student to understand reasonably.

The review paper itself will involve summaries and comprehension of the readings, but it also requires students to describe relations among the readings and draw inferences to arrive at tentative conclusions. Drawing inferences and relating the readings to a more general theme is an aspect often missing from students' review papers. Some papers resemble a kind of grocery list—a series of paragraph summaries with no connection drawn between paragraphs, and conclusions representing a short-list repetition of what was found in the paragraphs. Some of the emphasis on relations can be provided in discussing students' article choices, but attention should also be directed toward what should be included in the paper. Constructing an outline of a paper improves the quality of writing (Kellogg, 1987).

Critiques can take several forms, but I have in mind here an argumentative essay on a controversial topic. This kind of writing is exemplified by letters to the editor in the popular press and by commentaries on published articles in a variety of professional journals. There is some target article to which one writes a response. Compared to the three paper types discussed earlier, students tend to find critiques to be daunting, even a bit mystifying. Here are two reasons for such reactions. First, students are inclined to view their tasks as requiring comprehension or acquisition and reproduction (as critics have suggested, this orientation might be favored by instructors). The students' goal is to show that they have learned what has been assigned. Doing so is quite different from assessing the merits of what one has read or arguing for a point of view. The intellectual task of assessment and argument is unfamiliar to them. In addition, there is a perceived status difference between student and the professional author of an actually published article that could be intimidating. A second reason is that a critique has little identifiable form. Book reports, research reports, and literature reviews are not only more familiar but also have fairly obvious general forms. But what does a commentary look like? In assigning critiques, I have found it essential to provide students with a number of sample commentaries and to discuss the examples so that students can gain an idea of the various ways in which critiques can be fashioned. Because of the analytic nature of critiques, these papers reflect students' relevant knowledge base and reasoning abilities.

SETTING THE ASSIGNMENT

It seems inevitable that writing assignments will be ill-defined to some extent. It is very difficult to anticipate all of the questions that students might have (whether they will or will not ask them). Nonetheless, it is to the instructor's advantage as well as the students' for the assignment to be described in some detail so that misinterpretations of the assignment as well as questions seeking clarification might be minimized. Among the main descriptors of a writing assignment are these:

The purpose of the assignment; what is most important about the assignment
What is to be included in the paper (sections, topics)
The format and style to be followed
The minimum number and type of required references
The minimum or maximum number of pages
Opportunities or requirements for preliminary review
How the paper will be graded; opportunities or requirements for revision

Figures 7-1 and 7-2 present sample descriptions of writing assignments. These are offered, not as ideal types, but rather as reasonable descriptions that were developed over successive writing assignments.

Paper Limits. Instructors frequently require minimal lengths for students' papers, presumably to indicate the importance of the paper and the amount of work that should go into it. Here I want to emphasize setting maximum limits for student papers. Students tend to employ a disorganized writing strategy in which they include everything they can think of that is related to the topic and hope that the reader, namely the instructor, will grasp the good aspects of what they have written and give them credit for having included them. By imposing maximum length limits on a paper, students must think more carefully about the topic and about what they're going to include in their papers. Length limits require writers to be efficient—to say what needs to be said and avoid unnecessary embellishments.

Writers do not like limitations on how much they can say. Even professional writers know that to meet relatively strict length limitations requires considerable work. By placing a reasonable length limit on students' papers, instructors will help students to improve both their thinking and their writing processes.

FEEDBACK, GRADING, AND REVISING

Most commonly, if student papers are required, they are submitted toward the end of the term and receive overall grades and perhaps some comments. Grading written assignments is notoriously unreliable, both across graders and within a grader over time. It is time-consuming for instructors to provide extended comments on students' papers. The fact that the students are seldom required to or have the opportunity to revise their papers is unfortunate because, with reasonable feedback on first drafts, revising their papers will both improve their writing skills and their understanding of the material they are writing about. Ideally, an instructor would have a meaningful feedback system that could be used to provide guidance to students that would help them revise their first drafts of papers and that would guide the instructor when determining grades for final versions of papers.

This paper focuses on summarizing research articles and relating them to one another. Your paper will be based on three research articles in psychological journals: one (target) article that you must choose from the list given below, plus two additional articles that are related to the target article.

Choose one of these two target articles:

: xxxxxx

Copies of the target articles are available at the reserve desk in the library.

Selecting Two Additional Articles

1. The task is to select two articles that are meaningfully related to the target article, so that the three articles form a cohesive set.
2. Each article you select must have a publication date that is later than the target article. For example, if you choose the xxx target article (published in 1984), your other two articles must have been published in 1985, or later.
3. Each article must be a research report in a professional psychological journal. If you are not sure that an article you have found meets this criterion, ask the instructor. You will be told if any articles seem to be inappropriate for this assignment and get suggestions for finding usable articles.

Rules for Preparing and Submitting Drafts and Final Papers

1. All rules described in the course syllabus apply.
2. Your paper must contain (a) an introduction in which you describe the theme of your review, (b) a summary of each of the three articles, and (c) a discussion section in which you explain the relations among the articles and what they collectively tell us about the topic.
3. The maximum allowable length of the text of your paper is five pages. Papers exceeding this limit will be rejected; if drafts, without comment, if final versions, with zero points.
4. You must attach, to the end of your paper, copies of the first page of your two additional articles (and the abstract or summary, if it is not on the first page).

Grading criteria are described on the reverse side of this page.

Figure 7-1   Instructions for the Literature Review Paper

This paper focuses on evaluating the argument or thesis presented in a psychological article of a type usually called secondary sources. That is, the target article is not a report of original research; rather, it is a (possibly selective) literature review in which the author presents a specific viewpoint on a psychological topic. Your task is to prepare a commentary on a target article. Although your paper must summarize the target article to some degree, the emphasis should be on analyzing and critically evaluating the content of the target article.

Choose one of these two target articles:

:   xxxxxx

Copies of the target articles are available at the reserve desk in the library.

General Suggestions

1. It is crucial that you thoroughly understand the target article. Gaining that understanding may require additional reading. Beyond comprehension, it is important to carefully scrutinize the argument presented in the target.
2. A commentator is not required to clearly disagree with the target's author. You may agree, embellish, or supplement the author's argument, just as you may disagree or offer an alternative view of the topic. You may have a mixed reaction, in which case be sure to specify the strengths of your agreements and disagreements.
3. The target author's argument can be evaluated from any of several perspectives: completeness of the literature review, interpretation of cited results, logical consistency of the several steps in the argument, implications, and more.
4. It is alright to introduce additional literature. Perhaps the target author missed a key reference—perhaps a later publication brings a new perspective to the argument. However, you are not required to add any references for this paper; focus on analysis of the quality of the argument made by the target author.

Rules for Preparing and Submitting Drafts and Final Papers

1. All rules described in the course syllabus apply.
2. Maximum allowable length of your paper is five pages of text. Papers exceeding this limit will be rejected; drafts, without comment, final versions, with zero points.
3. There should be no abstract for your paper.
4. You must attach to the end of your draft and final paper, copies of the first page (and abstract, if on another page) of any articles you add to your paper.

Grading criteria are described on the reverse side of this page.

Figure 7-2   Instructions for the Critical Analysis Paper

A scheme that we have found useful makes use of a set of rating scales for both feedback and grading. Because students receive, in effect, a set of grades, the feedback they receive is more specific than overall grades and can direct them toward aspects of the papers that are strong as well as those that are weak and need improvement. Some rating scales are obviously specific to the particular paper being written, whereas others refer more generally to characteristics of the students' writing. In Figures 7-3 and 7-4, the point values assigned to different ratings and rating scales are idiosyncratic to the instructor. They merely illustrate how such a system might be implemented. When using rating scales to evaluate student papers, graders have their attention directed toward relatively specific aspects of the papers, which facilitates grading by a providing a set of easier-to-answer questions compared to an overall assessment. Because evaluation of a section of the paper, for example, the introduction, is likely to be more reliable than an overall assessment of the entire paper, rating scales can make paper grading more reliable. Because each student receives multiple ratings on a paper, there is at least some moderately specific feedback. If the scales are used to provide feedback on first drafts, students can then use the initial ratings to direct their efforts at revising their papers. Any written comments on the papers add feedback but are not required to bear the full feedback burden.

Revising.   In addition to giving students useful feedback about their drafts of papers, instructors will find it helpful to instruct students directly on the best ways to revise papers. Novice writers such as students have been found to revise papers differently, compared to expert writers. Experts focus first on global problems that might exist in a paper—they attack the larger issues of revising and only later address details. Novices tend to focus on details (Hayes & Flower, 1986). Therefore, feedback to students should guide them toward addressing more global aspects of their papers.

There are two kinds of difficulties that students might face in trying to improve a paper. First, those whose writing skills are not well developed can have difficulty in identifying weaknesses in a paper, especially one of their own. Feedback provided by instructors or other paper evaluators can help students see weaknesses. The second difficulty is that, even with specific feedback, such that some weakness is identified, students might not know how to correct the weakness and improve the paper. We have found it helpful both to show students examples of well-written papers and to have students practice evaluating papers and receive feedback about their evaluations (Dominowski, Dallob, & Penningroth, 1994). Exercises were structured as follows: First, students were shown an example of a good (part of a) paper together with comments indicating what was good about that paper; any weaknesses were also discussed. Then, students were given two sample papers chosen to be relatively good and relatively weak. The students were asked to evaluate these papers and to indicate which was better and which was worse. After doing so, students then received the evaluations of the sample papers

Name_____   Grader_____
                    Draft__   Final __

TITLE PAGE	−2	OR	0
	INCORRECT		CORRECT FORM

LOW		**MEDIUM**		**HIGH**

OVERALL CLARITY OF INTRODUCTION
1	2	3	4	5

ACCURACY AND CLARITY OF ARTICLE SUMMARIES
1	2	3	4	5

DEGREE TO WHICH THE REFERENCES ARE COORDINATED/RELATED
1	2	3	4	5

CLARITY AND QUALITY OF CONCLUSIONS OFFERED
1	2	3	4	5

DEGREE TO WHICH INDIVIDUAL SENTENCES ARE UNDERSTANDABLE
1	2	3	4	5

DEGREE TO WHICH RELATIONS AMONG SENTENCES (PARAGRAPHS) ARE UNDERSTANDABLE
1	2	3	4	5

EFFECTIVENESS OF ORGANIZATION (SEQUENCE) OF THE SENTENCES AND PARAGRAPHS WITHIN THE PAPER
1	2	3	4	5

DEGREE TO WHICH EACH SENTENCE CONTRIBUTES TO DEVELOPMENT OF THE TOPIC (GLOBAL COHERENCE)
1	2	3	4	5

PRECISENESS OF WORDING/ABSENCE OF AMBIGUITY
1	2	3	4	5

EXTENT TO WHICH REQUIRED STYLE IS FOLLOWED *NOTE SCORING
−1	0	1	2	3

BASIC GRAMMAR/SPELLING/PUNCTUATION/PARAGRAPHING *NOTE SCORING
−2	−1	0	1	2

MAXIMUM POINTS=50

Figure 7-3   Grading Key for Essay

Name_____   Grader_____

TITLE PAGE   −2   0   +2

Bonus   WRONG-FORMAT   CORRECT   EXCELLENT

LOW   **MEDIUM**   **HIGH**

DEGREE TO WHICH PAPER SHOWS UNDERSTANDING OF TARGET ARTICLE
1   2   3   4   5

ACCURACY AND FAIRNESS OF REPRESENTATION OF TARGET ARTICLE
1   2   3   4   5

LOGICAL DEVELOPMENT OF THE IDEAS EXPRESSED
1   2   3   4   5

DEGREE TO WHICH IDEAS WERE ELABORATED WHEN NEEDED
1   2   3   4   5

PERSUASIVENESS/EFFECTIVENESS OF COMMENTARY
1   2   3   4   5

DEGREE TO WHICH INDIVIDUAL SENTENCES ARE UNDERSTANDABLE
1   2   3   4   5

DEGREE TO WHICH RELATIONS AMONG SENTENCES (PARAGRAPHS) ARE
UNDERSTANDABLE
1   2   3   4   5

PRECISENESS OF WORDING; ABSENCE OF AMBIGUITY
1   2   3   4   5

GLOBAL COHERENCE: EXTENT TO WHICH EACH SENTENCE CONTRIBUTES
TO THE THEME
1   2   3   4   5

EXTENT TO WHICH REQUIRED STYLE IS FOLLOWED **NOTE SCORING
−1   0   1   2   3

BASIC GRAMMAR/SPELLING/PUNCTUATION/PARAGRAPHING **NOTE SCORING
−2   −1   0   1   2

MAXIMUM POINTS=50

Figure 7-4   Scoring Key for Commentary

that were made by the graders. The essential idea was to show students examples of well-written papers and to help them develop their own paper-evaluating skills. Students' revisions of their papers showed substantial improvement in writing quality.

PLAGIARISM

The obvious purpose of writing assignments is to help students demonstrate that they have completed the assignment, as well as to provide students with the opportunity to improve their writing skills. If students do not do the work, the intended purpose is thwarted. Plagiarism is offering another's thoughts and writing as one's own, with no identification of the original source. Concern over plagiarism has frequently been expressed (Standing & Gorassini, 1986); the question facing instructors is what, if anything, might be done to minimize its occurrence. Plagiarism can occur in different ways. Complete papers can be purchased from commercial establishments or downloaded from the Internet. Text from published material can be incorporated verbatim or near-verbatim into a student's paper. One student can copy another's work. Because plagiarism can take different forms, efforts to combat it also vary.

To reduce the chances of students using already existing papers, instructors can take steps to make their papers unique to their courses. Rather than requesting a general paper on some generally available source, an instructor can include in the assignment directions that require students to refer specifically to course material in writing their papers. For courses that are taught repeatedly, instructors who change their writing assignments from one offering to the next limit opportunities to use existing papers.

Perhaps the most difficult form of plagiarism to deal with exists when students copy text from published sources without proper citation. The first problem is that the plagiarism might be unintentional! Students cannot copy another's work, word for word, without being aware of doing so; although it seems unlikely that college students would be unaware of the requirement to use quotation marks in such cases, a brief reminder from the instructor would clarify proper usage. More troublesome is superficial modification of another's words, versus proper paraphrasing of the ideas contained in the original text. Roig (1997) found that undergraduate students, given an original text and various rewritten versions of it, made the mistake of judging plagiarized (superficially modified) versions as properly paraphrased. In addition, students might not know how to properly cite an author when they do use their own words to paraphrase an author's ideas. For example, if a student writes a paragraph summarizing another's innovative analysis of some issue but merely includes the other's paper in a reference list, the student has not cited properly the source of the ideas in that paragraph. The solution to problems of misunderstanding is prevention—a brief but enlightening lecture on issues of plagiarism that clearly spells out proper methods of citation.

The second general problem concerns detection and verification of plagiarism from published sources. In some cases, the stylistic differences between the published material and a student's own writing might be noticeable enough that one's suspicions are aroused. Nonetheless, tracking down the source of the imported material will be at least time-consuming and might be impossible. How does the instructor determine whether a student has actually written some part of the paper or copied it from a published source? The instructor might interview the student, asking questions about various parts of the paper in an attempt to assess the student's understanding of the written material. Another proposed technique is to employ what is called a cloze test. This procedure calls for deleting, say, every fifth word from a prose passage. The modified passage, with blanks (which should be the same size) where the deleted words used be, is then given to a person with the task of filling in the missing words. Cloze tests have been used simply to determine how predictable a prose passage might be. In the present context, the underlying assumption is that a person will be better able to fill in the blanks for a passage he or she has written, compared to the success rate for a passage written by someone else. Research using this procedure (Standing & Gorassini, 1986) has shown that students tend to score higher (about 85%) in filling in passages they have written compared to completing passages written by another (about 60%). However, there is variability in scores such that a relatively low score could be obtained even when completing one's own prose if there has been some delay between creating the passage and filling in the blanks. A very high score, on the other hand, is likely to be a good indication that the student has written the passage.

Even if very accurate plagiarism assessment techniques were available, students might not agree to cooperate with such post-hoc procedures, and refusal is not proof of guilt (Standing & Gorassini, 1986). If an instructor included on the course syllabus a statement to the effect that the instructor reserved the right to conduct plagiarism assessments before accepting papers, perhaps the procedure would be seen as justified. Such an announcement might also have a deterrent effect.

One somewhat cumbersome but effective technique for deterring plagiarism is to require students to append copies of their cited references to submitted papers. Possession of the sources allows a grader to compare a student's paper to cited text, whether to check for possible plagiarism or for the quality of the student's description and use of the cited material. Examining copies of potentially interesting articles can help instructors select materials for subsequent offerings of a course. If the number of references per paper is more than a few, this procedure will be wasteful and infeasible. It also is ineffective for detecting when students use a source that they do not cite in their papers. Nonetheless, for shorter papers, the requirement to append copies of cited articles can be useful.

SUMMARY

Writing assignments allow students to consider their thoughts on a topic, and improving writing skills improves thinking. Expressive writing assignments are short and ask students to react to course material; the goal is to help students to understand a topic, and such assignments are often not graded. Persuasive writing assignments such as term papers, lab reports, and critiques require students to carefully formulate and organize their thoughts to produce coherent papers. Clear instructions regarding writing assignments, including information about how papers will be evaluated, should be provided in handouts. Writing assignments are most beneficial when students receive feedback on papers and submit revisions. Written comments and ratings on multiple scales dealing with different aspects of a paper provide guidance for revising. Students also need exposure to examples of good writing to improve their papers. Steps to reduce plagiarism include class presentations on plagiarism, constructing assignments so that they are course-specific, and requiring students to submit copies of relevant parts of reference materials.

8

Test Construction

Constructing tests is a critical part of teaching. In selecting the content to ask questions about and choosing what questions to ask, the instructor tells the students what is really important about the course. From students' perspective, exam content is what matters because test scores directly affect their academic lives, and they rightly expect test questions to reflect what has been stressed by the instructor and textbook authors. Therefore, a fundamental principle for instructors to follow when constructing tests is to ensure that test questions are related to instructional objectives.

In addition to deciding what to ask about which topics, test constructors also face the issue of how to assess students' knowledge, what kinds of test items to use. Multiple-choice, true-false, short-answer, and essay questions, even though they might be directed toward the same topic, do not tap identical forms of knowledge. It is not the case that one question type is necessarily better than another; basically, the types are just different, and each has strengths and weaknesses, as we shall see. The choice of question type reasonably can be based on two broad concerns: relation to instructional objectives, and practical considerations. As an example of the influence of instructional objectives, if an instructor wants students to be able to discuss issues of some complexity, essay questions seem most appropriate. Because instructors often have multiple goals for student learning, exams frequently contain questions of different types. Also, equity considerations support using a mixture of testing techniques, because some students perform better on multiple-choice exams than on essays whereas others have the opposite performance pattern (Bridgeman & Morgan, 1996)

Practical considerations also play an important role in test construction. The creation and eventual scoring of tests take up noticeable amounts of time, and instructors are busy people, especially when teaching a course for the first time. The size of the class and the presence or absence of teaching assistants place strong constraints on testing practices. For example, a faculty member teaching a class of 100 students, without assistants, might believe that essay questions are the most appropriate assessments for a particular course. Suppose that, for a given exam, four questions, each likely to yield a two-page answer, would provide adequate coverage of the course material. Even if the instructor could grade each answer in five minutes (which seems unlikely), scoring the 100 exams would take over 33 hours without allowing any time for anything but reading and scoring answers—not even resting one's eyes! It's doubtful that an instructor could allocate a week's work to nothing but grading an exam, except under very special circumstances such as a very important end-of-year exam with no other duties once the exam is given. In the normal course of events, something will have to give—fewer questions or a different question type. A rough rule regarding course testing is that exam forms that take less time to grade will take more time to construct, so instructors pay the price in any case. Because faculty members usually expect to teach courses more than once, time spent creating easy-to-grade exams is likely to lead to time saved later, if the exams can be used again.

Course objectives and time-and-effort issues are not the only matters that influence test construction. For example, the reliability of scoring is an important consideration. Our discussion of the various question types will include strengths and weaknesses as well as techniques for avoiding problems and creating tests that assess students' knowledge to a reasonable degree.

MULTIPLE-CHOICE QUESTIONS

A multiple-choice item consists of a stem that directly or indirectly poses a question and a set of alternatives from which the answer is selected. These questions frequently are cued-recognition tests of memory, although test items can be constructed to require identification of new examples, complex comparative judgments, or even lengthy calculations. Fundamentally, multiple-choice items involve discrimination among the presented alternatives, so the relevant question for analysis is "What does one need to know to select the correct alternative?" It is important to recognize that answering these items rests on discrimination among alternatives, so that the kind of discrimination dictates what is required.

To illustrate this point in a fundamental way, consider the two multiple-choice items shown below. Both are based on the proposition "The standard deviation is a measure of variability," but they are not identical questions:

A. The standard deviation is a measure of
   1. central tendency.
   2. variability.
   3. skewness.
   4. extremity.

B. Which of the following is a measure of variability?

1. Median
2. Standard Score
3. Geometric Mean
4. Standard Deviation

Item A provides "standard deviation" and asks, in effect, which of the four alternatives is most closely associated with that term. Item B provides "variability" and asks which of the alternatives is most closely associated with this term. Although a person who firmly knows the underlying proposition would answer either question correctly, a student with less-secure knowledge could succeed on one item but fail the other. For example, instruction might have first presented "variability" and then "standard deviation" as one such measure among others. As a result, the connection from variability to standard deviation might be stronger than the reverse connection from standard deviation to variability.

Types of Questions.   Many kinds of questions can be asked using a multiple-choice format. One general distinction among question types is between lower level and higher order questions. Operationally, the answer to a lower level question can be found in one place in a textbook (or good set of notes), whereas higher order questions typically refer to information from two or more locations. Lower level questions concern definitions of terms or simple facts. Higher order questions are relational, calling for comparisons or inferences to be made. Multiple-choice questions successfully can tap knowledge at different levels (Hancock, 1994). There are, of course, multiple question types within these broad levels. Here's a nonexhaustive list, described in terms of what they ask the student to do:

Identify a verbatim statement (from textbook or lecture notes)
Identify a paraphrase of a statement
Identify a previously presented example of a concept

"Which of the following is an example of ...?"

Identify a new example of a concept
Select/execute the solution to a previously presented problem
Apply a previously presented solution to a new, analogous problem
Compare two concepts or theories

"What is a major difference (similarity) between ...?"

Relate a theory to a research finding or other observation

"Which finding supports the theory ...?"

Relate an observation to two or more theories

"Which theory best explains the finding that ...?"

Explain or draw inferences regarding a concept, theory, or procedure

"How does the ___ theory explain the finding that ... ?"

As the questions become more complex, requiring greater knowledge and more reasoning, the use of a multiple-choice format seems less appropriate. Because a student might guess the correct alternative, and because a student might have considerable relevant knowledge but miss one aspect and thus the question, the simple record that is obtained—did or did not choose correctly—might seem an inadequate index of the knowledge in question. For such complex questions, instructors might prefer a different format, to be discussed later.

Similarity of Distracters.   Because multiple-choice items require discrimination among alternatives, the similarity of distracters to the correct alternative plays a strong role in determining item difficulty. As an extreme example, suppose that Item A above were modified as follows:

A. The standard deviation is a measure of
   1. personality.
   2. variability.
   3. height.
   4. political affiliation.

A student in a statistics course probably would reject alternatives 1, 3, and 4 as not statistical terms, or simply as yielding no feeling of familiarity from this course, and thus correctly select alternative 2 even if unable to pass the original item form. Focusing on alternatives' similarity can be a good way to construct multiple-choice items by leading instructors to consider precisely what discrimination they want the students to make.

Number of Alternatives and Guessing.   A weakness of multiple-choice items is that they can be answered correctly without having any relevant knowledge, simply by making a lucky guess. Two comments are in order here. First, because of the chance element, using multiple-choice questions for very complex questions or extensive calculations seems wasteful. For example, suppose a problem requires a four-step calculation; if students can successfully complete the four steps, they will be able to choose the correct numerical answer. A student who knows three steps will fail, just as a student who knows no steps will do. Of course, a student might just guess the correct answer. If an instructor wants to know if students can complete the computation, it seems better to ask them to show their calculations, even though evaluating their protocols will be more time-consuming than scoring a multiple-choice item.

The second comment applies to test construction as well as grading decisions. By simple formula, the probability of correctly guessing the answer to a multiple-choice item is $1/n$ where n is the number of alternatives presented. With four alternatives, "chance" is 25%, with five, 20%. But for the vast majority of actual multiple-choice questions, the number of viable alternatives—those that might be chosen by a student with weak knowledge of the relevant material—is less than the number presented. Quite commonly, only one or two distracters are endorsed by students who fail to select the correct alternative. The basic reason for this phenomenon is that there are seldom three or four really good distracters for a test item.

Consider how alternatives for a multiple-choice question might be created. First, there is the correct alternative. Second is a highly similar alternative, one that might be confused with the answer by students whose knowledge is shaky; in some circumstances there might be two such items. A third alternative is a more weakly associated entry, perhaps in the general topic area but not really related to the specific topic of the question. The fourth alternative might then be very weakly related, a fifth even more so. Students with weak knowledge of the particulars of a question nonetheless are likely to be able to reject really distant alternatives, so these are seldom chosen. They might as well not be there. Indeed, that is my advice to test constructors. As long as you can think of "good" distracters, compared to the correct alternative, add them. When you reach the point where you can't think of additional, idea-based distracters, stop. There is no requirement that all items have the same number of alternatives—it's your exam, and it can have any "look" you desire. Indeed, three-alternative questions might be preferable to four-alternative items (Landrum, Cashin, & Theis, 1993). Rather than spending time adding weak distracters that the least-knowledgeable students will reject, spend the time doing something more valuable or enjoyable. Perhaps this advice will be easier to follow after creating items all having the same number of alternatives and seeing how many are virtually never endorsed.

Multiple-choice questions work best when there is only one correct answer. Using items where, in the instructor's view, there are two or three correct answers, with students instructed to "select all correct alternatives," introduces factors unrelated to students' knowledge of course material. Independently of how much or how firmly they know relevant material, students differ in their personal criteria for endorsing alternatives. That is, two students might have equal relevant knowledge for a possibly multiple-correct-alternative item, but if one is more reluctant than the other to mark two (or three) alternatives as correct, their scores will differ, but not because their knowledge differs. For the same general reasons, when each question has a single correct alternative, students should be instructed to answer all questions, that is, to "select the best alternative" for each item. In this way, individual differences in willingness to endorse alternatives, which are unrelated to differences in knowledge, will not affect students' scores.

Item Structure.   What follows is a list of comments that are intended to facilitate the construction of good questions, to help avoid poorly written questions, and to describe some issues that arise in relation to item structure. Some concern the stem of the question, others the alternatives.

1. The main question should be clearly phrased in the stem. Stems that end in question marks are usually quite clear.
   Poor: Craik and Lockhart
   a. developed a theory of child development.
   b. argued that short-term memory is not distinct from long-term memory.
   c. etc.....
   Better: What was Craik and Lockhart's contribution to cognitive psychology?
   a. A theory of child development.
   b.....

2. Avoid lengthy, run-on sentences in the stem. Use several simple sentences, if necessary, with the last clearly stating the question.
   Poor: What book did D. H. Lawrence, an English novelist, write that led to a famous trial and influenced writing and publishing thereafter?
   Better: D. H. Lawrence was an English novelist. What book did he write that led to a famous trial and influenced writing and publishing thereafter?

3. Minimize the use of completion items, especially those with two or more blanks. Determining what is required for such items can be unnecessarily difficult for students. Use direct questions instead. If using single-blank completion items, try to place the blank at the end of the sentence.
   Poor: _____ and _____ are hormones that serve as neurotransmitters.
   Better: What two hormones serve as neurotransmitters?

4. All alternatives should have the same grammatical relation to the stem. Typically, the correct alternative fits grammatically with the stem; if some distracters do not fit, they might be rejected for that reason, making the item "too easy."

5. More generally, avoid extraneous differences among alternatives, such as name vs. no name, short vs. long alternatives, that might cue correct responses. For example, if the correct alternative is distinctly longer (or shorter) than the distracters, it will stand out for that reason and thus be more likely to be chosen.

6. Avoid terms such as "frequently" or "often" because their meanings are not clear, so they create ambiguity (Case, 1994).

7. Avoid the use of the alternatives "All of the above" and "None of the above." Ordinarily, these alternatives cannot be used very often, so their appearance is marked. When used, they often can be selected or rejected without complete knowledge of relevant material. For example, suppose a student must select the best alternative for a five-alternative item, the last being "All of the above." If the student is confident that two alternatives fit the stem, then "All" can be chosen without knowledge or careful consideration of the other

alternatives. If the student is confident that one alternative is incorrect, then so is "All" (so it might as well not be there).

8. The more complex the item, the greater the influence of reading and reasoning abilities will be. Some students might know the relevant material sufficiently well but have difficulty working their ways through the question. Consequently, the item will not distinguish such students from those who lack the basic knowledge, because both types will fail the question. Complex items thus serve as high-end discriminators.

Strengths and Weaknesses.   The great strength of the multiple-choice format is its ease and reliability of scoring. Checking answers is mechanical and requires neither interpretation nor special knowledge. Most commonly, multiple-choice exams are scored by machine; test-scoring offices at colleges typically also provide statistical information about the exam, such as item difficulty and item-test correlations (measures of how well each item separates those who scored better and worse on the exam as a whole). For these reasons, multiple-choice questions are popular among instructors teaching large classes.

Multiple-choice questions also offer the advantage of allowing different kinds of questions, at various difficulty levels, to be asked by manipulating the question posed and the similarity of alternatives. In addition, one can ask more questions when a multiple-choice format is used; because students do not have to construct answers, which takes time, they can answer more questions in a given time period. Using a greater number of questions is good because the set of questions provides better coverage of course material, and students' test scores are more reliable.

There are two major disadvantages to multiple-choice questions. First, they are time-consuming to construct. However, once constructed, multiple-choice questions can be used again, in either original or modified form. Maintaining exam security over time thus becomes important. If test items are re-used, the initial time cost in constructing them leads to time saving later on. The second weakness of this format is that correct alternatives can be guessed. To an extent, instructors can control the influence of guessing by carefully choosing distracter alternatives and thus controlling the level of knowledge one must possess to have a "good chance" of guessing correctly. Guessing correctly cannot be eliminated as a possibility; instructors often informally take guessing into account when setting the grade criteria for their courses.

SHORT-ANSWER QUESTIONS

As indicated by the name, short-answer questions require students to construct short, written answers. These questions are therefore cued-recall measures of memory for course material (multiple-choice questions require only recognition).

Because answers must be constructed, it is reasonable to assume that there is no chance of "guessing correctly." The problems that arise usually stem from ambiguously worded questions, which lead to scoring difficulties. Without such problems, scoring can be straightforward although somewhat time-consuming.

Instructors might use short-answer questions in place of multiple-choice questions because they want the students to recall the answer rather than merely select it from a set of alternatives. The stem (question) could be the same in both formats, and the answer could be quite short, even a single word. In such cases, because the answer must be recalled on the basis of only the cues present in the question, the short-answer version is likely to be more difficult than the multiple-choice version. Alternatively, the instructor might want students to construct answers of a few sentences in length, or having several, short parts.

Composing the question for a short answer requires even more care than constructing the stem of a multiple-choice item. With a multiple-choice item, ambiguities in the stem can, in part, be corrected by the set of alternatives, but instruction and cues for short-answer items must be contained in the question that is presented. Because students must construct answers, it is important to give them sufficient guidance regarding the form of answer to provide. Students face two problems in trying to formulate an answer: First, what type of information is being requested? Of the several things one might know about the topic mentioned in the question, which are most relevant? Second, how long an answer is required? Instructors might say that they prefer to leave such matters rather vague and see what students decide to do. That position is both unfair to students and a poor measurement technique. To the extent that a question is vague, students will interpret it differently. Differences among students in what they judge to be asked for and how much to write introduce difference in scores that can be unrelated to how much students know about the topic. The student who writes more than is needed for full credit is wasting time that could be spent on other exam questions.

Constructing Questions.   In asking short-answer questions, instructors will have an idea of the type of answer they want to see. For several reasons, it is best to phrase the question so that students will try to write the desired type of answer if they have relevant knowledge. Clarity is better for the students and minimizes grading problems for the instructor. The suggestions offered for constructing clear multiple-choice questions apply to short-answer questions as well. These include asking direct questions, minimizing the use of completion items, avoiding multiply mutilated sentences for completion items, and using two or more short sentences to pose the question, rather than a long, run-on sentence. Here are a few additional comments, based in part on the assumption that instructors use short-answer questions to increase item difficulty beyond that of multiple-choice questions.

1. Use paraphrases rather than literal textbook statements in posing questions; doing so makes the cues depend more on meaning rather than recognition of previously seen language.
2. If testing knowledge of definitions, give the term and ask for its definition rather than vice versa. Doing so requires the students to recall more, which is presumably a reason for using this question type.
3. If a specific number of points is desired in an answer, state that number in the question. Compare "What are the consequences of. ... ?" to "What are two consequences of ...?" In the latter case, students need not guess how long an answer should be.
4. Specify the terms in which answers should be given. "Where" is ambiguous; it is better to ask "In what city, or in what country ... ?" Similarly, "when" is ambiguous, and the question should indicate the desired term—year, century, specific date, and so on.
5. Contemplate "close-in" incorrect answers that might be given on the basis of incomplete knowledge. Ensure that the question clearly asks for more than such nearly correct knowledge.
6. In scoring answers, give credit when synonyms or equivalent paraphrases are used, except in the case of technical terms that need to be used precisely. Remember that the learning goal is conceptual understanding, not verbatim memorization.

Strengths and Weaknesses.   Short-answer questions are relatively easy to generate. Because they require students to construct answers, they provide more information about what students know than the selection of a multiple-choice alternative. Their disadvantages are related to grading: Question vagueness can yield interpretive problems, and even with quite clear questions, scoring answers requires time, relevant knowledge, and some judgment. Nonetheless, if instructors want to be sure that students can generate certain information and take pains to construct clear questions, then the effort is likely to yield the sort of information that instructors desire.

ESSAY QUESTIONS

Essay questions are distinguished from short-answer questions by their scope, the length of required answers, and the relative lack of specific cues for recall. Essay questions typically deal with larger issues and are based on information that is spread out, say, over a number of textbook pages or several lectures. The bare minimum essay question might be characterized as "Tell me what you know about (a stated topic)." Although test items this broad are seldom if ever used, the central point is that, relative to the amount of knowledge that is tapped and the length of answer that students must compose, they receive weak retrieval cues.

Students must generate their own retrieval cues for specific points to include in their answers, and their answers should reflect both how much they know about a topic and how well organized their knowledge is. Performance is also influenced by retrieval strategies, language abilities, and writing skills. For example, students who plan or outline their answers before writing produce better essays (Kellogg, 1987); knowing that a plan will yield a better answer is knowledge about writing rather than knowledge of the subject matter. Because essay questions and answers are comparatively complex, they tap more abilities than other question types. In addition to requiring considerable memory retrieval, essay questions often tap reasoning abilities because they ask for inferences and analyses. Not surprisingly, essay answers are the most difficult to grade reliably and the most time-consuming to evaluate.

Guidelines. When using essay questions, the goal is to pose a question that is clear enough that students can attempt to write the desired type of answer, and to have a scoring scheme that will yield reliable scores. The guidelines for short-answer questions generally apply to essay questions; here are some additional comments.

1. Relate essay questions to higher level instructional objectives that do not readily lend themselves to measurement with other formats.
2. Focus the question on a type of behavior that has been stressed as important to students. For example, if students have been told, directly or indirectly, that relating theories to data is important, test questions should reflect that emphasis.
3. Explicitly request desired analyses, interpretations, and other desired answer components. "Compare" is extremely vague and might be used only if any sensible comparison of any length will be accepted. Instructors have particular kinds of comparisons in mind, and they should include this information in the question. For example, "Compare the assumptions made by Theory A and Theory B" clarifies the student's task.
4. If multi-part answers are requested, indicate the relative importance of the components, for example, "Summarize the xxx theory (3 pts) and give two examples ... (2 pts)." With such information, students can allocate their time and efforts appropriately.
5. Give students sufficient time to write their answers, and consider telling them the approximate length of answer that is expected.
6. Before administering essay questions, consider how answers will be evaluated. Outline the desired model answer and other likely answers. Think about what will lead to answers being judged at different levels of quality. Doing so sometimes points to weaknesses in the question, which can then be rectified.
7. Sometimes instructors give students a choice of essay questions to answer. Allowing students to choose their questions presumably reduces anxiety

and makes the test easier, if students can accurately assess their knowledge relevant to the several questions (which they might not be adept at doing).

8. Accept the fact that scoring is time-consuming and difficult, and set up a system that will aid reliable scoring. Try to arrange a checklist, perhaps using the model answer, as a part of the scoring system, to facilitate consistency. At the same time, be sensitive to answers that do not fit the scoring scheme so that they can be evaluated on their merits.

9. Score a given question on all exams before going on to the next question. Preferably, read all answers to a question before assigning a score to any. The reasons for using this procedure are to minimize the influence of "halo effects" whereby the score on one question is influenced by the score on another, and to minimize the influence of shifting criteria as one goes through the sequence of answers. One technique is to place the answers (exam booklets) in piles representing different judged levels of quality, then to briefly review and adjust the placement of individual answers before assigning scores.

The fundamental reason for posing essay questions is to see what students can do with larger, more complex or more encompassing questions. The essential weakness of essay questions is that they can be ambiguous (underspecified) and are always time-consuming and difficult to score, requiring scorers to have substantial relevant knowledge. Because such questions typically require extensive knowledge as well as analytic and writing skills, they perhaps are best suited for deciding who are the best students in a course.

TRUE-FALSE ITEMS

The essential true-false item presents a statement for which students are to choose one of the two alternatives. Because of the binary option, the formal chance level of responding correctly is 50%. The high rate of guessing correctly means that a relatively large number of true-false items is needed to allow for reasonable identification of above-chance performance. However, just about any content can be used for a true-false item, so generating a large number of items is not especially difficult, although constructing good items can be time-consuming.

Ambiguities.   There are two general problems with true-false items. First, the truth value of many statements that might be used is ambiguous, subject to the type of interpretation that is applied, or depends on subtle aspects of the statement. For example, consider the statement "The United States became independent of the British crown in 1783." True or false? In part, the answer depends on how one interprets "became independent." The Declaration of Independence was signed in 1776, fighting stopped in 1781, and a peace treaty was signed in 1783. Also, is it appropriate to speak of "the United States" prior to the adoption of the

U.S. Constitution in 1789 (is it a trick question?)? Simple statements of fact, such as those pairing authors with book titles, are likely to be unambiguous (barring a debate about true authorship). But many meaningful statements are somewhat unclear with respect to truth value.

A second problem concerns individual differences in criterion setting regarding when to mark a statement "true" or "false." If a person is supremely confident that a statement is, say, "true," choosing an answer would seem obvious. But students will have varying degrees of confidence that statements are true, so they must decide "how confident they should feel" to mark a statement as "true." The essential point is that two students, having the same "feeling of confidence" about a statement, might well adopt different criteria for answering "true," so that one marks "true" and the other marks "false." Their feelings of confidence are imperfect indicators of their knowledge about the statement; assume here their knowledge is equal. Yet, their answers are different because one is more likely than the other to mark a statement "true." These differences in criterion setting affect test scores but are not based on knowledge of the material. Students' differences in tendencies to respond "true" or "false" can invalidate scores on true-false exams (Grosse & Wright, 1985).

Test Instructions.   There is a simple way to alleviate problems stemming from ambiguity regarding statements' truth values and individual differences in criterion setting, namely, to tell students the percentage of test statements that are true. To provide for maximum discrimination, the test should be constructed so that 50% of the statements are true. When students have this information, they know that they should be marking "true" for half the items, so personal differences in criterion setting should play little role in determining test scores. In effect, the students' task is to mark "true" for the 50% of statements that seem "truest" to them. Statement ambiguity can still be a problem, but less so than when the percentage of "true" statements is unknown. To minimize problems due to ambiguity, instructors should keep test statements as direct as possible and should encourage students to ask questions about perceived ambiguities when taking a test (really for any kind of test item). A good instruction is to tell students that they should ask any questions they have about a test, with the understanding that the "worst" that can happen is to be told that a particular question fairly cannot be answered. When students inquire about test items, instructors must decide what, if anything, is reasonable to tell students. In my experience, making that judgment is usually easy. If a student plainly asks for a clarification, a good policy is to honor that request; on occasion, a student's question has brought an ambiguity to my attention such that I have announced the clarification to the entire class. If, however, a student asks for information that the instructor believes students should know, the appropriate answer is "I can't tell you that."

True-false items are easy to construct, at least initially, and easy to score. They can concern any sort of content, including higher order interpretative statements, such as the form "A major problem for the theory. ... " The weaknesses are a high level of correct responding by chance, and ambiguities regarding statements' truth status and criteria for marking "true." As noted above, the ambiguities can be alleviated by informing students of the percentage of "true" statements.

TESTS BASED ON JUDGMENTS OF ASSOCIATION

Two test formats, one traditional and one novel, are based on the sound idea that what a person deems associated or similar depends on what the person knows about the items in question. For both matching tests and what are here called relatedness tests, instructors use their knowledge of course material to construct test materials that they consider more or less related. When the test is given to students, the essential question concerns the extent to which students' judgments correspond to those of the instructor.

Relatedness Tests.   Standard true-false items require students to choose between two alternatives; as noted above, if students know that 50% of the items are to be considered "true," they should so mark the half of the items for which their confidence in an item's truth value is highest. Diekhoff (1984) proposed a type of binary-choice test for which the question is not about truth value as such; rather, the test is intended to assess students' conceptual organization of a section of course material.

To explain, cognitive psychologists have shown that judgments of relatedness between pairs of terms belonging to a domain of knowledge reflect a person's overall understanding of that domain. For example, suppose one identified 30 terms, concepts, or phrases that are the most important items in a section of material, say, a chapter in a textbook. Each of the items could be paired with every other item, and people could be asked to judge how related the two items are. The number of pairings quickly becomes large—435 for 30 items. Judges' ratings of relatedness for all pairs can be analyzed with statistical techniques that describe the structure of a person's knowledge of the content area. Basically, the techniques show how items are clustered and separated, depicting a "relatedness space" to characterize the organization of knowledge. In research on such relatedness judgments, the relatedness spaces of experts, that is, faculty, are quite different from those of novices—students beginning the study of the subject matter. As student learning proceeds, their relatedness judgments come to resemble those of the experts (Schoenfeld & Herrmann, 1982). The essential point is that relatedness judgments reflect knowledge. What is measured is not accuracy of recall of some specific point, but how the person mentally organizes a knowledge domain. When students' patterns of judgments match more closely the instructor's, they are displaying greater knowledge of the relational aspects of the domain. Put differently, relatedness judgments tap relatively high levels of students' knowledge of a domain.

Instructors might well want to know something about how their students organize course material. In part, essay questions are used to tap broad relational knowledge, as we have seen. Relatedness judgments could also be used, but the research procedure of rating all possible pairs and employing abstract analyses is too time-consuming and cumbersome for course use. But, here is where Diekhoff (1984) offers a practical alternative. His suggestion is as follows: The instructor selects a number of important items (terms, concepts, phrases, etc.), perhaps 20 to 30, from a section of course material, perhaps a chapter, more or less depending on the density of important items. The next, critical step is then to form 20 to 30 pairs of items such that half contain strongly related items and half weakly-related items in the instructor's view. The pairs (properly intermixed, of course) are given to students with the instruction to mark half highly related ("true") and half weakly related ("false"). The result is an easily scored test that assesses students' knowledge of conceptual relations in course material.

The scope and the difficulty of such relatedness tests can be controlled by the instructor. The larger the difference in relatedness between "high" and "weak" pairs, the easier the test will be. If the test covers a larger amount of material, it is likely that weakly related pairs will be weaker and thus more different from highly related pairs, resulting in an easier test. Although relatedness tests might not have the "face validity" of broad essay questions, they do offer an alternative method of assessing students' overall grasp of course material.

Matching Tests. Another testing format that makes use of judgments of association or relatedness is the matching test. The set-up is simple: There is a list of items to be matched and a list of alternatives to match to them. Here's a short example, using movie facts; select the correct alternative (movie) for each item (actor):

___Tom Cruise	a. Legal Eagles
___Robert Redford	b. Forrest Gump
___Tom Hanks	c. Back to the Future
	d. Top Gun

As illustrated, the number of alternatives need not be equal to the number of test items, although equal numbers might be the most common form. Implied here, each alternative is to be used just once, and there is only one alternative matching each item. Indeed, to avoid unnecessary ambiguity, matching tests should be constructed so that each item has only one matching alternative, and each alternative matches only one item, and students should be informed of this fact. As with other ambiguity-reducing procedures, the rationale is to prevent individual differences in nonknowledge-based tendencies, here, to use an alternative more than once, from affecting test scores.

Matching tests can be fairly easy to construct, especially if one adopts a "thematic" approach to the format, for example, actors with movies, authors with novels, theorists with theories, historical events with dates, and so on. A key to constructing a good matching test is adhering to the one item—one alternative matching rule. After (initial) construction but before copying and use, matching tests should be checked to ensure that multiple correct matches have been avoided. When mixed types of items and alternatives are used, there's a greater chance of there being multiple matches that might be missed by the test constructor. Having multiple matches when one does not desire them is not a disaster, but it does modify the scoring system and might result in the instructor's failing to get information about students' knowledge of an item of interest.

Regardless of the number of items and alternatives, the expected number of matches to be obtained by chance is one. For example, with 10 items and alternatives, the expected guessing score is one correct; with 20, the expectation is still one correct. With, say, at least 10 items, the influence of guessing on scores is quite small. Of course, what one needs to know to complete matches correctly depends on the nature of the test items. As the degree of association between items and their matching alternatives increases, and as the item-alternative pairs become more different from one another, the test becomes easier. To the extent that each item is somewhat associated with more than one alternative and each alternative is somewhat related to more than one item, the test will be difficult. If the items and alternatives are taken from a narrow slice of course material, the cross-match associations will be substantial and the test will be difficult. The method is fundamentally flexible in that the nature of the connection between an item and its matching alternative can take any form the instructor desires, and can change from one pairing to another.

Strengths and Weaknesses.   Relatedness tests are relatively easy to construct and easy to score. The instructor's work in creating the test is to consider the chosen concepts and terms and ponder how they relate to one another; the exercise can be stimulating. Once the highly related and weakly related pairs have been selected, there should be few problems. Scoring the test is quick and mechanical. A disadvantage is the high, 50% probability of guessing correctly, as with true-false tests.

The construction of matching tests starts with the instructor choosing item-alternative pairings, which should not be especially difficult. Substantial work can be required to check the test for multiple correct matches and to modify the test to reduce the problem. Scoring matching tests is simple, and as noted earlier, guessing correctly will have little influence.

Both formats are flexible in allowing different kinds of associations to be the proper basis of responding. Both formats differ from, say, multiple-choice tests in two ways: First, no direct question is ever posed; rather, only a vague question is implied—"How related do the members of a pairing seem to be?" Second, students really cannot consider items separately; rather, they must coordinate their answers to multiple test items. This means that, with these formats, instructors do not get specific information regarding what students don't know (well enough) when they make mistakes.

The lack of a specific question does not seem problematic for relatedness tests because the pairs are predetermined and the student's task is clearly to divide the pairs into two groups differing in degree of within-pair association. For matching tests where there is a consistent "theme," again the task is clear. For example, if the task is to match authors with books, the implicit question is obvious: Which book did each author write? But when the kinds of connections between items and alternatives are varied, a matching test can be ambiguous and cumbersome. If there are, say, 15 items of different sorts having varying connections to 15 alternatives of different sorts, a considerable amount of test interpretation and decision making can be required. For the first item a student considers, the situation is like a 15-alternative multiple-choice test with no clear question having been asked. For the second item, it's a 14-alternative, vaguely cued choice, and so on. In these circumstances, students can spend substantial time trying to figure out how they should select matches. A portion of that time might be considered wasted. Matching tests can be kept relatively unambiguous by making items distinct from alternatives and having a consistent type of connection for correct matches. Doing so might tend to lead to tapping rather low-level knowledge with matching tests, such as authors with books, or events with dates. More penetrating tests, however, can be produced with some ingenuity, such as having theoretical concepts as items and important research findings as alternatives.

USING TESTS TO PROMOTE LEARNING

Although tests ordinarily are seen as a means of assessing students' knowledge and assigning grades, they can also be excellent sources of learning. The idea that tests are strong contributors to learning was discussed in Chapter 3, and the idea is well worth repeating. Dempster and Perkins (1993) identified four conditions of testing that promote learning through testing: (1) testing soon after learning, (2) testing frequently, (3) spacing tests over time, and (4) making tests cumulative. The first three ideas were discussed in Chapter 3. The last, making tests cumulative, is intended to promote longer term retention of course material. The cumulative final examination is well known. Cumulative testing, however, can be done on an ongoing basis, by including in each test after the first, some questions about material from prior tests. Quite clearly, students should be informed of the inclusion of questions about "old" material and encouraged to review earlier tests. After any test, instructors can address questions for which there appeared to be relatively widespread knowledge deficiencies; in addition, students should be encouraged to review their own test record to correct any personal misunderstandings. Including a cumulative component in a course testing scheme changes the atmosphere toward a focus on learning for the longer term, which is more productive than an attitude of meeting only shorter term goals.

SUMMARY

Course goals, ease and reliability of scoring, and practical considerations affect the kinds of tests instructors employ. Multiple-choice questions involve recognition memory; the stem should pose a clear question, and difficulty depends on the similarity of distracters to the correct alternative. Constructing good multiple-choice questions is demanding, but scoring is simple. Because guessing can yield correct answers, using this question type for complex questions or calculations is questionable. Short-answer questions require recall and production of the answer; the key to good questions is posing clear questions. Essay questions concern larger, more complex issues and require substantial recall and organization of relevant knowledge. Scoring answers is time-consuming and notoriously difficult to accomplish reliably. True-false items are easy to generate but engender problems due to ambiguity and a high level of guessing correctly. To avoid extraneous influences on scores, it is essential to tell students the percentage of true and false items in the set. Tests requiring students to discriminate between strongly and weakly associated items tap knowledge of the structure of a topic area and offer an easily scored means of assessing higher level knowledge, although in an unusual form. Matching tests can require knowledge of different types and different levels but must be constructed carefully to avoid ambiguity. Tests should be used to promote learning as well as to assess students' knowledge; frequent tests, with feedback, and a cumulative component to testing serve this goal.

9

Grading Systems

Choosing Component Weights
Grading on a Curve
Criterion-Based Grading
Special Considerations

Grading schemes apply to individual items, tests, assignments, and whole courses. Here I will focus on determining course grades (which involves determining test grades, etc.).

The final outcome of assessment ordinarily is the assignment of grades on a scale from A to F, with D the minimum grade required to receive credit for a course. Pass-fail systems simply collapse grades A to D to one grade of Pass. The use of $+/-$ grading increases the number of levels and decreases the differences between adjacent grades but doesn't change the basic issue. A grading system should be fair, reliable, understandable to students, and should reflect course goals. An instructor must use intuition or judgment in devising a grading system—there is no completely mechanical method. This fact may be taken as an advantage, allowing you to use your best judgment in determining grades.

Grading is not an intrinsic element of teaching, despite the ubiquitous administrative requirement to assign grades and the amount of time and effort devoted to the process. Instruction, assessment, and feedback are fundamental tasks for a teacher, but assessment and feedback do not require the assignment of grades. Telling students which exam answers were right and wrong, or which aspects of a paper were good and which showed weaknesses, provides feedback to students about their performance. In principle, instructors could provide such feedback without ever assigning grades. It might seem that grades are an alternate form of feedback; however, by themselves, grades provide vague feedback. For example, receiving a grade of B on a paper tells a student that in some way the paper could have been better without indicating which aspects were weak or the kinds of improvements that are desired. Course grades are similarly fuzzy, perhaps even more so, because they reflect multiple components. Rather than directly providing feedback designed to guide learning, grades supply an evaluation relative to some criterion. How to define grades is a matter of some discussion, as we shall see shortly.

Constructing a grading system is an important task for instructors, primarily because grades are important for students. Instructors might view grading as a

129

required nuisance and bemoan students' focus on grades, but Covington (1999) argues that pursuing grades and developing an interest in course material are not necessarily incompatible. It is reasonable for students to care about grades because grades affect their lives. Quite separate from the personal meaning of a grade to a student, various agencies use grades to allocate resources to students. Colleges deny access to further courses when students' grades fall below a desired criterion. Access to the next level of education, in a graduate school or a professional school, is partially dependent on students' having sufficiently high grades. Scholarship support often depends on grades, and parents might make their financial support contingent on the level of grades achieved. For reasons such as these, instructors should take grading seriously.

Grading systems also affect students' reactions to a course and instructor. If students are unhappy with or confused by a grading system, they might participate less or with a less positive attitude. Some analysts have concluded that students prefer low workloads and easy graders (e.g., Greenwald & Gillmore, 1997b). Others, however, have found no association of low workloads with high student evaluations of teaching (Marsh & Roche, 2000) and have argued that the grade-rating data support the idea that more successful teachers earn higher ratings from their students (Howard & Maxwell, 1982). Students' evaluations of teaching have been found to be most strongly related to how much they think they have learned (Marsh & Roche, 2000). Students' evaluations of instructors also are strongly related to their perceptions of the fairness of the grading system (Rodabaugh & Kravitz, 1994). Fairness has multiple facets, including the relations between course goals and course requirements, the weights given to different requirements and their relation to the importance and effort associated with the requirements, and the way in which grades are related to students' performance. For students to view a grading system as fair, they must understand how the system functions, which means that instructors must explain the schemes that they use.

Deutsch (1979) pointed out that fairness can be defined in many different ways and that grades might reflect any or several of these meanings. Among the alternatives he discussed were assigning grades on the basis of effort, performance, improvement in performance, the social value of contributions, performance in relation to ability, and equality of outcome (give all the same grade). Some of these value systems might seem more familiar or more acceptable than others, but all of them, and others, could be argued to be fair systems. Most actual grading systems employ some mixture of underlying values; for example, performance and effort. Values are reflected in both the weights given to requirements and the way in which grades are related to performance.

CHOOSING COMPONENT WEIGHTS

Decisions must be made regarding the weights to be assigned to various course components. Perhaps some instructors believe that course grades should reflect only what students know, as indicated by exams. That view can limit grades to memory assessments and is too restrictive. As discussed in Chapters 3 and 4, knowledge can be expressed in many different ways, and being able to apply knowledge to new situations can be more important than memory retrieval. Furthermore, grades on class assignments completed during a course have been found to be better predictors of very long-term memory for course material than scores on a comprehensive final exam (Conway, Cohen, & Stanhope, 1992). So it should be the norm that courses have multiple types of requirements. Even if the requirements all are exams, or all are papers, issues of weighting components arise.

Weights can be shown in two ways. Fractional or proportionate weights can be assigned to each requirement. For example, suppose students are required to write three papers, each of which will be graded on a scale from A+ to F. Students might be told that the three papers will be weighted equally, or perhaps because the third paper requires more work and is more central to course goals, the weights for the papers might be 1/4, 1/4, and 1/2, or some other scheme. To determine final grades, letter grades need to be converted to numerical form. For example, a scale including three levels of each grade category A through D and one F category would have 13 levels and could readily be converted to 13 numbers (A+ = 13, A = 12, A− =11, B + = 10, and so on). Applying the weights to the numerical values will yield the final average. If a student had received grades of B, C+, and A−, the numerical values would be 9, 7, and 11, respectively. If equal weights were used, the average grade would be $1/3 (9+7+11) = 9.0$, a final grade of B. With unequal weights (like those above), the average grade would be $.25(9)+.25(7)+.50(11)=9.5$, which is midway between B and B+.

An alternative weighting method is to base final grades on point totals and indicate weights for components by point values. Equal weighting for the three papers might be indicated by stating that each paper will be worth (a maximum) of 20 points (or some other, equal number). Unequal weighting is shown in unequal point values, for example, "the first two papers are worth 20 points each, the third paper is worth 40 points." Either a points scheme or a weighting equation will do the job. The popularity of points schemes suggests that they might be a bit easier to use. Students will interpret the weights given to course components as indicators of importance and will adjust their efforts accordingly. For example, if the course requirements are three tests each worth 100 points and a paper worth 20, relatively little attention will be given to the paper. The amount of effort students will devote to a task will depend on its weight in the grading system.

Weights should reflect both the amount of effort required by a component and the importance of the component to course goals. More work or more difficult work would ordinarily merit more weight. However, an instructor must make decisions regarding importance and decide how much emphasis and grade weight to give to each component, keeping in mind the fundamental soundness of a work-weight relation. Maintaining a proper relation between work and weight is an important part of fairness. If, for example, students were required to write a paper that involved a great deal of library research or data collection as well as writing, but counts very little in the grading scheme, they would resent the requirement. If an instructor, say, wants students to read journal articles and write a paper about them, but doesn't want to give the paper much weight in the grading system, the instructor must find a way to structure the assignment so that the likely workload fits the grade weight.

These decisions occur in different ways at multiple levels, for example, weighting a test versus a paper: How long a test, what kinds of questions? How complex a paper, how much effort is required to get needed information? On a smaller scale, weighting items on a test: If a multiple-choice answer is worth 1 point, how much is a short written answer worth? The answer here clearly will depend on the relative complexity of the questions and the required length of a written answer. More complex questions and longer answers warrant more points. Weighting choices also can have subtle, unintended consequences. Consider the weighting of lectures and textbook as sources of questions for exams. If nearly all exam questions come from lectures, why should students read the textbook? Why were they required to buy it? If nearly all exam questions come from the textbook, why should students come to class? Instructors should have answers to such questions.

Decisions about component weighting exist with any grading system. The second critical aspect of grading is the manner in which grades are related to student performance. There are two "popular" systems, grading "on a curve" or using "fixed criteria." As I have a distinct bias on this issue, I will state it: I see many problems with "curve" grading and prefer a fixed-criterion system. Although I will discuss each approach in detail, here are two differences between them that lead me to prefer fixed criteria:

1. A curve system places students within a class in competition with one another for grades; a fixed-criterion system does not do so.
2. A fixed-criterion system can be described to students at the outset of a course (e.g., 90% will be an A, etc.), so they know what will be expected of them. A curve system cannot be comparably described because grade criteria will be set only after requirements are completed.

GRADING ON A CURVE

This approach rests on the assumption that the meaning of a score depends on its placement in a distribution of scores and is seen in the development of standardized tests: A domain of knowledge is defined, a population of relevant items is identified, and a sample of those items is used on a test. The basic assumption is that discriminating among test-takers is the primary goal, with the added assumption that a proper, normative group of test-takers has been identified, and the corollary that placement of scores on the original scale is not important. Thus, curve grading essentially implies assessing performance (test, paper, or other assignment), obtaining a distribution of scores, and applying a set of cut-points to the distribution. The cut-points must be intuitively derived by the grader. This could be done on a completely ad hoc basis by looking at the score distribution and deciding to separate the As from the Bs here, the Bs from the Cs there, and so on. Alternatively, in an a priori rigid system, it might be assumed that there should be 10% As, 20% Bs, 40% Cs, 20% Ds, and 10% Fs (where such percentages come from is a mystery). With such a scheme, one simply finds the cut-points that produce the desired percentages. With a rigid system, and perhaps also with an ad hoc system, grades do not reflect the overall level of performance for the group, only differences in scores within the group. For example, suppose an instructor gives a 100-point test and the highest, average, and lowest scores for the group are 95, 83, and 72, respectively. A curve system is applied to the scores, and there will be As, Bs, and so on. Now suppose that high, average, and low scores were 80, 60, and 40. A curve system would again yield As, Bs, and so on even though almost this entire distribution of scores is below the first example. A student with a score of 75 might get a grade of F if in the first group but get an A if in the second group.

Curve grading is applied to a distribution of scores. In a college course, instructors obtain multiple distributions of scores, one for each requirement. A complete curve system would require that each component be graded on a curve, and that some way be found to put together all the curved grades to compute a final course grade. That is a messy, difficult way to grade, and probably nobody attempts such a scheme.

The most common "curve" system is one in which points are given for each component, with points summed (perhaps with weights) to produce "point totals" to which "a curve" is applied. Such schemes involve considerable instructor intuition, and distributional notions arise, weakly, only in the final step. Why are such systems used? Among possible reasons are these:

1. "Points" are easy to communicate as scores to students.
2. Instructors want to have control over where the cut-points will be but don't have enough confidence in their tests to select the cut-points in advance. Or, they have general expectations about cut-points but don't want to commit themselves in advance.
3. Instructors accept "weak" distributional notions, for example, "Everybody can't get an A," "Most students should get a C."
4. (compared to using fixed criteria) Less attention needs to be paid to test construction.

Test Analysis. In any curve system, because the goal is to discriminate among students, evaluation of test items uses item-test correlations—roughly, comparisons of performance on an item of high versus low scorers on the whole test. College test-scoring services typically provide instructors with information about item difficulty and item-test correlations. Items that do not discriminate, or those that reverse-discriminate (lows better than highs) can be eliminated, with official test scores based on the remaining, "good" items. Keeping nondiscriminating items probably will do little harm, but noticeable reverse discriminators should be discarded if item difficulty lies in the broad middle range. For very easy items and very difficult items, item-test correlations are rather meaningless because the vast majority of students are getting the same score, and the correlation is determined by the small number of students who get the alternate score ("wrong" for a very easy item, "correct" for a very difficult item).

Evaluation.   Using a "typical" curve system in which students accumulate points for various requirements and grades are "curved" using the total points distribution is fairly easy and allows instructors to keep their options open regarding grade criteria until the end of the course. At the same time, curve systems make it difficult for instructors to inform students of their progress during the course. Suppose a student, after the first test, says "My score was 26 out of 35—how am I doing?" The instructor can tell the student whether that score was above or below the average, by how much, and perhaps give additional information about the distribution. This feedback is meaningful but incomplete. If the student then says "But was my score a B, or C+, or maybe an A?" what can the instructor say? If the instructor says that it's hard to answer that question because grade criteria won't be decided until the end of the course, the student will be dissatisfied and should be. The instructor could tell all students that, if he or she had to give grades for just this test, what the cut-points would probably be. That information is useful although still tentative. To give students an idea of their grade progress during the course, the instructor needs to compute the distribution of "total points so far" after each completed requirement and tell students where the "if I had to grade now" cut-points would be in that distribution. To give students information about their progress, the instructor has to engage in another round of curve grading each time another requirement is completed. Not giving students such information would leave them ill-informed about their progress, which would be extremely poor practice.

As noted earlier, curve systems place students in competition with one another for grades. This competition has two undesirable consequences. First, it discourages cooperative learning, students helping one another. With respect to learning, it makes perfectly good sense that a student who is learning faster or understands better can aid another student to learn course material. Students of roughly comparable ability can help one another in many ways, through discussions of course material as well as cooperative informal testing sessions in which students can sharpen their knowledge. Although competitive grading does not rule out such help, it does discourage it. Second, curve grading reduces students' control over their outcomes because their grades depend not only on how well they perform but also on how others perform. It is considered desirable for students to develop an internal locus of control, the belief that their outcomes depend on their efforts, rather than on luck or immutable abilities. Tying grades to what others do discourages such development.

In addition to these difficulties, two other problems arise when using curve systems. A basic problem with curve grading is that a proper reference group is not used. Relative scoring systems assume that a large, appropriate normative group has been identified and assessed. In course grading, the reference group is only those who completed a particular class, a biased sample rather than a well-defined population. The grading sample is biased because it does not include students who have dropped a course, most commonly because they were having trouble with the course. More fundamentally, we know that samples vary, thus we can infer that curved grades will vary in part because of sample variation rather than individual performance. This leads to problems such as "curve breakers" or the same achievement level leading to different grades because of what others in the group score. The appropriate reference group is larger than a single class, which makes class-limited curve grading fundamentally flawed.

Curve grading can also produce conflict with instructor intuitions. All instructors have at least general notions about grades, and conflicts can arise between instructor intuitions and the results of curve grading. Suppose an instructor gives a test with the general expectation of an average grade around 65% and a range from 40% to 95% (the source of the expectation is irrelevant). If the obtained distribution differs, the instructor may feel uneasy about, say, giving an A to a score of 65% (if the distribution is "too low") or about giving a D to a score of 80% (if the distribution is "too high"). More formally, instructors may not accept the curve-grading assumption that placement of the distribution on the original scale is irrelevant. Shouldn't we expect instructors to give reasonable answers to questions about "what a student should know or be able to do to get a grade of ___?" Indeed, some "curve-grading" instructors adjust their grades on the basis of their intuitions about what should be required for any particular grade, so they really use a mixed system. They would be better off using a fixed-criteria system.

CRITERION-BASED GRADING

Fixing the performance criteria for grades in advance allows instructors to describe the system to students at the outset of a course and avoids placing students in direct competition for grades. Each student's grade will depend entirely on how well they meet the established standards. An instructor who initially uses a curve system, after teaching a course several times, might gain sufficient confidence in his or her tests to switch to a fixed-criteria system, announcing grade criteria in advance. In effect, the instructor is informally using information from multiple classes to set criteria.

This approach, of course, does not help an instructor teaching a course for the first time. Is there a viable alternative to curve grading in the absence of cumulative distributional information? I think there is.

The core of a fixed-criteria system is to establish grade criteria in advance, on judgmental grounds. With this kind of system, one does not really care what the distribution looks like; rather, the numbers of A, B, C, and other grades will simply reflect how students perform against the criteria. This approach can be used casually but properly requires instructors to construct tests carefully and to use their intuition somewhat more formally. There are elements of a mastery orientation underlying this approach, although it is not, as such, a mastery system.

The key to success with criterion-based grading (and, I believe, with all grading) is that the instructor is satisfied with the criteria that are established. If a student earns an A, the instructor should see that as appropriate, and similarly for the other grades. Just as the cut-points for a curve system must be chosen intuitively, so must the standards for criterion-based grading. Instructor intuitions about grade standards stem from their own experiences and, preferably, from discussion and reflection on the issues. In my seminar over the years, a number of novice teachers seem to have imported a "90/80/70/60" scheme for grades, perhaps from high school. One can ask, "90% of what for an A?" It's a good question, and a proper response is to arrange assignments and tests, and their grading schemes, so that 90% represents appropriate performance for an A. Below, I describe a relatively formal method of determining grade criteria, as a guide to thinking about the issue. Less formally, an instructor should be comfortable with and able to justify grade criteria. New instructors might be hesitant to announce grade criteria in advance because they are not confident that they will succeed in devising tests that will make the criteria appropriate. I do not believe that this is a serious problem. Instructors can tell students the grade standards that they intend to use while indicating that slight adjustments might be needed when test results are examined; any adjustment should be slight. In fact, adjustment for test inadequacies can be made without perceptible change in the announced criteria, as described later under test analysis.

Setting the Criteria.   What should be the criterion for a grade of A? Perfection (100%) is obvious but impractical; thus, one needs to decide "how much imperfection" one will allow. Consider the criterion for D (minimum performance yielding credit for the course). Any of several intuitions might be used: For multiple-choice or true-false tests (which allow "chance" computations), one possibility is to define minimum D as the lowest score allowing rejection of the hypothesis of guessing with high confidence. For example, with a 40-item, 4-alternative test (ignoring the existence of useless alternatives, etc.), pure guessing leads to an expected score of 10 correct (25% of 40), and 19 is the lowest score allowing rejection of guessing with high confidence, so 19 would be minimum D. Some instructors use 50% as the minimum D, believing that one's performance should be more "knowing" than "not knowing" to get credit (some others use this for minimum C). Having identified criteria for minimum A and minimum D, one needs to find a way to set the intermediate criteria. The entire process is helped if the instructor has made multi-level judgments of the importance of course material and uses these in test construction and grading. An example:

> I try to make my tests 80% material that everyone should learn and 20% material that I expect only the better students to get correct. My general allowance for imperfection is 10%. Thus, minimum A=90%. I strongly feel that a student should know at least 60% of the basic material to get credit for the course. Thus, minimum D=60% of 80%=48%. A solid (middle) C student should know the basic material. Thus, (allowing for imperfection) middle C=90% of 80%=72%. A B student should know the basic material and at least half the "better student" material. Thus, minimum B=90% of 80% +50% of 20% = 82%. If I decide to make the C range symmetric around middle C, my grading scheme is complete:
> A=90% and up   B=82–89%   C=63–81%   D=48–62%   F=47% or less

Remember, this is just an example, illustrating the thought processes. This approach can readily be applied to nontest components such as papers. One decides what features an A (or B, etc.) paper should have and then assigns point values to correspond to the overall scheme. For example, if 85% has been defined as a minimum A, then on a 20-point paper, a student who writes an A paper receives at least 17 points (85% of 20). In this way, students can determine their grade progress on any requirement.

Test Analysis.   A scheme like that above assumes that tests will do what the instructor intends. What if they don't? What if some items have flaws? As with curve systems, reverse-discriminating items are problematic and should be ignored. Nondiscriminating items are intrinsically neutral, however. Two special problems can arise.

1. An item is "too easy." From a criterion-based perspective, this does not mean simply that most everyone got it right. That outcome can be absolutely fine, an indication of successful instruction. Rather, "too easy" means that one can get the item right without knowing what the item was intended to assess, that is, the item was poorly constructed. In practice, it may be impossible to tell if an easy item is "too easy," and there's probably nothing that can be done after the fact. The only "solution" is to avoid such items in the first place.
2. An item is "too difficult." This means that students who in some sense know the material get the item wrong, practically that even the best students don't score well on the item. The most sensible inferences are that either the item was poorly constructed, or the preceding instruction (lecture, text) was ineffective. Identifying such an item rests on examining the performance of the best students (defined by total test score). For example, if

the top group of students average 88% on the test as a whole but score only 40% on a particular item, that would be a "too difficult" item. Such items should not be counted as required and the grade standards should be based on the remaining "good" items. If a 40-item test seems to include 3 bad (= too difficult) items, grades should be based on a maximum of 37 items. In a strict system, performance on bad/discarded items should be ignored. Alternatively, an instructor may decide to let those who got the correct answer to "bad" items keep those points, using these items in effect as bonus items.

SPECIAL CONSIDERATIONS

Extra Credit

Each instructor must decide whether to allow bonus credits (e.g., extra-credit questions on tests, bonus projects) and, if allowed, how much weight such credits should carry. The main reason for extra credits is to allow students to raise their grades above what they would be on the basis of standard requirements. College faculty hold different opinions about the appropriateness of allowing extra credits (Palladino, Hill, & Norcross, 1995), and the issue is related to what wants grades to represent. Without question, extra credit opportunities must be related to course material and goals. Bonus test questions would be items of very high difficulty, such that an instructor does not feel justified in requiring them of students. Bonus projects require extra effort above what is deemed reasonable to require of students and might require dealing with more difficult material. Difficulty-based bonus items will benefit better students, if anyone, whereas effort-based bonus projects can benefit students throughout the range of grades.

The amount of extra credit made available should be determined by deciding how much possible upward movement the instructor wants to permit, for example, a whole grade category, half a category? Suppose a course requires four exams worth 30 points each and a cumulative final worth 80 points, for a total of 200 points as the basis of grading. If the grading scheme were 90% for A, 75% for B, 60% for C, and 50% for D, then the minimum point totals would be A—180, B—150, C—120, and D—100. Suppose further that the instructor will allow students to write an extra-credit paper based on library research. How many points (maximum) should the bonus paper be worth? Perhaps the instructor is reluctant to let a bonus project be worth a whole grade category, which is 20 to 30 points in the example. Perhaps the instructor is comfortable with the bonus paper being worth about half a grade category, say, 15 points maximum. If so, then students whose exam totals place them in the upper half of a grade category could earn the next higher grade by earning bonus points. For example, a student with a C+ exam point total of 140 could move up to a B by earning 10 or more extra credits. The instructor simply must decide how much potential grade movement to allow. Having done that, the instructor must then structure extra-credit assignments so that the amount and difficulty of the work is appropriate for the chosen point value. If extra credit is allowed, it must be made available to all students in an equitable fashion (see Chap. 10). Also remember to establish grade criteria before adding bonus credits to students' scores.

Borderline Cases

In determining course grades, "problems" can arise with respect to students who "just miss" the cut-point/criterion for a grade category (however that is set). The potential problems are complaints from students and a bit of anguish for the instructor. Such problems can be reduced by obtaining more measurements. The more "points" involved in a course, the less likely it is that students will be a small number of points below a grade criterion.

One method for dealing with "just missed" students is to accept the fact that some people will "just miss" and give them the lower grade that the system dictates. This approach is defensible but can lead to complaints or pleas for reconsideration. An alternative is to define a range of uncertainty below each grade criterion so that students falling in this range will receive a second look before final grade assignment. The second look should be a systematic method of deciding whether or not such students will be given the higher grade. One might ask if dropping the lowest test score and recomputing overall percentage, or dropping the first test score and recomputing, would result in the student's meeting the criterion for a higher grade. If a cumulative final exam was given, an instructor might give the higher grade if the student met the criterion on the final. Still another method is to allow students to earn bonus points to compensate for poor performances, making no further adjustment. Whatever scheme is used, it must be applied equitably to all students, not just those who might ask for reconsideration, and it is best if students are informed of the instructor's system.

SUMMARY

Grading policies deserve attention because grades are important to students. Fairness in grading is critical. The weights given to various course requirements should reflect course goals and the difficulty level and effort required by the requirements. Weights frequently are indicated by the points assigned to each requirement, with course grades based on point totals. Curve grading is a matter of applying intuitively derived cut-points to a distribution of scores. Although easy to use, curve grading makes grade progress difficult to assess and places students in competition for grades, thus discouraging cooperative learning. The assumptions underlying curve grading in a course are questionable. Criterion-based grading requires instructors to announce grade criteria in advance and then assess performance in accordance with the stated plan. Criteria can be set with varying degrees of formality but should reflect the instructor's beliefs about the performance levels appropriate for different grades. Extra-credit opportunities are at the instructor's discretion; if allowed, they must be equally available to all students. Similarly, an instructor's method for dealing with borderline grades must be applied uniformly.

IV

Professional Issues and Concerns

10

Ethical Issues and Special Situations

In the Classroom
Equitable Assignments
Rules and Exceptions
Socializing
Academic Integrity
Students with Disabilities

Teaching takes place in multiple contexts—classroom, the college or university, and the larger society. Instructors therefore have multiple sets of expectations or constraints that they must respect when teaching their classes. Instructors have responsibilities to their students, to the department and college, to their discipline, and to society's laws and customs. Most of the ethical issues, situations, and problems that instructors face concern interactions with the students in their classes. Dealing with the variety of issues and problems that are presented by individual students requires instructors both to have well-thought-out policies and to act flexibly and fairly in finding solutions to particular situations.

Instructors both teach and assess the students in their classes. Because instructors assign grades, and grades can have significant impact on students' lives, instructors hold relative power over their students. At the undergraduate level, it is essentially impossible for the teacher-student relationship to be between equals. Instructors need to be aware of the imbalance of these relationships, in part so that they don't do unintended harm. For example, a sarcastic remark made while bantering with friends might be the desired interaction, but a comparable remark to a student can be devastating—it carries different meaning because of the social imbalance.

In dealing with students, the essential criterion is fairness. Students must have equal opportunities to learn, to complete assignments, and to earn credits that might influence their grades, insofar as these are controlled by the instructor. Obviously, grades must be assigned in an equitable manner. To a great extent, these issues can be handled satisfactorily by having a clearly described and well-publicized grading system and by requiring quite ordinary assignments that students complete on their own time. Nonetheless, issues of inequity can arise, often quite suddenly, and such issues will be discussed here.

Before considering the several kinds of issues that concern interactions with students, I will briefly describe the responsibilities that arise in a somewhat more formal sense.

Institutional Constraints.   Departments, colleges, and disciplines relevant to a course generate expectations regarding what the course will be like. Although instructors are typically given considerable leeway in deciding what the content and requirements of a course will be, there are nonetheless constraints on what might be acceptable to relevant institutions. Instructors are expected to select course content that is reasonably consistent with the course title and catalog description and with general expectations of those working in the area of study. When a course is prerequisite to another course in a department's program, the constraints on course content are usually stronger. Instructors are also expected to assign readings that are appropriate to the course content. Selecting readings and, indeed, choosing course content and assignments should also be appropriate to the background knowledge of the students and goals for the course. In practice, instructors are given great latitude with respect to this constraint, although repeatedly pitching a course at an inappropriate level for the students who take it can have negative repercussions.

There are other institutional expectations that we perhaps seldom think about but that exist nonetheless. Instructors are expected to be competent to teach any course to which they are assigned and to be adequately prepared for each class session. Although instructors are, indeed, assumed to have reasoned opinions about course material and allowed if not encouraged to express their views, they are also required to present course material fairly and to avoid requiring students to agree with them about controversial topics. At a more mundane but still important level, they are expected to place orders for textbooks and other materials in a timely manner. They are expected to assess students' performance in a reasonable way and to assign grades in a manner consistent with institutional policies. They should also be reasonably prompt—at some schools the tradition is to wait no more than 10 minutes for a full professor, proportionately less for teachers of lower ranks. Undergraduates often don't know their teachers' academic ranks, but a tardy, new instructor should not be too surprised to find some empty seats upon reaching the classroom.

IN THE CLASSROOM

As mentioned in the chapter on lecturing, instructors need to monitor their behavior so that they communicate with students in all parts of the classroom. Some students will be more active, ask better questions, and give more frequent or better answers to questions posed to the class. Because these student behaviors are reinforcing to instructors, there's a tendency for instructors to direct much of their presentation to especially active students. What is required is that instructors give other students ample opportunity to participate in the class. Patience is required, as well as encouragement of students who might be reluctant to speak out in public situations. It is also important to be gentle in responding to students' comments, questions, and answers. Students are reluctant to speak in classes because they fear looking foolish or uninformed. The worst thing that can happen is for the instructor to react negatively to a student's statement, that is, to give the impression that he or she considers the student to be foolish or uninformed. Instructors need to walk a delicate line, balancing gentle encouragement of students' participation with accurate and clarifying responses to the content of what students say. No good will come from students' forming the impression that the instructor treats some students better than others.

It is claimed by some that instructors tend to respond more positively to participation by male students compared to female students. Such biases, if they exist, are usually considered to operate unconsciously, so that the person is not aware of treating people differently. Members of minority groups, however minority might be interpreted in a given classroom, might be sensitive to any perceived differences in an instructor's responses to members of different groups. Indeed, members of the majority group, again however defined, might feel that special attention is given to minority-group members. Focusing on possible student perceptions of discriminatory behavior can lead instructors to raise their arms or eyebrows in despair—"Please just let us teach our classes!" Indeed, well-intentioned instructors are unlikely to encounter problems. Nonetheless, it is worthwhile to take small amounts of time to encourage participation from all class members and to listen and respond to each student's participation with care. Doing so should avoid possible problems of perception of bias; it is also good educational practice.

Another area that requires consideration is discipline in the classroom. In order for course goals to be achieved, there must be a minimum level of discipline during class meetings. The basic criterion is that behavior is relevant to and supportive of the aims of the course, rather than being disruptive. In a classroom that is functioning well, lively discussions with widespread participation take place and might well include periodic injections of humor, but it will be obvious that the vast majority of behavior is relevant to the current course topic. In addition, the participants will abide by generally accepted standards of reasonably polite social interaction. It is the instructor's job to monitor the situation and to act so that a productive atmosphere pervades the classroom.

Two situations that can be troublesome are considered by Goss (1995). One concerns students who disagree openly with the instructor. The question here is whether the students' disagreement is a legitimate questioning of the course content or a challenge to the instructor's authority. It is appropriate for students to question course material rather than simply accept everything that is presented. When faced with a challenge, the instructor's first task is to carefully analyze the student's comment or question. A good working assumption is to treat the student's challenge as an honest approach to course material. Perhaps the comment can be rephrased so that it contributes to the development of the topic at hand. If the student's point is relevant but not appropriate for class-time discussion, the instructor should acknowledge the student's comment and suggest a brief meeting after class or during office hours to discuss the matter. If the student's challenge is inappropriate or if the student wants to prolong the discussion, the instructor must take control. Goss (1995) suggests, in addition to expressing interest in a nonclass discussion with the student, emphasizing the need of the class as a whole to return to the day's material. More generally, coping with an overly active student might include a gentle bypass of the student ("Let's give others a chance") or a private discussion of appropriate behavior. If these steps do not suffice, it might be necessary to ignore the student in class, but only as a last resort.

Another possible problem concerns angry students. Students might become angry with an instructor because of a bad outcome—a low test score or paper grade, or they could get angry with one another during a class discussion. Outbreaks of anger are rare and should be so. Overt anger in a classroom is unacceptable because it contradicts the goal of reasoned discourse that is central to a college or university. Goss (1995) suggests prevention regarding grade-based anger; informing students in advance that they are welcome to discuss grades with you outside of class. She further suggests devising and announcing schemes through which students may question a grade, for example, by citing textbook material supporting their answers. Having clear, well-described grading systems helps to avoid problems.

When confronted by an angry student in or out of the classroom, it is essential for instructors to maintain a calm, professional demeanor. A calm instructor provides a useful model for the students and, by refusing to contribute to the tense atmosphere, helps to defuse the situation. Student anger is unlikely to last long in the presence of an attentive, calm instructor. When a calmer atmosphere prevails, the specific issue can be addressed, most preferably in private.

EQUITABLE ASSIGNMENTS

The description of a course in the timetable tells students where and when they will be expected to appear if they enroll in the course. Students will be required to do work outside of official class meetings, but studying or completing the class assignments ordinarily is scheduled by students on an individual basis. Occasionally, issues of equity arise when instructors make assignments that can be completed only at a particular time and place outside of class. For example, requiring students to attend a special talk and write a report on the presentation causes problems for students who have other commitments at the time of the talk. A student who has to work or who has another class at the time of the talk is placed in a dilemma by the assignment and is at a disadvantage with respect to completing it. It does not matter whether the assignment is required or is a means of earning extra credit—the issue is the same. The solution to the problem is to make available an alternative assignment that does not impose a specific time requirement on the student or to arrange an alternative way to complete the assignment, for example, by having a videotape of the talk available for students at other times.

A similar problem can arise with respect to opportunities for getting help with the course, such as the timing of instructors' office hours. Again, the clear solution is to make available a reasonable opportunity to schedule a meeting at another time. In considering the issue of making alternatives available, one might be inclined to want to know a student's reason for needing an alternative arrangement. The idea is that an instructor might consider some reasons legitimate but others insufficient. My advice is to ignore this step because one is perhaps never able to make an accurate assessment of stated reasons. It is simpler and better to make alternatives available on a regular basis.

RULES AND EXCEPTIONS

Instructors must devise policies for a number of situations that might arise during a course. The issues include items such as late assignments, makeup tests, extra credits, incomplete grades, and changing grades. An exam is scheduled for a particular class meeting. What will happen if a student misses the class and therefore misses the exam? Under what circumstances will students be allowed to take a makeup exam? What will be the nature of the makeup exam—will it be different from the original exam? Similar questions arise with respect to assignments. Will assignments be accepted after the due date? What will be the penalty for late assignments? A student who's not doing well in the course might approach the instructor and ask if there is anything he or she can do to earn extra credits. Toward the end of the course, a student might well make a multiple request for more time to complete assignments combined with a grade of incomplete and an opportunity to earn extra credits.

Instructors need to think about all these issues prior to beginning a course and to establish the rules they will apply to such situations. New instructors often are inclined to set simple rigid rules in the hope that they won't have to make any decisions. No makeup exams will be given. No late assignments will be accepted. Although such policies are reasonable, they are unlikely to be administered in the all-or-none fashion that is initially intended. Suppose a test is scheduled for Friday at 1:00 p.m. At 11:00 a.m., a student calls to report that she is sick and will be unable to take the test—may she please take a makeup test on Monday? Or a student arrives at the test site at 1:45, indicating that he had an accident on the way to school—may he please take the test now and have the regular allotted time? Or a student calls on Thursday to report an illness, and so on. The possibilities are many, and it is rarely the case that an instructor will treat them all alike. Instructors should try to establish reasonable policies, think about the procedures they want to follow in considering exceptions, and allow themselves to make adjustments on the case-by-case basis.

It is important that the relevant policies and procedures are communicated to all students. It is especially important to give students guidelines regarding requests for exceptions. For example, if a student will miss a test, what should the student do with respect to informing the instructor and possibly asking for a makeup test? Suppose the stated policy is that no makeup tests will be given. Two students are sick; one decides to call the instructor and take a shot at getting a makeup test. The instructor decides "Oh, OK, I'll give you a makeup." The other student, less assertive, believes that nothing can be done and thus does not contact the instructor. Most people would consider this instructor's policy as administered to be unfair. If the instructor will make exceptions to the basic rules, that fact should be communicated to the students. In addition, procedures to follow for requesting exceptions should be described. It is not possible to anticipate the variety of situations that might arise. Instructors should make a good-faith effort to describe their policies and procedures to students so that students in similar circumstances will be treated similarly.

Illness and Family Crises.   Instructors' policies regarding makeup exams, late assignments, and grades of incomplete typically assume that students will face only minor, short-term life problems while taking a course. When a student has a protracted illness or must deal with a family crisis such as the death of a parent, ordinary policies do not provide adequate treatment. The situations involve temporally extended obstacles to devoting adequate attention to studying and to completing course requirements. The best course of action is often not clear. It is relatively easy to give a student extended time to complete an assignment; however, a very long extension can pose problems. Allowing more than the usual number of makeup exams or a greater delay before taking the makeup can be done but might not be the best course of action. Will the student be able to prepare adequately to take the exams? Suppose the student will miss a third or half of the class meetings—is it reasonable to assume that the student will know enough to attempt to earn course credit or a reasonable grade?

In trying to find a reasonable solution to such situations, it is important for instructors to work with the student to explore alternatives. Doing so requires that students inform instructors when special situations arise, preferably early. For that to happen, instructors might need to explicitly encourage students to tell them of any circumstances that might impair their course performance. It is to the instructor's advantage to know about any such situations, and early information facilitates finding solutions. Without an explicit statement from the instructor, some students will be inclined to provide that information when need arises, but others might be reluctant to do so. An up-front announcement can save trouble later.

Plans of action must be constructed on a case-by-case basis. Relevant factors include the expected length of the disruption as well as its severity, the likelihood of aftereffects, the student's course performance to date, and the number and types of requirements that will require adjustments. If something happens early in a term and will be long-lasting, the likely best solution is for the student to drop the course. Indeed, I would consider a course drop as a primary alternative whenever a substantial disruption is expected, even if the school's official deadline for such actions has passed. In my experience, administrators will relax the rules if an instructor makes a sensible argument for doing so in a particular case. In trying to assess the length and severity of a disruption, it's worth keeping in mind that emotional upheaval is likely to have noticeable aftereffects. Difficulty in concentrating on schoolwork might persist longer than the student anticipates.

Instructors must decide what kinds of crises will lead them to make major adjustments in their course policies. Specific criteria realistically cannot be anticipated so that they will cover the variety of situations that might arise. Rather, instructors need to evaluate specific cases that are presented to them. A good procedure to follow is to take some time before communicating a decision. For example, if a student appears during office hours to describe a problem and request special treatment, a useful response is to express concern and to suggest another meeting, perhaps the next day, to discuss details. The delay gives the instructor time to consider the situation as well as possible alternatives before committing to a plan of action. The delay is likely to lead to a better decision.

SOCIALIZING

Interactions between instructors and their students will not be restricted to the classroom, nor should they be. Discussing course material during office hours and providing guidance regarding academic matters are important ways in which instructors contribute to the student's education. Difficulties can arise when teacher-student relationships are mixed with social interactions.

Students like teachers who are friendly and easy to talk to, who appear interested in students. For instructors, breaking through the anonymity of class rosters and having pleasant conversations with students makes teaching much more enjoyable and fulfilling. Having good rapport with students increases the effectiveness of class meetings—students pay more attention to what is being said, and students' participation increases. There is no sensible criticism of students and teachers liking one another. Questions concern the kinds of social behavior that are acceptable.

Because instructors are in the power position and students are not, responsibility for keeping relationships within acceptable limits falls undoubtedly on the shoulders of instructors. Teachers want to be liked—perhaps new teachers especially want students to like them as a sign that their teaching is going well. However, instructors must keep in mind that they are not teaching classes to be liked, that their primary mission is to teach. Unlike ordinary friendships, which are between equals, student-teacher relationships are unbalanced; instructors need to keep this in mind.

Consider some typical behaviors in ordinary friendships: Asking for or giving small favors, such as a ride home. Lending small amounts of money. Offering or accepting an invitation to a party. Going out for coffee, a meal, or drinks. Giving and accepting gifts. Hugging each other. In Tabachnick, Keith-Spiegel, and Pope's (1991) survey of psychology faculty, responses to these items in relation to instructor–student relationships were mixed, with substantial percentages of "ethical" and "unethical" ratings. There was one exception: Although "accepting a student's inexpensive gift" received more ethical than unethical ratings, "accepting a student's expensive gift" received 88% unethical ratings. The survey items did not distinguish clearly between undergraduates and graduate students. Because graduate students are older and interact with the faculty in different ways (e.g., as assistants) over extended periods of time, the above activities are likely to be viewed as more acceptable with graduate students, less appropriate with undergraduates. The general point is that what might otherwise be unremarkable activity between friends can be questionable when it occurs between instructors and students.

Instructors need to protect their positions of responsibility. Grades must be assigned fairly, and policies must be administered fairly to all students. "Giving a break" to a friendly student is inappropriate. Although there is widespread agreement that it is unethical to allow one's liking for a student to influence such decisions, it is very difficult to avoid that influence. In addition, the appearance of favoritism is detrimental to teaching effectiveness. As Keith-Spiegel (1994) suggested, large-group activities are unlikely to raise ethical issues. Small groups and repetitive activities are more dangerous.

Amorous Relationships.   Sometimes, instructors find themselves attracted to students, and vice versa. Should instructors date their students, get involved in sexual relationships with them? Regarding graduate students, the general answer is no. The difficult case is that between an advisor and advanced-graduate-student advisee where the two people have worked together for years and where it might be academically dubious for the faculty member to stop supervising the student's research. Even here, many believe that the faculty member may supervise but should not participate in any evaluation of the student's work. With respect to students in undergraduate classes (including independent study), the answer is simple: No. This proscription applies to regular faculty, part-time teachers, and teaching assistants. One who will grade, supervise, or otherwise make decisions about a student should avoid an amorous relationship. The dangers are clear and serious.

Because of the imbalance of a teacher-student relationship, the legitimacy of the student's "free consent" can be questioned. Should the relationship end, any claim of coercion will be taken seriously. The possibility of bias is obvious, as is the likelihood of perception of bias even if decisions are based on merit. Psychological damage can occur. Reputations can be harmed. In light of laws on sexual harassment and the dangers inherent in teacher–student amorous relationships, many schools prohibit them.

What about dating after the course is over and the grade submitted? The power imbalance is muted but still exists, because the instructor might be involved in making recommendations or nominating students for awards. Some believe that general status differences between instructors and students inevitably create a power imbalance. It's not surprising that opinions on this issue were mixed, although "unethical" ratings were twice as frequent as "ethical" (Tabachnick et al., 1991).

ACADEMIC INTEGRITY

Academic honesty is a core value of colleges and universities and is expected of both students and faculty. Instructors are expected to present accurate information and to deal fairly with controversial issues, and to treat students equitably. Students are expected to earn their grades and credits by doing their own work. Cheating on exams and plagiarizing assignments are unethical student behaviors. Also proscribed are bribery, threats, and alteration of records. Instructors are the first line of monitoring and sanctions with respect to students' violations of academic integrity. Put simply, instructors are expected to enforce the rules, and many consider an instructor's ignoring strong evidence of cheating to be unethical (Tabachnick et al., 1991).

According to surveys using anonymous self-reports by students, cheating is widespread (e.g., Newstead, Franklyn-Stokes, & Armstead, 1996). Reported cheating is more common among males and among students with lower grades. The primary reason for cheating is, not surprisingly, to improve one's grade. Students whose focus is on learning, rather than on getting good grades, might be less likely to cheat. Although a lower level of cheating was reported at a college with an honor code (May & Loyd, 1993), inclusion of an honor pledge in course materials did not lessen cheating (Gardner, Roper, Gonzalez, & Simpson, 1988).

Although instructors are charged with detecting (and punishing) cheating, they are often reluctant to act in this capacity (Keith-Spiegel, Tabachnick, Whitley, & Washburn, 1998). Dealing with academic dishonesty is seen as the worst aspect of an instructor's job. While deploring cheating, faculty members see themselves as scholars and teachers rather than "academic police," so they are disinclined to adopt the enforcement role. The primary reason given for not pursuing possible instances of cheating was lack of sufficient evidence. Suspicions of cheating outnumber demonstrations of cheating. Other reasons given for overlooking possible cheating included stress, the excessive time and effort required, fear of retaliation or lawsuit, and the belief that cheaters would fail anyway (Keith-Spiegel et al., 1998). These reasons are understandable, yet protecting academic integrity is part of an instructor's job. What to do?

Instructors readily can employ methods to prevent cheating. Short written answers or essays are more difficult to copy than multiple-choice selections. Multiple forms of exams, distributed so that no student is seated next to another with the same form, make copying virtually impossible. Constructing two forms of every test is an onerous task and does not stem from pedagogical considerations; instructors justifiably might reject use of this technique. A modest type of alternate forms can be constructed by rearranging the pages of an exam into two different orders. To do this, questions may not overlap pages, which they should not do in any case. Question numbers need to be done twice, but this is a small and mundane task compared to creating a complete second set of questions. As mentioned in the chapter on writing assignments, making assignments unique to the course and requiring copies of source materials to be submitted reduces the likelihood of plagiarism from external sources.

Academic integrity might also be promoted in other ways. Extolling the virtues of learning and demonstrating the satisfaction that comes from mastering course material can help students adopt a learning orientation rather than a grade orientation. Having an honor code and perhaps having students sign it for each test or assignment might promote self-monitoring and deter cheating. During exams, instructing students to keep their answer sheets covered except when they are writing on them can reduce opportunities and temptations to copy. Gently repeating this instruction as needed and moving around the room while monitoring can also help.

It can be very difficult to monitor students' behavior during exams in large classes. It is not possible for instructors to be aware of the many external sources that students might use inappropriately in writing course papers. Occasionally, suspicions of cheating might arise because of unusual similarity of two students' exams or papers, perhaps because of striking changes in writing style within a student's paper. At such points instructors must decide whether to pursue the matter, what procedures to follow, and how much effort to give to the pursuit.

In considering possible cheating, it is important to exercise caution both mentally and procedurally and to consider alternative explanations. Obviously, exam copying is feasible only when the student are physically near each other in a monitored test environment. Even if students sitting next to each other produce remarkably similar answer patterns on, say, a multiple-choice test, copying might not be involved. For example, suppose two adjacently seated students both make eight errors on a 40-item test, with six of the mistakes on the same items and five being the same exact wrong alternative. On many if not most multiple-choice tests, regardless of the number of alternatives presented, only a couple receive high frequencies of endorsement—the correct alternative and a popular error. So people who miss the same question might be quite likely to pick the same wrong answer. In well-constructed tests, high-scoring students are likely to miss only the most difficult questions, meaning that they might well miss the same questions. In short, apparently amazing similarity of answer patterns might not imply copying. One way to test this idea is to examine the answers of a third student with a comparable score but known to be seated in a different part of the room. If this student's answer pattern shows high similarity to the others (it need not be identical), the ambiguity of similar answer patterns is demonstrated, and no solid basis for further investigation exists.

It's also important to remember that students are not as predictable as instructors might like to think. Middle-range students inevitably learn some material better than others and might often score better on one test than another or write one paper better than another. So the simple fact that a student's performance is better than his or her past record does not mean that something untoward has occurred. Students' relevant knowledge and effort vary, so outcome quality might be expected to also vary. In addition, a student's in-class writing might well differ from writing done outside of class. In class, writing typically is spontaneous and not rewritten, whereas a longer term assignment allows for extra time and revision. A student who is not a good spontaneous writer still might produce better papers written over a long time. Again, simple inconsistency with past behavior is not a sound basis for hypothesizing that a student has cheated. Also, as discussed in the chapter on writing assignments, students might not have a clear understanding of the differences among quoting, citing, and plagiarizing. This problem can be alleviated by appropriate instruction early in the term.

One important rule to follow is to make no public accusations of cheating. If a suspect exam or paper is to be discussed with a student, it should be done in private. Confronting a student with the suspicious evidence in the hope of obtaining either an acceptable explanation or a confession might be tried, but the usefulness of this technique is unknown. Instructors might be inclined to ask students to explain exam answers or to discuss points made in a paper. A problem here is a lack of baseline information about the quality of students' explanations. It's possible that any student simply isn't good at explaining multiple-choice answers or defending statements to a higher status individual in a tense and threatening situation. Therefore, weak explanations are ambiguous, but good explanations should be taken as indicating that the student did the work in question. Of course, a student might refuse to answer such questions on the grounds that other students have not been asked to explain or defend work they have submitted.

An instructor might include in a course syllabus a statement reserving the right to obtain additional information, at the instructor's discretion, in order to accept an exam or assignment. Indicating that questions of authorship must be resolved before work will be accepted alerts students to the seriousness of the matter and could be part of a larger presentation on academic integrity.

In dealing with cases of possible cheating, it is advisable for instructors to consult with their colleagues to gain information and perspective. Such consultation should be done without revealing the name(s) of the students involved. If an instructor decides that the evidence justifies the conclusion that cheating has occurred, the question of sanctions must be addressed. Colleges' policies on this issue vary, so it is important to learn what those policies are. Single instances of cheating on a test or assignment commonly lead to a grade of zero or failure on that requirement; assigning a failing grade for the course is also a possibility. More serious consequences such as suspension or dismissal from the college are likely to require more serious transgressions and will surely involve additional administrative entities, for example, department head, college dean, perhaps a formal review panel. For any sanction beyond failure on a single exam or assignment, instructors should definitely consult with their department heads.

STUDENTS WITH DISABILITIES

Instructors face substantial challenges when their classes include students with disabilities, especially those that affect communication. Visual and hearing impairments require adjustments in the way in which information is communicated. Disabilities also affect the methods used to assess student performance. Teaching students with disabilities requires considerable effort on the part of instructors; the experience is likely to produce better teachers.

It is essential for instructors to be aware of any special needs that students in their classes might have. As in the case of illnesses, a specific request that students with a disability contact the instructor at the very beginning of a course is an important step. Including a statement to this effect on the course syllabus is a good idea.

There are technological means of compensating for some disabilities, for example, braille lecture notes, text reading audio output computer systems, or sign language interpretation of oral presentations. Instructors are unlikely to be able to provide such enhancements, but some might be available from other sources. Instructors should insure that students have contacted the school's office of disability services to obtain whatever help might be available. Here we can consider what instructors can do in a more low-tech fashion to produce important effects.

Visually impaired students might be blind or have weak vision. Those with weak vision require enhanced visual presentations—large print for example. Such students may have difficulty reading what is on a blackboard or overhead display; providing a large-print paper copy of such presentations can be quite helpful. Making course assignments available in electronic format is useful if the student has computer access to adjust the visual parameters to their needs. Large-print versions of course exams will be needed; alternatively, special testing arrangements could be made that allow the test to be projected to a viewable size for the student. The student is very likely to require extra time to complete exams.

Blind students require a substitute for visual presentation. Instructors must become aware of what information is being presented only visually and try to describe that information auditorily. Graphic material needs to be described in detail; pointing and verbal equivalents such as "this line" will be insufficient. It also becomes important to speak very clearly, because the blind student has no supporting visual context to help interpret unclear speech. Allowing, encouraging, or making tape recordings of lectures will provide the students with the reviewable record of class sessions. Because blind students will need considerable lead time if they will have Braille or audiotape recordings made of reading assignments, it is important for instructors to specify assignments as early as possible. (A little reflection leads to the realization that doing these things would be beneficial to all students.) Blind students will require special testing arrangements both for presenting test questions and providing answers. The test might be given orally with questions being read by an examiner who also records answers. A computer with voice recognition software could be used to provide an imperfect but usable text record of the student's answers to essay questions.

Hearing-impaired students require visual augmentation to provide information that is ordinarily presented auditorily. Most hearing-impaired students read lips to a reasonable degree. For instructors, what becomes critical is to face the students when speaking to them and to speak clearly. Using informative gestures will also be helpful. There's also a need to find a way for the student to communicate to the instructor. Hearing-impaired students' ability to speak will vary with the extent and developmental timing of their disability. The use of e-mail for questions and discussion can provide substantial help.

Teaching students with disabilities requires instructors to become self-conscious with respect to their classroom behavior. This is a good kind of self-consciousness because it makes instructors more aware of the strengths and weaknesses of different presentation methods and more aware of various ways to do things better. Preparing handouts, using tape recordings, communicating with e-mail, and devising different ways of assessing students also broaden an instructor's repertoire of useful teaching techniques. Quite often, what is done to accommodate a student with a special need is a good thing to use more generally, perhaps with some modification. In these ways, coping with special situations produces better instructors.

SUMMARY

Instructors have multiple professional and ethical responsibilities. In the classroom, patience and consideration of students' self-respect are required, and efforts should be made to foster equitable participation. Disruptive students require a calm, professional approach. Assignments, whether required or optional, must be designed so that all students have fair opportunities to meet requirements and gain extra credit. Rules regarding matters such as late assignments and makeup tests should be announced, while recognizing that special circumstances such as extended illnesses will require modifications. Socializing between instructor and students is dangerous because of status and power differences, and amorous relationships must be avoided. Instructors are responsible for upholding academic integrity and should take steps to deter cheating. Students with disabilities present special teaching challenges; adjusting to their needs can result in discovering techniques that improve instruction for all students.

11

Student Evaluations and Improving Instruction

Factors Affecting Evaluations
Collecting Evaluations
Feedback and Improving Instruction

It is now commonplace for students to complete course evaluation forms at the end of the term. Such evaluations might be optional or be required by the school's administration. There is a long-lasting and continuing debate over the validity of students' evaluations of courses and instructors. Some faculty members see them as nothing more than popularity contests. Others believe that students' opinions are valuable; I belong to this camp. Regardless of one's individual opinion on the matter, administrative emphasis on student evaluations is strong and increasing, so it behooves an instructor to pay attention to them. Beyond any external consideration, students' comments about a course can be very useful to instructors. Student evaluations are hardly a recent phenomenon; for many years at some colleges, student groups have collected course evaluations and published the results as a registration guide. Students naturally would prefer to take good courses and to avoid those they will not like. At least some instructors might be surprised that students do not necessarily equate good with easy. Indeed, most summaries of course evaluations don't include information about grade distributions, although they typically do include ratings of the amount of work required and the fairness of exams. Whether one accepts or bemoans the ways in which students might judge courses, one understandable purpose for student evaluations is to allow students to share their opinions with one another on a more widespread basis than simply talking to friends.

Administrative reasons for promoting course evaluations are several. Students constitute a major part of the college community, and it makes sense that in some way they should express their views. Students are, so to speak, the consumers of instructional programs, so their evaluations of courses provide a kind of index of customer satisfaction. Administrators also need information about the quality of instruction in their schools for internal and external reviews. Students' course evaluations represent only one possible indicator of instructional quality, albeit a rather obvious one. Other possible sources of information about instruction include reviews of course materials, students' performance on external exams (for example, the GRE), observation of classroom performance by other members of the faculty, retrospective interviews with students or faculty about a particular course or a whole program, as well as observations or reviews by external examiners. Each of these sources has strengths and weaknesses, and some require considerable expenditures of time and money. For example, students have more experience with a course than the other possible evaluators, but they might lack perspective and be affected by grade considerations. Classroom observations by other faculty members suffer from inadequate exposure (perhaps just a single class meeting) and take the observers away from other responsibilities. It seems obvious that a combination of methods should be used, that it would be a mistake to rely too heavily on any single source.

The most contentious use of student evaluations of courses and instructors is using them to assess the teaching effectiveness of individual instructors. It is perhaps a combination of academic and self-interest that has led to a virtual litany of criticisms of student evaluations. There should be no doubt that, at best, student evaluations are imperfect indicators of teaching effectiveness. At the same time, there is no reason to dismiss student evaluations. Research has shown that student evaluations are at least moderately related to other measures of teaching effectiveness including instructors' self-assessments (Howard, Conway, & Maxwell, 1985). Student evaluations are potentially susceptible to influences that can lead to interpretive difficulties, which will be described shortly, but they nonetheless represent one viable measure of instructional quality. As noted above, the danger lies in naive reliance on students' ratings as the sole or primary indicator of teaching effectiveness. What instructors need to do is to compile their teaching portfolios, including descriptions of course syllabi, sample tests, and any special materials prepared, as well as student evaluations. These portfolios will provide evaluators with a much more complete record of teaching efforts and should reduce problems of overreliance on a single, convenient measure such as student evaluations.

Last but not least, another reason for collecting students' evaluations is to provide feedback to instructors. All instructors have opinions of their own strengths in teaching (and perhaps also weaknesses), of what has worked well and not so well. Finding out what their students think about various aspects of the course can provide instructors with confirmation of their own views, alert them to possible problems, or simply surprise them by drawing attention to something not previously considered.

FACTORS AFFECTING EVALUATIONS

Students' ratings of courses and instructors are related to a number of variables. These correlations can be viewed either as confounding influences on student evaluations or as understandable influences that should be taken into account in interpreting their ratings. For example, students' ratings tend be positively related to measures of students' performance, in the most perplexing case, that students receiving higher grades tend to give higher course ratings. The simplest explanation of an achievement-evaluation relation is that students who have gotten the most out of a course will be most satisfied with it. In short, instructors who produce more successful students deserve higher ratings. A counterargument is that instructors who grade more leniently will inappropriately receive higher ratings (Greenwald & Gillmore, 1997a). Even granting a leniency influence, there appears to be ample evidence that ratings are related to achievement as they should be (Cohen, 1982).

Student evaluations have sometimes been found to vary with the size of classes, with larger classes tending to yield lower ratings (Gilmore, Swerdik, & Beehr, 1980). Also, gender sometimes seems to matter; in one study, ratings of male instructors were unaffected by student gender whereas female instructors tended to receive high ratings from female students and lower ratings from male students (Basow, 1995). The magnitude of influence of these and other variables on the students' evaluations is not clear. It is worth noting that overall ratings of effectiveness have also been found to be related to factors such as presenting material clearly and being well prepared for class (Tang, 1997). The point is that student evaluations, although imperfect and subject to possible biases, are consistently related to factors that we would expect and want to influence them.

COLLECTING EVALUATIONS

Assuming that student evaluations will be collected, relevant questions concern what to have the students evaluate and how to have them do it. In some settings there might be an official form that is specified by the administration or a student organization. In these cases, instructors should supplement such forms with their own evaluation scheme as they see fit. Frequently, official forms do not provide information that can be most useful to instructors, and some of the included information has ambiguous meaning. Evaluations should deal with important aspects of instruction, some of which apply to virtually any course whereas others are course specific. General forms typically miss the specific aspects, so that an evaluation scheme tailored in part to a particular course is a good idea.

Items to Evaluate.   The general rule is to have students evaluate all aspects of the course that are deemed important or interesting. Figure 11-1 shows items that are commonly included.

Students usually are also asked to provide overall evaluations of the course and the instructor, and might be asked the specific question "Would you recommend this course to other students?" Evaluation forms typically also ask for

Interest level of course content
Clarity of course objectives
Amount of work required
Usefulness of homework or other assignments
Quality of textbooks and other materials
Relation between exams and course objectives
Fairness of examinations
Clarity of presentation of concepts and theories
Instructors ability to explain
Quality of instructors answers to students' questions
Instructors facility with English
Quality of interaction between instructors and students
Availability of instructor for consultation

Figure 11-1   Likely Items on a Course Evaluation

biographical information such as school class (freshman, etc.), reason for taking the course (required or elective), expected grade in the course, and perhaps gender and overall grade point average.

Notice that the list of items is generally applicable and generally worded. As such, some of the items are likely to be ambiguous. For example, suppose the course materials have included a textbook, a book of readings, explanatory material written by the instructor, and worksheets of one sort or another. Asking students to rate "instructional materials" will not yield very useful information. It is much better to obtain separate evaluations of each type of course material. For another example, consider the meaning of asking students to evaluate the fairness of exams. There are at least two components to exam fairness, the appropriateness of the questions asked and the manner in which answers were graded. Again, directing students' attention to these components is likely to yield more informative responses.

There is, of course, a limit to the number of items that students can be asked to evaluate. Asking them for too many judgments can lead to boredom, inattention, and uninformative responses. If students believe that their evaluations will receive attention, they will be willing to spend a short while providing their judgments.

Ratings or Comments

Most evaluation forms I have seen asked students to make ratings of a list of items. This multiple-choice format yields numerical responses that are easy to summarize; by scanning the forms into a computer, ratings distributions and average ratings can be obtained with relative ease. The obvious weakness of ratings is that they tell you nothing whatsoever about the reason for any rating. From the perspective of feedback to instructors, ratings can provide little guidance. Very high ratings of an item imply that students found no weaknesses, but lower ratings do not indicate what students did not like.

Rating Scales.   Despite their weaknesses regarding quality of information, the convenience of rating forms makes them a popular choice. If course ratings will be collected, one question concerns the kind of rating scale to be used. How many points should the scale have and how should the points be labeled? Five-point scales are common and are probably adequate; people generally can distinguish five levels of most any attribute but might have difficulty reliably using many more than five. The familiarity of the five-category grade scale might also provide a frame of reference for the judgments. Indeed, students are sometimes asked to assign grades (A, B, ...) for each item to be rated. The use of plus and minus grades (B+, C−) suggests that more than five points could be used, but it is unclear how reliably these apparent refinements would be used in making overall, retrospective judgments such as "How well did the instructor explain things?"

Labeling the rating scale involves a choice of both the kind of labels to use and the number of points to be labeled. That is, with a five-point scale, one could attach a verbal label to each point or just label the endpoints of the scale. These two methods of labeling are illustrated below:

1	2	3	4	5
Very Poor	Poor	Average	Good	Very good

1	2	3	4	5
Very Poor				Very good

The second method leaves the meanings of the interior points implicit, which might seem to be a weakness. However, labeling just the endpoints is a method that usually yields reliable ratings. Two comments are relevant. First, the meanings of verbal labels such as "Good, Poor" and the like vary from one person to the next, so attaching a verbal label doesn't guarantee that any rating value will be used more reliably. Second, what is implicit in virtually any five-point rating scale is that two of the ratings on one side (here, the left side) are negative, the middle is some kind of reference point, and the two ratings on the other side (here, right) are positive. The more extreme the rating, the more positive or negative it is. So what goes on in a person's head when making a rating might be something like "Do I want to make a positive or negative rating? Ok, positive— but not the highest rating." This person would choose 4, whether or not 4 has a verbal label. As it's simpler and easier to label just the endpoints, with no clear loss of reliable information, doing so would be a sensible choice.

What labels should be used, and should the labels change depending on the nature of the item being evaluated? For example, for the item "What is your overall rating of the instructor?" a scale from 1 = "Very poor" to 5 = "Excellent" seems readily understandable. But, for an item such as "How beneficial were the homework assignments?" "Very poor" to "Excellent" seems at least ungrammatical, and labels such as "Just busy work" to "Very helpful" fit the item better. The essential question is whether students respond differently, depending on the choice of labels, and there is no clear relevant evidence. Anecdotal observations suggest that students have no trouble using a general "Very poor to Excellent" scale for all items including those for which the labels don't fit nicely. A related question concerns the specific labels used on a general good-bad scale. Would students respond differently to a scale of 1 = Very poor to 5 = Excellent, compared to 1 = Very poor to 5 = Very good? Because "Excellent" appears to be better than "Very good," we might expect that there would be more ratings of 5 with the first scale. Again, there is no clear evidence that this difference in labels matters. The argument outlined above suggests that the particular verbal labels won't matter much. The idea is that the rater will give, say, the highest rating only if that is what raters desire, regardless of what label is attached to the highest rating. Because there is no clear evidence that slight differences in verbal labels matter much, the best guideline for constructing a course rating scale is to use endpoint labels that are reasonably attainable and that also represent reasonable endpoints. End labels such as "Worst ever" or "Perfect" are not useful because they, logically, will seldom be used. Also uninformative would be end labels that don't realistically imply understandable extremes, such as "above average" as the highest possible rating.

Comments.   In contrast to using rating scales, asking students to comment on various aspects of a course yields much richer information that is more difficult to compile and summarize. If, for example, students are asked to comment on the textbook, their responses will indicate not only whether their overall opinions are positive or negative, or mixed, but also what they did or did not like about the textbook (in many cases). Students' comments are much more informative than students' ratings. Comments can be categorized as positive or negative, possibly with distinctions such as "very positive" (for example, "best instructor I've had") versus "positive" ("did a good job"), or mixed (for example, "presentations were over our heads, but she did usually answer questions"). To do this, the comments must be read and categorized, based on their content. As is true in many measurement situations, effort expended is directly related to information gained. A numerical index of student sentiment can be constructed by calculating the percentages of positive and negative (and neutral/mixed) comments for an item, and the content of the responses provides more detailed information.

The only major weakness of using comments as evaluations is the time required to review all the comments received. With very large classes, the review would be cumbersome; for ordinary purposes, a random sample of comments could be reviewed. For medium and small classes, obtaining students' comments seems the best alternative. A mixture of both rating scales and comments could be used, providing rating scales where comments are unlikely to add useful information and requesting comments on aspects where more detailed information is desired.

Open-Ended Questions.   Asking students to evaluate specific components of a course is a good general principle. Obtaining a few overall evaluations is also reasonable. One very informative technique is to ask students, usually at the end of the response form, to describe "up to three things that they really liked about the course" and "up to three things that they disliked and should be changed." In answering these questions, students will indicate what they think is most important about the course, both positively and negatively. Tallying these responses provides an interesting picture of the course from the students' perspective. Because students tend to list only items that are most salient to them, they commonly list fewer than three items in both categories. A count of the number of likes and dislikes gives an overall view of the course. We would prefer to see likes exceed dislikes; for a well-received course, the positive difference will be quite large. Repeated entries provide further information about course aspects and naturally form lists of "what to keep" and "what to consider changing" in future offerings. As a guide to future course offerings, instructors probably should attend only to opinions for which there is considerable inter-judge agreement.

Procedures

When should course evaluations be collected? For purposes of obtaining students' overall judgments of the course and its various aspects, the general answer is obviously toward the end of the course. More specifically, final evaluations are best obtained during a class meeting as close as feasible to the end of the course, for example, during the last week of instruction. Class time should be allocated to students' completing evaluation forms. Asking for evaluations after the final exam is less satisfactory because students are likely to be fatigued and desiring to leave, which will lead to a lower percentage of completion and more cursory responses. The goal is to get subjectively accurate responses from all or nearly all the students in a course. Informing students in advance when evaluations will be collected might increase the percentage of students who provide information. A two-stage collection procedure also can be useful, having a designated day on which class time will be allocated to giving evaluations followed by a "second chance" to participate after the next class meeting.

Evaluations should be given anonymously, to minimize any student's desire to "please the instructor" because of concerns about the course grade. Having no names or other identifiers on the evaluation forms results in anonymously prepared forms. Having students then place completed forms in an envelope or other container so that evaluation forms are effectively mixed makes it unlikely if not impossible that the instructor could identify the source of any evaluation.

In some situations where evaluations are collected by a student organization, a student, rather than the instructor, collects completed evaluation forms and takes them away for processing. This procedure is quite reasonable but can produce a problem for instructors, namely a sometimes substantial delay in getting the information back to instructors. In addition to simply desiring more immediate feedback, instructors sometimes need evaluation information for near-term course planning. For example, suppose an instructor teaches the same course in the spring and the following fall; in such cases, student input about textbooks, other readings, perhaps a new testing or assignment scheme could be very useful in planning the fall offering. The information is needed soon rather than after, say, a term's delay. One solution is for the instructor to ask the students for selected evaluations on a separate sheet. The content of the instructor's form would depend on the nature of the external student-government form, addressing what the other form does not and focusing on the items for which information is most urgent.

FEEDBACK AND IMPROVING INSTRUCTION

We would be shocked to discover that the best course, or best lecture, or best just-about-anything had occurred on a person's first attempt. Teaching requires a complex, multifaceted set of skills that is quite open-ended and has a learning curve with no definitive endpoint. No matter how successful a teacher has been, whether in a specific episode or over a longer time frame, the answer is "yes" to "Could it be better?" I am not calling for the pursuit of perfection; rather, I wish to emphasize that opportunities to improve instruction are abundant. Early in a teaching career, there are many things to learn, but even after years of experience there are new alternatives to explore.

Teaching is not a repetitive activity. Each class period, each course, each group of students requires adjustment and adaptation. Analogously, each experience can be the basis of learning which facilitates the next effort. The first lecture can help the second, the first two can help the third, and so on, even though the content is always changing. Constructing the first test and reviewing the results should help in constructing the second test. Having taught a course once and coping with the many tasks and organizational demands will help in teaching the next course whether it is the same as or different from the first. Because instructors regularly face similar but not identical tasks, they are following learning-to-learn functions, which typically show the largest gains early in the series of tasks. Teaching for the second time, although still requiring much effort, will be noticeably easier than the first time; subsequent general improvements will be smaller although still important.

Obtaining and making good use of feedback is an important part of learning. Student evaluations are one source of feedback that could be used to improve instruction. People generally follow a "Win stay, lose shift" strategy, also known as "If it ain't broke, don't fix it." For example, if students indicate in end-of-course evaluations that they thought the textbook was pretty good, using it again is quite reasonable. If, in contrast, they gave the book low ratings, that's a signal to look for an alternative. Poor evaluations are a cue for considering change, but making a change requires generating an alternative to the status quo. Ratings fall short in this respect. For example, suppose an instructor's lectures receive ratings that are lower than desired; the ratings neither tell the instructor what the students found lacking nor suggest a change that might be tried. If, however, students frequently commented that "lectures were too abstract," that implies a call for presenting more examples to flesh out the meaning of abstract concepts. In general, comments are likely to provide more guidance regarding what kinds of changes might be considered.

There is no reason for instructors to wait until the end of a course to obtain feedback from students. From a learning perspective, feedback is better obtained while there is a chance to use it to modify performance. In-progress feedback can be obtained in different ways varying in formality. For example, an instructor might have students complete a lecture-assessment form like the sample presented in the chapter on lecturing and compare the students' judgments to a self-assessment. Where there are discrepancies between the instructor's and students' judgment, a brief class discussion might be held to clarify the matter and perhaps to suggest changes. It's not necessary to use an evaluation form; students could simply be asked to write on a sheet of paper their likes and dislikes, or "what's going well" and "what's going not so well."

There are sources of student feedback that do not involve directly asking for students' opinions. Assessing, informally, the level of student attention and participation in class provides feedback. Reactions to questions posed to the class are informative. One highly regarded teacher had students write answers to two questions in the last minute of class: What is the most significant thing you learned today? What question is uppermost in your mind at the end of this class session (Wilson, 1986)? Reviewing the answers told the instructor if students were understanding lectures and if there were any questions worth addressing the next time.

Although the idea of using feedback to improve instruction is eminently sensible, assessments of its effectiveness are not all positive. For example, instructors who received detailed lecture assessments during a term received post-feedback student ratings of their lectures that were comparable to those of faculty who had received no feedback (Murray, 1985). Faculty who taught the same course twice, receiving multiple-item student evaluations after the first offering, showed no change in evaluations at the end of the second offering (Wilson, 1986). When students' ratings and comments were combined with consultation, discussion, and suggestions for change from professional staff, instructors did show improvement. Even here, improvement was uneven; it appeared that more concrete, behavioral suggestions that instructors could readily put into practice were more likely to lead to improvement (Wilson, 1986). These studies focused on some of the aspects of lecturing that were discussed in Chapter 6.

As emphasized throughout this book, there is much more to teaching than lecturing. A broader focus is implied in the earlier example of evaluating a textbook and considering whether a change might be in order. Any aspect of teaching is a candidate for change and improvement. An instructor might change exam format, assignments, the frequency and timing of exams, homework, handouts, or how students are prepared for exams (say, scheduling review sessions), as well as other possibilities. Shifting attention away from classroom behavior to these other aspects of a course has the benefit of more clearly stressing the real goal of instruction, which is student learning. How one lectures, conducts discussions, or answers questions is an important contributor to student learning, but becoming a better classroom performer is not the only way to increase students' learning. Asking what might be done to increase students' understanding of course material is a key to improving instruction, as well as considering changes that concern any aspect of a course. Based on the principle that active learning is deeper and longer lasting than passive learning, a solution might be to have the students do more intellectual work, rather than the instructor making better presentations. These alternatives are not in conflict, as both could be implemented. The central point is that attempting to improve one's instruction can involve much more than improving classroom presentations.

It's not realistic for instructors to try to carry long lists of "things to do" in their heads. Of course, when considering a specific issue (for example, how to best present a complex of information in tomorrow's class), alternatives can be generated and evaluated, using references such as this book for help. The general goal stated earlier—improve student learning—provides some guidance but is perhaps too general. It would be helpful for an instructor to have a short list of intermediate-level goals that characterize an approach to teaching. Each instructor needs to develop a personal goal set, which will evolve with experience. As an example, here are five guidelines suggested by S. C. Erickson (1998):

1. Emphasize knowledge that will be worthwhile to students in the future. This judgment affects the choice of reading materials and methods of evaluation as well as class content.
2. Help students develop enthusiasm for learning, especially enthusiasm for intellectual curiosity. Erickson suggests that instructors do this by exemplifying such enthusiasm; he also says that being enthusiastic about ideas doesn't require a flamboyant style and readily can be shown in a low-key fashion. Focusing on questions and complex issues is recommended.

3. Teach so that students remember, by which Erickson means directing students' attention to what you want them to learn and making the students active learners by having them discuss issues and write about central topics. He adds that overlearning through extended practice is important (see Chap. 4)

4. Teach students to manage concepts by requiring them to make accurate semantic distinctions, by using multiple examples of concepts, and by helping students to understand how concepts provide a framework for interpreting events.

5. Use tests and assignments as teaching tools. Here, Erickson refers to ideas mentioned in several chapters of this book, such as asking clear questions about important material on exams, using writing assignments to develop understanding, providing comments on papers, and giving frequent tests, graded or ungraded, to maintain focus and monitor progress.

Erickson's guidelines are eminently reasonable and clearly compatible with the orientation of this book. No such list is exhaustive, and an instructor's personal list might well differ in content or in the language used to capture an idea. What's important is to have a set of guidelines that are meaningful and thus useful. As I said at the outset, teaching is a complex and difficult activity. It is also a very important activity to the lives of one's students. Striving to teach well, in its many meanings, will lead to great satisfaction.

SUMMARY

Student evaluations of instruction are a fact of life for most instructors, and evaluation summaries form an important part of teaching portfolios. Although students' evaluations might be subject to some biases, analyses suggest that they generally are sensibly related to the quality of instruction. Evaluations should be requested for each course component, as well as obtaining overall assessments. Rating scales yield data that are easily summarized, but written comments provide better information about students' opinions. Requesting comments about course components supplies detailed data, whereas answers to more open-ended questions about likes and dislikes indicate what is salient to students and influences their overall impression. Students are useful sources of feedback about teaching techniques, and instructors need not wait until the end of a course to check students' reactions to an instructional effort. Improving instruction depends on attention to feedback, willingness to try new approaches, and creativity in devising possibly better procedures.

Closing Note

I hope that you have found the ideas in this book to be stimulating and useful for making your teaching more effective and enjoyable. I trust that you will revisit some of these pages from time to time, to review a topic or to seek assistance in dealing with a new situation. In closing, I want to encourage you to do three things.

First, remember that teaching is a creative activity that is productively approached as a series of experiments in instruction. Each course, each class meeting is an opportunity to try out teaching ideas. The goals of instruction change from course to course and from class to class; one day the goal might be learning a new concept, another day the focus might be on solving problems. Not every experiment will be a rousing success; any weakness in outcome implies that a better technique could be found. When things don't work as well as desired, the sensible response is to try a new approach, guided by consideration of the learning goal and what was done. Sometimes a small change can yield excellent results. Even though we understand the fundamentals of learning, memory, and thinking, we sometimes can forget to put sound principles into practice. Perhaps the cuing of critical information could be sharper, perhaps a handout would be more effective than an overhead, perhaps a learning goal would be better achieved with a different assignment. Trying out ideas makes teaching more fun and will lead to better instruction, whether sooner or later.

Second, consult with others and allocate some time to seek out information about teaching. Periodic conversations with colleagues provide mutual support and can stimulate ideas. There are journals devoted to issues of general interest to college faculty, such as *Research in Higher Education* and *Journal of College Student Development*. Because teaching is a natural topic of interest in psychology and education, teaching journals in these areas are potentially valuable to instructors in any specialty. For example, many of the articles in *Teaching of Psychology* are not specific to psychology; they are about teaching. There also are many sources of articles on instructional issues in particular disciplines, such as *American Journal of Physics*, *Journal of Research in Mathematics Education*, *French Review*, and *Nature*. In all areas, there are professional organizations concerned with teaching, either as special groups or sections of national organizations. These resources can provide both information and invigoration.

Last, your comments about this book, your questions and experiences, will be appreciated. My own experiences and many discussions with new college teachers were the foundation for selecting topics to include. I have tried to show how research-based knowledge of learning, memory, and thinking can inform teaching practices and guide the selection and invention of specific techniques. In addition to offering useful ideas, I hoped to provoke your thinking about teaching so that your choices are made with awareness of issues and alternatives. There might be other topics you would like to have included; the exposition might be improved at some points. Your feedback will help to guide revision of the text.

Please send your comments to me in care of:

Editorial Department/Education Editor
Lawrence Erlbaum Associates, Inc., Publishers
10 Industrial Avenue
Mahwah, NJ 07430–2262

Thank you and best wishes for success.

Roger Dominowski

REFERENCES

Adams, J. A., & Montague, W. E. (1967). Retroactive inhibition and natural language mediation. *Journal of Verbal Learning and Verbal Behavior, 6*, 528–535.

Anderson, J. R. (1982). Acquisition of cognitive skill. *Psychological Review, 85*, 369–406.

Ansburg, P. I., & Dominowski, R. L. (2000). Promoting insightful problem solving. *Journal of Creative Behavior, 34*, 30–60.

Applebee, A. N. (1984). Writing and reasoning. *Review of Educational Research, 54*, 577–596.

Appleby, D. C. (1994). How to improve your teaching with the course syllabus. *APS Observer, 7*, 18–19, 26.

Baddeley, A. D. (1999). *Essentials of human memory.* Hove, UK: Psychology Press.

Baddeley, A. D., & Longman, D. J. A. (1978). The influence of length and frequency of training sessions on the rate of learning to type. *Ergonomics, 21*, 627–635.

Bahrick, H. P. (1984). Semantic memory content in permastore: Fifty years of memory for Spanish learned in school. *Journal of Experimental Psychology: General, 113*, 1–24.

Baker, L., & Lombardi, B. R. (1985). Students' lecture notes and their relation to test performance. *Teaching of Psychology, 12*, 28–32.

Barnes, C. P. (1983). Questioning in the college classroom. In C. L. Ellner & C. P. Barnes (Eds.), *Studies of College Teaching.* Lexington, MA: Lexington Books, pp. 61–81.

Basow, S. A. (1995). Student evaluations of college professors: When gender matters. *Journal of Educational Psychology, 87*, 656–665.

Berardi-Coletta, B., Buyer, L. S., Dominowski, R. L., & Rellinger, E. R. (1995). Meta-cognition and problem solving: A process-oriented approach. *Journal of Experimental Psychology: Learning, Memory, and Cognition, 21*, 205–223.

Bower, G. H. (1970). Analysis of a mnemonic device. *American Scientist, 58*, 496–510.

Bower, G. H., Clark, M. C., Lesgold, A. M., & Winzenz, D. (1969). Hierarchical retrieval schemes in recall of categorized word lists. *Journal of Verbal Learning and Verbal Behavior, 8*, 323–343.

Brandwein, A. C., & DiVittis, A. (1985). The evaluation of a peer tutoring program: A quantitative approach. *Educational and Psychological Measurement, 45*, 15–27.

Bransford, J. D. (1979). *Human cognition: Learning, understanding, and remembering.* Belmont, CA: Wadsworth Publishing Company.

Bridgeman, B., & Morgan, R. (1996). Success in college for students with discrepancies between performance on multiple-choice and essay tests. *Journal of Educational Psychology, 88*, 333–340.

Britton, B. K. (1978). Incidental prose learning. *Journal of Reading Behavior, 10*, 299–303.

Burke, R. J. (1969). A comparison of two properties of hints in individual problem solving. *Journal of General Psychology, 81*, 3–21.

Buyer, L. S., & Dominowski, R. L. (1989). Retention of solutions: It's better to give than to receive. *American Journal of Psychology, 102*, 353–363.

Caldwell, E. C. (1985). Dangers of PSI. *Teaching of Psychology, 12*, 9–12.

Case, S. M. (1994). The use of imprecise terms in examination questions: How frequent is frequently? *Academic Medicine, 69*, S4–S6.

Catrambone, R. (1994). Improving examples to improve transfer to novel problems. *Memory & Cognition, 22*, 606–615.

Chatman, S. P., & Goetz, E. T. (1985). Improving textbook selection. *Teaching of Psychology, 12*, 150–152.

Check, J. F. (1986). Positive traits of the effective teacher–negative traits of the ineffective one. *Education, 106*, 326–334.

Cohen, P. A. (1982). Validity of student ratings in psychology courses: A research synthesis. *Teaching of Psychology, 9*, 78–84.

Conrad, R. (1964). Acoustic confustions in immediate memory. *Journal of Experimental Psychology, 92*, 149–154

Conway, M. A., Cohen, G., & Stanhope, N. (1992). Why is it that university grades do not predict very-long term retention? *Journal of Experimental Psychology: General, 121*, 382–384.

Covington, M. V. (1999). Caring about learning: The nature and nurturing of subject-matter appreciation. *Educational Psychologist, 34*, 127–136.

Craik, F. I. M. (1979). Human memory. *Annual Review of Psychology, 30*, 63–102.

Craik, F. I. M., & Lockhart, R. S. (1972). Levels of processing: A framework for memory research. *Journal of Verbal Learning and Verbal Behavior, 11*, 671–684.

Crouse, J. H. (1971). Retroactive interference in reading prose materials. *Journal of Educational Psychology, 62*, 39–44.

Dallob, P. I., & Dominowski, R. L. (1992). *Erroneous solutions to insight problems: Fixation or insufficient monitoring?* Paper presented at the annual meeting of the Western Psychological Association, Portland OR, April.

Davis, M., & Hult, R. E. (1997). Effects of writing summaries as a generative learning activity during note taking. *Teaching of Psychology, 24*, 47–49.

Deffenbacher, J. L. (1978). Worry, emotionality, and task-generated interference in test anxiety: An empirical test of attentional theory. *Journal of Educational Psychology, 70*, 248–254.

Dempster, F. N., & Perkins, P. G. (1993). Revitalizing classroom assessment: Using tests to promote learning. *Journal of Instructional Psychology, 20*, 197–203.

Deutsch, M. (1979). Education and distributive justice. *American Psychologist, 34*, 391–401.

Dewey, R. A. (1995). Finding the right introductory psychology textbook. *APS Observer*, March, 32–33, 35.

Diekhoff, G. M. (1984). True-false tests that measure and promote structural understanding. *Teaching of Psychology, 11*, 99–101.

Dominowski, R. L. (1969). The effect of pronunciation practice on anagram difficulty. *Psychonomic Science, 16*, 99–100.

Dominowski, R. L. (1973). Required hypothesizing and the identification of unidimensional, conjunctive, and disjunctive concepts. *Journal of Experimental Psychology, 100*, 387–394.

Dominowski, R. L. (1990). Problem solving and metacognition. In K. J. Gilhooly, M. T. G. Keane, R. H. Logie, & G. Erdos (Eds.), *Lines of thinking: Reflections on the psychology of thought* (Vol. 2). Chichester, England: Wiley, pp. 313–328.

Dominowski, R. L. (1995). Content effects in Wason's selection task. In S. Newstead & J. Evans (eds.), *Perspective on thinking and reasoning: Essays in honour of Peter Wason*. London: Erlbaum, pp. 41–65.

Dominowski, R. L. (1998). *Required retesting in a statistics course*. APS Annual Institute on the Teaching of Psychology, May.

Dominowski, R. L., & Buyer, L. S. (2000). Retention of problem solutions: The re-solution effect. *American Journal of Psychology*, *113*, 249–274.

Dominowski, R. L., Dallob, P. I., & Penningroth, S. (1994). *Emphasizing analytic skills in teaching students to write about psychology*. 1st APS Annual Institute on the Teaching of Psychology.

Dominowski, R. L., & Rice, H. V. (1999). *Error correction as homework: A useful alternative to retesting*. APS Annual Institute on the Teaching of Psychology, June.

Erdle, S., & Murray, H. G. (1986). Interfaculty differences in classroom teaching behaviors and their relationship to student instructional ratings. *Research in Higher Education*, *24*, 115–127.

Erickson, S. C. (1998). Self-knowledge of a job well-done: Reflections on a teacher's self-appraisal. *APS Monitor*, Jan., 24–26, 48.

Ericsson, K. A., & Hastie, R. (1994). Contemporary approaches to the study of thinking and problem solving. In R. J. Sternberg (Ed.), *Thinking and problem solving*. New York: Academic Press, pp. 37–79.

Evans, J. St. B. T., (1989). *Bias in human reasoning: Causes and consequences*. Hove, UK: L. Erlbaum, Assoc.

Evans, J. St. B. T., Barston, J. L., & Pollard, P. (1983). On the conflict between logic and belief in syllogistic reasong. *Memory & Cognition*, *11*, 295–306.

Fischoff, B. (1975). Hindsight ǂ foresight: The effect of outcome knowledge on judgement under uncertainty. *Journal of Experimental Psychology: Human Perception and Performance*, *1*, 288–299.

Flanagan, M. F. (1978). A strategy for increasing class participation. *Teaching of Psychology*, *5*, 209–210.

Gagne, R. M., & Smith, E. C., Jr. (1962). A study of the effects of verbalization on problem solving. *Journal of Experimental Psychology*, *63*, 12–18.

Gardner, W. M., Roper, J. T., Gonzalez, C. C., & Simpson, R. G. (1988). Analysis of cheating on academic assignments. *Psychological Record*, *38*, 543–555.

Gick, M. L., & Holyoak, K. J. (1983). Schema induction and analogical transfer. *Cognitive Psychology*, *15*, 1–38.

Gilhooly, K. J., Logie, R. H., Wetherick, N. E., & Wynn, V. (1993). Working memory and strategies in syllogistic-reasoning tasks. *Memory & Cognition*, *21*, 115–124.

Gilmore, D. C., Swerdik, M. E., & Beehr, T. A. (1980). Effects of class size and college major on student ratings of psychology courses. *Teaching of Psychology*, *7*, 210–214.

Glover, J. A., & Corkhill, A. J. (1987). Influence of paraphrased repetitions on the spacing effect. *Journal of Educational Psychology*, *79*, 198–199.

Goetz, E. M., & Gump, P. V. (1978). Whole class settings and part class settings. *Teaching of Psychology*, *5*, 93–95.

Goldwater, B. C., & Acker, L. E. (1975). Instructor-paced, mass-testing for mastery performance in an introductory psychology course. *Teaching of Psychology*, *2*, 152–155.

Goss, S. (1995). Dealing with problem students in the classroon. *APS Observer*, Nov., 26–29.

Greenwald, A. G., & Gillmore, G. M. (1997a). Grading leniency is a removable contaminant of student ratings. *American Psychologist*, *52*, 1209–1217.

Greenwald, A. G., & Gillmore, G. M. (1997b). No pain, no gain? The importance of measuring course workload in student ratings of instruction. *Journal of Educational Psychology, 89*, 743–751.

Griggs, R. A. (1999). Introductory psychology textbooks: Assessing levels of difficulty. *Teaching of Psychology, 26*, 248–253.

Grosse, M. E., & Wright, B. D. (1985). Validity and reliability of true-false tests. *Educational and Psychological Measurement, 45*, 1–13.

Hacker, D. J. (1998). Self-regulated comprehension during normal reading. In D. J. Hacker, J. Dunlosky, & A. C. Graesser (Eds.), *Metacognition in educational theory and practice*. Mahwah, NJ: L. Erlbaum Assoc.

Halpern, D. F. (1997). *Critical thinking across the curriculum*. Mahwah, NJ: L. Erlbaum Assoc.

Halpern, D. F., Hansen, C., & Riefer, D. (1990). Analogies as an aid to understanding and memory. *Journal of Educational Psychology, 82*, 298–305.

Hamilton, R. J. (1989). The effects of learner-generated elaborations on concept learning from prose. *Journal of Experimental Education, 57*, 205–217.

Hamilton, R. J. (1997). Effects of three types of elaboration on learning concepts from text. *Contemporary Educational Psychology, 22*, 299–318.

Hancock, G. R. (1994). Cognitive complexity and the comparability of multiple-choice and constructed-response formats. *Journal of Experimental Education, 62*, 143–157.

Harris, R. J. (1977). The teacher as actor. *Teaching of Psychology, 4*, 185–187.

Hayes, J. R., & Flower, L. S. (1986). Writing research and the writer. *American Psychologist, 41*, 1106–1113.

Helsabeck, F., Jr. (1975). Syllogistic reasoning : Generation of counterexamples. *Journal of Educational Psychology, 67*, 102–108.

Herrman, D. J. (1987). Task appropriateness of mnemonic techniques. *Perceptual and Motor Skills, 64*, 171–178.

Hettich, P. (1976). The journal: An autobiographical approach to learning. *Teaching of Psychology, 3*, 61–63.

Howard, G. S., Conway, C. G., & Maxwell, S. E. (1985). Construct validity of measures of college teaching effectiveness. *Journal of Educational Psychology, 77*, 187–196.

Howard, G. S., & Maxwell, S. E. (1982). Do grades contaminate student evaluations of instruction? *Research in Higher Education, 16*, 175–188.

Hyde, T. S., & Jenkins, J. J. (1969). Recall for words as a function of semantic, graphic, and syntactic orienting tasks. *Journal of Verbal Learning and Verbal Behavior, 12*, 471–480.

Johnson-Laird, P. N., & Byrne, R. M. J. (1991). *Deduction*. Hove, UK: L. Erlbaum Assoc.

Kahneman, D., & Tversky, A. (1982). On the study of statistical intuitions. *Cognition, 11*, 123–141.

Kaplan, R. M., & Pascoe, G. C. (1977). Humorous lectures and humorous examples: Some effects upon comprehension and retention. *Journal of Educational Psychology, 69*, 61–65.

Keith-Spiegel, P. (1994). Ethically risky situations between students and professors outside the classroom. *APS Observer*, Sept., 24–25, 29.

Keith-Spiegel, P., Tabachnick, B. G., Whitley, B. E., Jr., & Washburn, J. (1998). Why professors ignore cheating: Opinions of a national sample of psychology instructors. *Ethics & Behavior, 8*, 215–227.

Keller, F. S. (1968). Good-bye, teacher ... *Journal of Applied Behavior Analysis, 1*, 79–89.

Kellogg, R. T. (1987). Writing performance: Effects of cognitive strategies. *Written Communication, 4*, 269–298.

Kiewra, K. A. (1985). Students' note-taking behaviors and the efficacy of providing the instructor's notes for review. *Contemporary Educational Psychology, 10*, 378–386.

Kiewra, K. A. (1987). Notetaking and review: The research and its implications. *Instructional Science, 16*, 233–249.

Kintsch, W. (1986). Learning from text. *Cognition & Instruction, 3*, 87–108.

Klugh, H. E. (1983). Writing and speaking skills can be taught in psychology classes. *Teaching of Psychology, 10*, 170–171.

Koriat, A., Lichtenstein, S., & Fischoff, B. (1980). Reasons for confidence. *Journal of Experimental Psychology: Human Learning & Memory, 6*, 107–118.

Kramer, T. J., & Korn, J. H. (1996). Class discussions: Promoting participation and preventing problems. *APS Observer*, Sept., 24–25, 27.

Kyllonen, P. C., & Christal, R. E. (1990). Reasoning ability is (little more than) working memory capacity? *Intelligence, 14*, 389–433.

LaBerge, D., & Samuels, S. J. (1974). Toward a theory of automatic information processing in reading. *Cognitive Psychology, 6*, 293–323.

Lamberth, J., & Knight, J. M. (1974). An embarassment of riches: Effectively teaching and motivating large introductory psychology sections. *Teaching of Psychology, 1*, 16–20.

Landrum, R. E., & Chastain, G. (1998). Demonstrating tutoring effectiveness within a one-semester course. *Journal of College Student Development, 39*, 502–506.

Landrum, R. E., Cashin, J. R., & Theis, K. S. (1993). More evidence in favor of three-option multiple-choice tests. *Educational and Psychological Measurement, 53*, 771–778.

Lehman, D. R., & Nisbett, R. E. (1990). A longitudinal study of the effects of undergraduate training on reasoning. *Developmental Psychology, 26*, 952–960.

Lockhart, R. S., & Craik, F. I. M. (1990). Levels of processing: A retrospective commentary on a framework for memory research. *Canadian Journal of Psychology, 44*, 87–112.

Lung, C. T., & Dominowski, R. L. (1985). Effects of strategy instructions and practice on nine-dot problem solving. *Journal of Experimental Psychology: Learning Memory, & Cognition, 11*, 804–811.

Lutsky, N. (1997) Teaching with overheads: Low tech, high impact. *APS Observer, May/June*, 26–28.

Markle, S. M., & Tiemann, P. W. (1970). "Behavioral" analysis of "cognitive" content. *Educational Technology, 10*, 41–45.

Marsh, H. W., & Roche, L. A. (2000). Effects of grading leniency and low workload on students' evaluations of teaching: Popular myth, bias, validity, or innocent bystanders? *Journal of Educational Psychology, 92*, 202–228.

Martin, R. C., & Caramazza, A. (1980). Classification in well-defined and ill-defined categories: Evidence for common processing strategies. *Journal of Experimental Psychology: General, 109*, 320–353.

May, K. M., & Loyd, B. H. (1993). Academic dishonesty: The honor system and students' attitudes. *Journal of College Student Develoment, 34*, 125–129.

McKeegan, P. (1998). Using undergraduate teaching assistants in a research methodology course. *Teaching of Psychology, 25*, 11–14.

Mikulincer, M. (1989). Learned helplessness and egotism: Effects of internal/external attribution on performance following unsolvable problems. *British Journal of Social Psychology, 28,* 17–29.

Miller, G. A. (1956). The magic number seven, plus or minus two: Some limits on our capacity for processing information. *Psychological Review, 63,* 81–97.

Morgan, C. H., Lilley, J. D., & Boreham, N. C. (1988). Learning from lectures: The effect of varying the detail in lecture handouts on note-taking and recall. *Applied Cognitive Psychology, 2,* 115–122.

Murray, H. G. (1985). Classroom teaching behaviors related to college teaching effectiveness. In J. G. Donald & M. Sullivan (Eds.), *Using Research to Improve Teaching.* New Directions for Teaching and Learning, No. 23. San Francisco, CA: Jossey-Bass.

Newstead, S. E., Franklyn-Stokes, A., & Armstead, P. (1996). Individual differences in student cheating. *Journal of Educational Psychology, 88,* 229–241.

Nodine, B. F. (1998). Why not make writing assignments? *APS Observer,* Nov., 20–22.

Novick, L. R. (1988). Analogical transfer, problem similarity, and expertise. *Journal of Experimental Psychology: Learning, Memory, & Cognition, 14,* 510–520.

Paivio, A. (1971). *Imagery and verbal processes.* New York: Holt, Rinehart, & Winston.

Paivio, A. (1991). Dual coding theory: Retrospect and current status. *Canadian Journal of Psychology, 45,* 255–287.

Palladino, J. J., Hill, G. W., IV, & Norcross, J. C. (1995). The use of extra credit in teaching. *APS Observer,* Sept., 34–35, 40.

Pascarella, E. T. (1989). The development of critical thinking: Does college make a difference? *Journal of College Student Development, 30,* 19–26.

Polich, J. M., & Schwartz, S. H. (1974). The effect of problem size on representation in deductive problem solving. *Memory & Cognition, 2,* 683–686.

Posner, M. I., & Boies, S. (1971). Components of attention. *Psychological Review, 78,* 391–408.

Postman, L. (1962). Retention as a function of degree of overlearning. *Science, 135,* 666–667.

Postman, L., & Underwood, B. J. (1973). Critical issues in interference theory. *Memory & Cognition, 1,* 19–40.

Quereshi, M. Y., & Buchkoski, J. E. (1979). Logical versus empirical estimates of readability and human interest of general psychology textbooks. *Teaching of Psychology, 6,* 202–205.

Radmacher, S. A., & Latosi-Sawin, E. (1995). Summary writing: A tool to improve student comprehension and writing in psychology. *Teaching of Psychology, 22,* 113–115.

Reigeluth, C. M. (1983). Meaningfulness and instruction: Relating what is being learned to what a student knows. *Instructional Science, 12,* 197–218.

Rhine, R. J. (1957). The effect on problem solving of success or failure as a function of cue specificity. *Journal of Experimental Psychology, 53,* 121–125.

Rodabaugh, R. C., & Kravitz, D. A. (1994). Effects of procedural fairness on student judgment of professors. *Journal of Excellence in College Teaching, 5,* 67–83.

Roig, M. (1997). Can undergraduates determine whether text has been plagiarized? *Psychological Record, 47,* 113–122.

Ross, B. H., & Spalding, T. L. (1994). Concepts and categories. In R. J. Sternberg (Ed.), *Thinking and problem solving.* New York: Academic Press, 119–148.

Scerbo, M. W., Warm, J. S., Dember, W. N., & Grasha, A. F. (1992). The role of time and cuing in a college lecture. *Contemporary Educational Psychology, 17*, 312–328.

Schallert, D. L., Alexander, P. A., & Goetz, E. T. (1985). What do instructors and authors do to influence the textbook-student relationship? *National Reading Conference Yearbook, 34*, 110–115.

Schneider, W., & Shiffrin, R. M. (1977). Controlled and automatic human information processing: I. Detection, search, and attention. *Psychological Review, 84*, 1–66.

Schoenfeld, A. H., & Herrmann, D. J. (1982). Problem perception and knowledge structure in expert and novice mathematical problem solvers. *Journal of Experimental Psychology: Learning, Memory, & Cognition, 8*, 484–494.

Sloman, S. (1996). The empirical case for two systems of reasoning. *Psychological Bulletin, 119*, 3–22.

Spelke, E., Hirst, W., & Neisser, U. (1976). Skills of divided attention. *Cognition, 4*, 215–230.

Standing, L. (1973). Learning 10,000 pictures. *Quarterly Journal of Experimental Psychology, 25*, 207–222.

Standing, L., & Gorassini, D. (1986). An evaluation of the Cloze procedure as a test for plagiarism. *Teaching of Psychology, 13*, 130–132.

Sternberg, R. J. (1988). *The psychologist's companion: A guide to scientific writing for students and researchers.* (2nd ed.) Cambridge, MA: Cambridge University Press.

Sternberg, R. J. (1997). *Successful intelligence.* NY: Simon & Schuster.

Tabachnick, B. G., Keith-Spiegel, P., & Pope, K. S. (1991). Ethics of teaching: Beliefs and behaviors of psychologists as educators. *American Psychologist, 46*, 506–515.

Tang, T. L. (1997). Teaching evaluation at a public institution of higher eduation: Factors relating to the overall teaching effectiveness. *Public Personnel Management, 26*, 379–389.

Tulving, E. (1986). What kind of hypothesis is the distinction between episodic and semantic memory? *Journal of Experimental Psychology: Learning, Memory, & Cognition, 12*, 307–311.

Tulving, E., & Osler, S. (1968). Effectiveness of retrieval cues in memory for words. *Journal of Experimental Psychology, 77*, 593–601.

Underwood, B. J. (1957). Interference and forgetting. *Psychological Review, 64*, 49–60.

Walker, C. J. (1980). An instamatic way of learning who is in your large class: A picture is worth a thousand names. *Teaching of Psychology, 7*, 62–63.

Ward, M., & Sweller, J. (1990). Structuring effective worked examples. *Cognition and Instruction, 7*, 1–39.

White, K. M., & Kolber, R. G. (1978). Undergraduate and graduate students as discussion section leaders. *Teaching of Psychology, 5*, 6–9.

Wilson, R. C. (1986). Improving faculty teaching: Effective use of student evaluations and consultants. *Journal of Higher Education, 57*, 196–211.

Zechmeister, E. B., & Johnson, J. E. (1992). *Critical thinking: a functional approach.* Belmont, CA: Wadsworth.

Zechmeister, E. B., Rusch, K. M., & Markell, K. A. (1986). Training college students to assess accurately what they know and don't know. *Human Learning, 5*, 3–19.

Name Index

A

Acker, L. E., 10–11
Adams, J. A., 41
Anderson, J. R., 28
Alexander, P. A., 72
Ansburg, P. I., 54, 57
Applebee, A. N., 99
Appleby, D. C., 16
Armstead, P., 151

B

Baddeley, A. D., 25, 41
Bahrick, H. P., 37–38
Baker, L., 88
Barnes, C. P., 90
Barston, J. L., 62
Basow, S. A., 159
Beehr, T. A., 159
Berardi-Colletta, B., 55–56
Boies, S., 22, 27
Boreham, N. C., 88
Bower, G. H., 35, 40
Brandwein, A. C., 14
Bransford, J. D., 45
Bridgeman, B., 112
Britton, B. K., 36
Buchkoski, J. E., 70
Burke, R. J., 53
Buyer, L. S., 53–55
Byrne, R. M. J., 59

C

Caldwell, E. C., 11
Caramazza, A. 46
Case, S. M., 117

Cashin, J. R., 116
Catrambone, R., 55
Chastain, G., 14
Chatman, S. P., 68
Check, J. F., 84
Christal, R. E., 58
Clark, M. C., 35
Cohen, G., 131
Cohen, P. A., 159
Conrad, R., 26
Conway, C. G., 158
Conway, M. A., 131
Corkhill, A. J., 80
Covington, M. V., 130
Craik, F. I. M., 29, 36–37
Crouse, J. H., 36

D

Dallob, P. I., 50, 98, 106
Davis, M., 99
Deffenbacher, J. L., 52
Dember, W. N., 88
Dempster, F. N., 127
Deutsch, M., 130
Dewey, R. A., 68
Diekhoff, G. M., 124–125
DiVittis, A., 14
Dominowski, R. L., 13, 26, 48, 50, 52–57, 61, 98, 106

E

Erdle, S., 94
Erickson, S. C., 166–167

Subject Index